THE CUBAN ECONOMY UNDER A MAGNIFYING GLASS

ESSAYS IN HONOR OF OSCAR ESPINOSA CHEPE

THE CUBAN ECONOMY UNDER A MAGNIFYING GLASS

ESSAYS IN HONOR OF OSCAR ESPINOSA CHEPE

Edited by Ernesto Hernández-Catá

In collaboration with Roger Betancourt and Jorge Pérez-López

Association for the Study of the Cuban Economy

Cover photo by Uva de Aragon

ISBN: 1497511976
ISBN 13: 9781497511972
Library of Congress Control Number: 2014906256
CreateSpace Independent Publishing Platform
North Charleston, South Carolina

CONTENTS

PREFACE:

ON OSCAR ESPINOSA CHEPE
(1940–1913)

Joaquin Pujol

When I first came across Oscar Espinosa Chepe's articles on the Cuban economy—often smuggled out of the Island by some visiting journalists or other visitors—I was very impressed by the amount of information he disclosed, the quality of the analysis, and the clarity of the writing. In 2007, at the request of Ernesto Betancourt, I assumed the responsibility for compiling the *Newsclippings* of the Association for the Study of the Cuban Economy. Since then I made it a point to search the Internet for Chepe's most recent articles and to ensure that they were incorporated into the *Newsclippings*.

Oscar graduated as an economist from the University of Havana in 1967 and later worked in a number of government agencies, including the Central Bank of Cuba. In 1968, when he was serving as an adviser to then-Prime Minister Fidel Castro, he was demoted and sent for two years to collect guano for fertilizer in bat-infested caves because he dared to question the economic policies of the government. From 1970 to 1984, he served as Chief of the Department in charge of managing Cuba's economic relations with Hungary, Czechoslovakia and Yugoslavia, and from 1984-87 as Economic Adviser to the Cuban Embassy in Belgrade. In 1987, having traveled back to Cuba on home-leave, he was barred from returning to his post in Belgrade and was assigned to the National Bank of Cuba until 1992, when he was accused of being a "counter-revolutionary" and expelled from all government jobs because of his critical views on the economic policies of the government.

He then started to work on his own as an independent economic journalist. In this capacity he authored scores of articles on the Cuban economy (for the most part smuggled out of Cuba), that were circulated through the Internet, and printed abroad in various publications, including: *Cambio 16, Expansión, El Nuevo Herald, The Miami Herald, El País* from Spain, *the Berliner Zeitung, Cubanet, Disidente Universal, Encuentro de la Cultura Cubana, Cubaencuentro, Vitral,* and many others in Europe and Latin America. He also participated by telephone on a pro-bono basis in a radio program on economic commentary broadcast out of Miami by Radio Martí.

In March 2003 Oscar was arrested together with 74 others in Cuba's crackdown on peaceful dissidents, in what became known as the "Black Spring". *Amnesty International* declared him a "prisoner of conscience." Sentenced to twenty years in jail, he was released temporarily after twenty months on medical parole, because of the deterioration to his health resulting from the conditions of the imprisonment. He remained subject to "house arrest". After that he received numerous invitations to present papers about the Cuban economy abroad but he was not allowed to travel outside of Cuba

In 2000, Chepe presented his first paper via remote access at the Annual Conference of ASCE in Miami. Over the years he presented 9 papers at these conferences: they can be found in the following volumes of *Cuba in Transition,* the Papers and Proceedings of ASCE's meetings: El estado real de la economía cubana, 2000; Cuba: la crisis se profundiza 2002; La crisis de la producción agropecuaria cubana: causas y posibles soluciones, 2006;

Cuba: opciones para un futuro digno 2007; Cuba ante un futuro incierto 2008; Crisis sobre crisis: la difícil situación económica, social y política de la sociedad cubana: probabilidades de su agravamiento, 2009; La economía cubana: ¿tiempos de esperanza? 2010; Situación económica, política y social de Cuba, 2011; and Situación de la economía cubana, 2012.

Several books collecting his writings have been published in the last 10 years. In 2003, *Crónica de un Desastre* was published by Editorial Hispano-Cubana, Madrid, and in 2007 *Cuba, Revolución o Involución*, Aduana Vieja, Valencia, Spain (edited by Joaquín P. Pujol). In 2011, *Cambios en Cuba: Pocos, Limitados y Tardíos* became available in digital form: (http://reconciliacioncubana.files.wordpress.com/2011/03/cambios-en-cuba.pdf.). His last publication, in collaboration with Ted Henken, saw the light shortly after his death in 2013, *Economics in Cuba* (edited by Ted A. Henken, Miriam Celaya, and Dimas Castellanos), Santa Barbara, California, ABC-Clio).

In 2013 Oscar Espinosa Chepe was finally allowed by the Cuban government to travel to Spain to receive medical treatment. He passed away on Monday, September 23, 2013 in Madrid, Spain. His wife, Miriam Leiva, was by his side. We will miss Oscar very much. He was a champion for freedom, democracy and good economic sense, un-beholden to the powers that be. He and Miriam displayed immense courage, speaking their minds and stoically accepting the consequences of the persecution imposed on them by the Cuban authorities.

Oscar Espinosa Chepe will be remembered as an honest, lucid and competent economic analyst who had the courage to express his views even in the face of persecution. We are honored to have had him as a member of the Association for the Study of the Cuban Economy.

INTRODUCTION

Ernesto Hernández-Catá

O scar Espinosa Chepe was a patriot and a man of immense dedication and courage. He was also a distinguished economist. I remember the day, several years ago, when he and I were interviewed on the radio by Antonio Gayoso. I was impressed by his honesty and his fairness: he would never hesitate to criticize government policies, sometimes severely, but he would also be prepared to recognize improvements when they occurred. Most of all, I was struck by his vast knowledge of the Cuban economy, his familiarity with statistics, and his capacity to analyze them intelligently.

The articles contained in this book have benefited from Oscar's knowledge and inspiration. They deal with many of the topics that interested him, and also with most of the issues and concerns that have confronted Cuban policy-makers: relations with Venezuela; the exchange rate system; international liquidity and external debt; productivity and growth; the problems of agriculture; the adequacy of education; and the political aspects of economic policy.

A common theme in most of the papers is the reform process started a few years ago by Raúl Castro's administration. These reforms have included the relocation of a large number of effectively unemployed workers from the state to the non-state sector; some liberalization of the labor market; the authorization of private purchases and sales of cars and houses, and the announcement and early implementation of a plan to gradually unify the exchange rate system. Some of the authors represented in this book believe that these reforms are insufficiently strong and excessively gradual, and they are not persuaded that they will not be partly reversed, as had been the case with past reforms. But I think most believe, as I do, that they are steps in the right direction.

♦ ♦ ♦

In *"The Growth of the Cuban Economy in the First Decade of the XXI century"* I try to explain the factors behind the astonishingly rapid expansion of the Cuban economy in the 2000s. In particular, I examine the possible contributions of macroeconomic and structural policies, the role of Venezuelan assistance, and the possible effect of data manipulation. The period under review is divided into 3 sub-periods: a moderate increase in GDP in 2000-02; exceptionally fast growth in 2003-06; and a pronounced slowdown in 2007-10. Performance is then evaluated using a growth accounting framework: capital formation and increased capacity utilization explain a substantial fraction of output growth in all three periods. However, the model fails to account for more than half of the very high growth of output in 2003-06. A simplified demand-side model suggested that the expansion of government current expenditure accounted for about half of GDP growth during that period, with domestic investment and exports of services accounting for much of the rest.

The article concludes that structural policies did not contribute to high growth. The share of the non-state sector in the economy declined from 2000 to 2010, as self-employment was discouraged by increasing taxation and regulation. In agriculture, the proportion of land in the hands of the cooperative and private sectors rose substantially, but this was not reflected in a major increase in production as non-state agriculture continued to be hampered by price controls, bureaucratic harassment, and uncertainty about the legal status of land tenure. The share of foreign trade in convertible currency fell, mostly because of the sharp rise in barter trade with Venezuela; and state enterprises were hindered by the obligation to centralize payment in a single account at the Central Bank. Altogether the first decade of the XXI century was one of counter-reform compared with the mid- and late 1990's.

The contribution of macro policies was ambiguous. Government expenditures provided a substantial stimulus, reflecting partly the growth of services provided to Venezuela, but the rise in the share of government crowded out other sectors, particularly in the middle years of the decade. The government continued to absorb domestic saving and, in 2008 it ran an unusually large fiscal deficit that probably contributed to a widening of the external current account and to a severe payments crisis. Monetary policy kept inflation low with the assistance of price controls, the fixed exchange rate, and the slow growth of wages. The Central Bank of Cuba helped to defend the fixed exchange rate—a goal of dubious value—by sterilizing part of its credit to the government through sales of foreign exchange reserves. Early in the decade, the period of dollarization was ended and a complicated multiple exchange system was introduced that involved serious distortions and discrimination against the export-oriented sector of the economy, as explained in Ed Canler's article in this book.

In searching for a satisfactory explanation of the country's apparently strong performance in the 2000s, the analysis turns to two factors: Venezuela and cheating. Real GDP growth, as officially reported, was almost certainly boosted in 2005 by a wild exaggeration of output growth in public health. To be sure, output in that sector increased rapidly in the 2000s, as Cuba agreed to provide the services of medical and teaching personnel in exchange for Venezuelan investments and the provision of oil to Cuba on highly favorable terms. The implementation of this accord made a substantial contribution to the measured expansion of output in Cuba. At the same time it increased the island's dependence on foreign largesse to levels unseen since the days of Soviet dominance and raised questions about the consequences of a possible end to politically-inspired foreign assistance.

◆ ◆ ◆

From the first decade of the XXI century, **Jorge Sanguinetty** takes us back to the early 1960's. Indeed he convincingly argues that understanding the current difficult problems of the Cuban economy and Raul Castro's policy dilemma, it is necessary to go back to the early days of Fidel Castro's government and to understand his dreams and objectives. Sanguinetty argues forcefully that Castro's goals were not economic but political. In fact, in Fidel Castro's mind the need to run the Cuban economy efficiently and to ensure a high standard of living for the population were distinctly secondary: his overriding objectives were to consolidate his grip on power, to project his image abroad, and to become a leader of third-word countries in the fight against capitalism and the United States.

In Fidel Castro's mind, there could be no trade-offs between his political goals and economic objectives. His speeches and his actions quickly demonstrated that his preferences were lexicographic: he nationalized industry and farms without concern for the consequences of lost human capital and managerial skills; he engaged in mass mobilization for literacy campaigns, failed sugar harvests, and political rallies without considering their enormous cost. He also eliminated political parties, the free media and the independent judiciary and the independent trade unions. Most importantly, he basically destroyed the institutions of the private market economy, replacing them by a system of rigid price controls and central planning.

But even central planning was too much of a constraint for Castro's freewheeling and politically obsessed mentality. Sanguinetty recalls how, as early as 1961, the Quadrennial Economic Plan was abandoned even before it was launched. With central planning gone, economic statistics became essentially a nuisance: Ernesto Guevara refused to accept the estimate of 1% growth of national income for 1961 and declared the National Accounts extinct; GDP was not heard of until the 1970's. Productivity growth suffered greatly from the lack of sensible direction of the economy. And the output of state enterprises was seriously hindered by the absence of a profit incentive, distorted prices, excessive centralization and the obligation to absorb unemployed workers in exchange for huge state subsidies. These subsidies had to go when, in the early 1990s, the Soviet Union eliminated its massive transfers to Cuba, giving rise to a crisis of major proportions which in 1994 forced the Cuban government to implement some modest reforms and to slash budgetary subsidies to enterprises. Less than a decade later, however, foreign subsidies re-appeared in the form of Venezuelan aid. As Sanguinetty rightly notes, reliance on foreign assistance remains an important aspect of Cuban economic policy, a way to fill the gap between the political aspirations of the leadership and the county's meager productive capacity.

Since he took charge of the management of the Cuban economy, Raul Castro apparently decided that important changes were needed to improve the performance of the Cuban economy and raise the standard of living of the population. I think this is, in itself, a significant change from the mentality of economic neglect that Sanguinetty describes in his article. But the reform process that has started will face strong opposition from the ideologically obtuse and from those who stand to lose from the reforms. For this reason among others, the faster the changes are implemented the better.

◆ ◆ ◆

The problems caused by Cuba's current multiple exchange rate system have been extensively discussed, both in the Island and abroad. In his article on *Pesos, Poverty and Perversions*, **Ed Canler** analyses the system, explains its distorting and discriminatory nature and offers suggestions for reform. He first recounts the history of the system dating back to the period following the elimination of Soviet aid in the early 1990. At that time, the authorities introduced a three-pronged scheme involving three currencies: the U.S. dollar, the inconvertible Cuban peso (which floated in secondary markets), and the convertible peso, or CUC. (The latter was fixed at one CUC/U.S. dollar and its value was fully backed by foreign exchange reserves, like in a currency board). The non-convertible Cuban peso (CUP) depreciated sharply after the post-Soviet crisis but later recovered and is currently set at 24 pesos per dollar. In the 1990's the system was modified though a (rather surrealistic) revaluation of the CUC against the dollar, but this action was subsequently reversed. Other changes involved the elimination of the currency-board features of the CUC and efforts to de-dollarize the economy including a 10% tax on conversions on CUP/$ transactions.

A crucial aspect of the present system is that the 1:1 Cuban peso/$ rate is applied to Cuban *enterprises* (and serves as a statistical conversion factor as well), while *households and tourists* must pay 24 pesos to purchase one dollar. Using a simple and ingenious diagram, Canler shows how the exchange rates for households and enterprises determine the quantities of dollars transacted in the market. The diagram also helps to understand how the system generates producer and consumer surpluses resulting from the huge difference between these two exchange rates. The system thus creates "winners" and "losers", comparing the present situation with that which would prevail under a unified free market system. To simplify a complex scheme, the winners are those that can buy one U.S. dollar for one Cuban peso, namely the official importers of food, medicines and fuel—goods that are subsequently sold to the population at subsidized prices. The losers are those who must pay 24 pesos per dollar: exporters and tourism enterprises, most agricultural producers, and, Cuban households whose salaries are mostly denominated in Cuban pesos. For a country with weak exports, a vulnerable external current account, and heavy dependence on oil and food imports, the system is precisely the wrong recipe.

Ed Canler naturally calls for the elimination of the current scheme, as I do, and its replacement by a unified market-determined exchange rate system. It is therefore heartening that in 2013 the Cuban authorities decided to move in that direction although, in my view, at an excessively slow pace. Canler proposes (and I agree) that, in the process of unification, the allegedly convertible CUC should be taken out of circulation, and he offers suggestions as to how this could be done in a safe way. As for the successor system, Canler argues persuasively that, since Cuba does not have enough international reserves and lacks the required credibility in world markets, it should go for a managed floating exchange rate system. Of course this will require the pursuit of disciplined monetary and fiscal policies.

◆ ◆ ◆

In their article, *Gabriel de Bella, Rafael Romeu and Andy Wolfe* tackle the most serious long-term problem faced by the Cuban authorities: the ageing of the population and its' implications for the social security system and the sustainability of the fiscal position. To be sure, the issue has been confronted for some time in many advanced countries (as well as in some developing countries like China) but Cuba is alone in Latin America in facing an acute form of this problem. The authors analyze the origins of the problem, evaluate its future evolution, and conclude with recommendations on how to deal with the problem.

Cuba's population has started to decline and the population of working age is projected to fall over the next 15 years. These developments are the result of two key factors: low birth rates and net negative migration. Since the onset of the revolution in the late 1950's Cuba has experienced a continuous decline in fecundity, with the number of daughters per woman falling below the zero population growth value of one in the mid-1980's. This factor, aggravated by large scale emigration, has set the stage for a decline in the population. At the same time, life expectancy at birth has increased markedly. These changes have resulted in a sharp increase the median age of the population, and they foreshadow a dramatic change in its age structure: the number of people 65 years and older would rise from 12% of the population in 2010 to 30% in 2030, with a corresponding increase in the number of people receiving social security benefits. At the same time, the share of the population between 25 and 66 years—those who contribute to social security—is expected to fall substantially.

Economic growth will play an important role in determining the future value of contributions and benefits. Therefore, in order to evaluate the outlook for Cuba's social security system and the prospects for fiscal sustainability, the authors construct a general equilibrium growth model which they combine with projections for key demographic variables (prepared by the United Nations) and for Cuba's social security system. The model is calibrated and projected on the basis of historical relationships and a number of assumptions. In particular, the rate of growth of productivity is assumed to remain unchanged from its average in the period 1970-2010 and tax rates are inversely related to interest-free foreign transfers (which the authors define to include exports of services to Venezuela).

In 2008, the Cuban authorities confronted the problem by raising the retirement age from 60 to 65 years for men and from 55 to 60 years for women. This measure postponed until 2029 the increase in beneficiaries that would otherwise have resulted from the aging of the population. Nevertheless, demographic and economic projections still envisage a substantial increase in social security beneficiaries, reflecting both the rise in the population aged 65 or more and their higher life expectancy. Together with the projected rise in the real value of benefits, this would result in a doubling of the ratio of social security outlays to GDP to a peak of 29% of GDP in the 2060s. As a result, cumulative fiscal deficits would surge to 140% of GDP by 2040 and 250% in 2050. Thus, on the basis of historical trends in productivity, the fiscal position appears to be unsustainable.

By simulating their model, the authors examine the consequences of alternative assumptions about key variables. On the bright side, higher growth of output in the long term would reduce social security outlays substantially. On the negative side, if external transfers were to disappear by 2020 (instead of remaining constant in real terms as in the baseline scenario) cumulative fiscal deficits would them balloon to more than 550% of GDP in 2050 and then keep rising. If the disappearance of external transfers were to be accompanied by increases in tax rates, the impact on social security would be roughly the same as in the baseline scenario, but with significant adverse effects on investment, consumption and output growth.

My reading of this article is that the current and prospective aging of the Cuban population threatens the sustainability of the social security system and the country's fiscal position. Moreover, the outlook is dangerously sensitive to adverse changes in the external situation and particularly in the level of transfers received by Cuba, which depends critically upon the politically- inspired largesse and uncertain future of the Venezuelan regime. Of course, the Cuban government could reduce future social security benefits by increasing further the retirement and/or the level of contributions (measures unlikely to be very popular). It could also improve the fiscal position in other ways by reducing unnecessary budget expenditures, improving the yield of the tax system, and possibly giving a role to the growing non-state sector in financing the system. However, as the authors convincingly argue, the best way to confront the problem is to bring about a major increase in the long-term growth of productivity and output by removing the many obstacles that continue to stifle development of a vibrant and competitive private sector.

♦ ♦ ♦

The article by **Luis R. Luis** examines the central problem of Cuba's external sector: its inability to generate sufficient foreign exchange to sustain growth in the presence of a weak export sector, the need to finance most of the country's fuel and food imports, and insufficient inflows of foreign capital resulting from a poor record of debt-servicing and an unhospitable investment climate. In this environment, political considerations have led Cuba to rely heavily on exports of professional services (in the areas of health, education and security) to Venezuela and a few other countries to finance its large oil import bill. These exports are part of a growing tendency to rely on barter trade.

In his analysis, Luis faces difficult problems related to the scarcity of data— problems that are common to most areas of Cuban economic statistics but are particularly severe in the external sector. He brings eclectic and imaginative solutions to these problems, for example by estimating flows of barter exports and imports on the basis of trade with countries like Venezuela, Ecuador, China and Russia, that are deemed not to require payment in cash for their exports to Cuba. He uses data on Cuban claims and liabilities vis-à-vis countries reporting to the Bank for International Settlements (BIS), and estimates for assets held in non-BIS countries. In the absence of published balance of payments data since 2009, he uses these estimates to construct a cash flow statement for the nation (essentially a balance of payments for convertible transactions). This allows him to derive residually a rough estimate of transfers, loans and investments received by

Cuba from Venezuela. These flows, together with Cuba's subsidized oil imports, illustrate the scale of island's dependence on Venezuela, which has allowed Cuba to use its limited cash flow resources to finance its convertible-currency imports. The dark side of the coin is that an interruption of this politically-inspired barter arrangement could result in a serious liquidity crisis.

Luis goes on to focus on Cuba's need for international liquidity. He builds a model in which the government's target for international reserves depends on two objectives: to support convertible trade; and to dampen the impact of external shocks related to the possible interruption of barter agreements. The analysis yields a table comparing actual levels of international liquidity in recent years with alternative target levels associated with various probabilities about the future occurrence of external shocks. The key result is that, in spite of a substantial increase in in recent years, actual levels of international liquidity fall short their target levels, even when the probability of a shock is as low as 20%. Given the deterioration of the economic situation in Venezuela, Luis concludes that external situation is dangerously vulnerable.

Of course, the Cuban authorities have used, and probably will continue to use other means to confronting troublesome external disturbances—such as the tropical storms, collapsing nickel prices, and world recession-induced decline in tourism that occurred in 2008—including foreign exchange controls and direct import restrictions. They also hope that Cuba's external position can be improved by boosting domestic oil production and reaching additional Venezuelan-style barter agreements with other oil exporting countries like Angola and Algeria. But these schemes are mostly patches that would perpetuate dependence and/or involve large efficiency costs. They are certainly no substitute for deep structural reforms that would expand export capacity and reduce Cuba's dependence on food and energy imports.

◆ ◆ ◆

In his article, *Lorenzo Pérez* tackles the difficult and politically sensitive problem of Cuba's foreign debt. Cuba defaulted on its external debt in the 1960's and did not try to renegotiate that debt for about 20 years. In the 1980s the country benefited from substantial assistance from the former Soviet Union, but this was eliminated in 1989-90; estimated arrears to Russia were reported to amount to over 21 billion rubles, with Russian officials claiming at that time that one ruble was worth one U.S. dollar. Since 1990 Cuba has engaged in bilateral negotiations with some of its creditors and until 2008 (when Perez' paper was published) it has honored most of its' debt-servicing obligations on new or refinanced credits. Debt to Russia (which took over the old Soviet debt) continued to be in arrears until recently. But in October 2013, Cuba and Russia announced that an agreement had been reached to write off 90% of that debt. Since the early 2000's Cuba has accumulated a large oil-related debt to Venezuela, although repayments until now have been very small because of the 10-year grace period specified in the Accord. Cuba affirms that it will re-pay this debt up to the last penny. "We shall see", was the comment of a senior Russian official.

At the end of 2006, the last year for which information was available when the article was finalized, the stock of Cuba's performing debt was $7.8 billion, most of which was medium- and long-term. The stock of non-performing debt was officially reported as $7.6 billion (most of which to Paris Club creditors) but this excluded arrears to Russia. Other sources report higher debt stocks, including $16.6 billion by the Economist's Intelligence Unit and 23.8 billion by the University of Miami. Turning to the indicators of debt sustainability, Pérez calculates Cuba's debt/GDP ratio at 40%, or somewhat below the ratios recorded by a sample of developing and transition debtors. However, when debt-sustainability is evaluated in terms of exports of goods and services, Cuban liabilities are much higher compared with the countries in his sample, suggesting a vulnerable external debt position.

Cuba can probably continue to muddle through for some time by continu-ing efforts to achieve bilateral agreements with some creditors and satisfying itself with very modest levels of external financing. However, achievement of external debt sustainability and resumption of satisfactory access to external finance will require a multilateral restructuring agreement with the Paris Club (which now includes Russia) and probably membership in the International Monetary Fund. Cuba will have to agree with the IMF on a comprehensive debt-sustainability exercise (which will involve the provision of heretofore unpublished economic statistics), and persuade the Paris Club that it will take the obligatory steps to eliminate the causes its payment difficulties. To the Cuban authorities these may appear to be strict conditions, but in fact they are in the county's clear long term interest. Without such an agreement Cuba may eventually face severe debt-servicing difficulties and be forced to reduce suddenly the gap between aggregate expenditure and income.

◆ ◆ ◆

G.B. Hagelberg passed away in 2011. He was a distinguished member of the Association for the Study of the Cuban Economy and an influential specialist on Cuba's agriculture. He will be sorely missed by friends and colleagues.

In his article on *"If it were only Marabú..."* Hagelberg paints a masterful, albeit depressing, picture of Cuban agriculture, and examines some relatively recent efforts to improve the situation. After years of neglect, stifling price controls, and reliance on heavy-handed bureaucratic procedures, the Cuban government began to recognize the need for changes aimed at arresting the Island's increasing dependence on food imports and the deterioration of its export-import food balance. Several measures were introduced after Raul Castro took over the reins of the economy, including the reimbursement of state debts to cooperative and private producers, some trimming of the inefficient and overstaffed Ministry of Agriculture, and some increases in procurement prices, notably for milk and beef. But these measures were modest, and in some cases were reversed: cancelled debts soon began to pile up again, and the rationalization of the Ministry of Agriculture was entirely insufficient.

A more important action was the large-scale grant in usufruct of idle state land to private farmers under decree-law 259 of 2008. The decree signaled, to quote Hagelberg, "the abandonment of the long-term held doctrine of the superiority of the state, large-scale, mechanized agriculture reliant on wage labor, of which Fidel Castro had been the foremost exponent in Cuba." Unfortunately, the potential benefits of decree 259 were weakened by the dense thicket of *marabú* that had invaded the land abandoned after the downsizing (*demolition* says Hagelberg) of Cuba's sugar industry. Another interesting measure was the introduction of the *Suburban Agriculture* program, which sought to reduce the distance between producers and consumers, to use men and animals instead of combustion engines, and compost instead of non-organic fertilizers. The announcement of the program gave rise to a flood of applications. But the task of the successful applicants was seriously complicated by the lack of hand tools, machinery and fuel, by insufficient bank credit, lack of experience, and by bureaucratic incompetence and harassment.

Of all the depressing stories about agriculture in communist Cuba, the tale of the sugar industry is among the most dramatic. In the crop year 2009/10, output had fallen more than 80% from its average level in the 1980's—a performance in line with Fidel Castro's assertion in 2005 that sugar was the "ruin" of the Cuban economy and belonged to the "era of slavery". The failure of the 2009/10 crop—the worst crop since 1905—was blamed on "bad organization" and "voluntarism". But Hagelberg observed that only half of the crops had been fertilized, only 3% irrigated, and that ceilings on sugar cane prices were the most repressive in the economy. In that area, as in others, the end of 'command and control' was the only real way to improve performance.

Hagelberg observed that the output in the major crops in 2009 was below its level in 2004, with the only exception of rice, although production of livestock had increased, except for poultry and eggs. He recognized, of course that it was too early to pass judgment on the effect of the recent reforms. But the data recently released by the National Statistical Office show a mixed picture: production in 2012 exceeded 2008 levels for rice, corn, beans, bananas and non-citrus fruits, but was below that level for horticultural crops, tubers and roots, tobacco and citrus fruits, justifying Hagelberg's view that optimism in the absence of further reforms was not justified.

The silver lining in the data is the clear over-performance of the non-state sector in most of the items listed in his Table 1: production of bananas, rice, corn, beans and non-citrus fruits increased in the non-state sector (in some cases substantially) while it fell in the state sector (dramatically in some cases); and output of horticultural crops, tubers and roots declined far less in the non-state than in the state sector. Only for citrus fruits was the drop in output equally severe in both sectors. From 2009 to 2012 deliveries for slaughter (in weight) remained virtually unchanged for beef and declined for pork (owing to a drop in state productions). The small increase in milk production was more than accounted for by higher output in the non-state sector. In evaluating these results, Hagelberg would have been confirmed in his strongly-held view that agriculture belonged in the hands of the private sector.

♦ ♦ ♦

In evaluating the prospect for market-oriented reforms most observers have stressed the difficulties associated with the country's distorted and command-driven economic regime. Among them, however, many believe that Cuba's relatively educated labor force is likely to be an asset in the reform process. In his article on *Schooling and Human Capital*, however, **Luis Locay** raises an important and intriguing question: how prepared is Cuba's labor force to operate in a market economy? At the outset Locay warns that it is difficult to answer this question, and that even if it could be answered it would not provide a simple guide for policy because the human capital requirements of a private economy cannot be predicted with any degree of certainty. He does believe, however, and he convincingly shows that the current distribution of occupations, knowledge, and skills in Cuba is very different from that prevailing in more market-oriented Latin American countries.

This finding should, at the least, temper the enthusiasm of those who believe that Cuba's alleged educational achievements have produced a labor force that is well prepared to operate in an environment where markets play an important role in allocating human resources. The source of that false optimism is in large measure the equation of "schooling" with human capital. Equating these two concepts may be legitimate in free economies, where investment in human capital is strongly influenced by the rewards and costs of education. But Cuba was, and remains, a command economy were decisions about key factors such as labor compensation, the fields of study, and the kinds of jobs that are available, are made largely by the government, often on the basis of ideological preferences. Choices are also severely restricted because individuals are prohibited from operating in the private sector in most key industries, including notably health care and education, reflecting the official view that, if the state financed your education you should work for the state and only for the state.

Locay's research concentrates on a broad comparison of Cuba and the rest of Latin America and shows that the distribution of employment by economic sector and by occupational categories is markedly different in Cuba than in other countries of the region. For example, the share of employment in the 'community and social services' sector is much higher in Cuba than elsewhere, while the shares of wholesale and retail trade, hotels and restaurants, financing, insurance, real estate and business services is considerably lower. In the same vein, Cuba has a relatively high proportion of workers in the professional and technical and in the administrative and managerial categories, but a below average proportion in the clerical and relate categories. In all these classifications, Cuba shows a significantly above-average deviations from sample averages, suggesting that the economic and professional distribution of its labor force differs appreciably from that of other countries.

Cuba also differs markedly from the rest of Latin America in terms of the distribution of University enrollment. In particular, the proportions of students enrolled in health care and education is well above the Latin American averages, while the shares of enrollment in commercial and business administration, social sciences, mass communication, and natural sciences are substantially lower than the regional averages. As a result, the proportions of doctor and educators in Cuba is much higher than elsewhere. Even bearing in mind the pitfalls in predicting the optimal distribution of jobs in a private economy, and even forgetting about the inadequacy of Marxist-trained teachers in such a system, it is difficult to escape Locay's conclusion: Cuba's concentration of employment in health and education cannot be sustained in a market-oriented economy.

Today, a large number of Cuban doctors and educators are working in 'friendly' nations. These professionals are generously compensated in the recipient countries— although, in line with a time-honored tradition, the Cuban government captures the bulk of that compensation. So the process is unjust, but it has helped to absorb the glut of medical and teaching personnel in Cuba. It also has helped, so far, to prevent the Cuban balance of payments from collapsing.

◆ ◆ ◆

The authors of the articles included in this book are all members of the Association for the Study of the Cuban Economy. I thank the Board of the Association for encouraging us to publish this book. I am also indebted to Roger Betancourt and Jorge Pérez López for helping me during the various stages of the publication process. They truly deserve the title of co-editors. Many thanks go to them and to the authors of this book for their dedication and their generous financial contributions that were indispensable to make this project a reality

1

THE CUBAN ECONOMY: A TIME FOR HOPE[1]

Oscar Espinosa Chepe

First of all, greetings to colleagues and friends participating in this important event. This Conference marks a period of 20 years of fruitful exchanges and arduous work on the part of our Association, a period during which valuable studies on the economy and other key aspects of the Cuban society have been accumulated. The wealth of knowledge collected during this period demonstrates the analytical and technical capability of our community residing abroad, which, together the one living in Cuba, will contribute substantially to the reconstruction of our Fatherland at the end of the long night of totalitarianism.

This conference takes place at a crucial moment in our country's history, when the economic situation, and the standard of living of the population are

---

[1] Presentation before the Annual Meeting of the Association for the Study of the Cuban Economy, August 2010.

worsening dramatically – which confirms the absolute failure of the development model applied for more than 50 years. Perhaps for that reason, the citizenry's awareness has matured considerably, and a consensus has emerged on the need for changes to shape a reconciled and non-exclusionary Cuba.

The sacrifices of the Cuban dissidence have contributed in large measure to this increased awareness—notably the cruel death of Orlando Zapata Tamayo, the persistent demands for the freedom of prisoners of conscience and peaceful political prisoners by the Ladies in White for more than 7 years, as well as Guillermo Fariñas' hunger strike. International support and solidarity have been very valuable, including the remarkable solidarity of our brothers abroad.

The Cuban Economy in 2009

The economy worsened in a striking manner in 2009. The growth of *real GDP* was reported to be 1.4%. But even this mediocre performance is hard to believe, given that on June 1 the production and services sectors reduced their consumption of energy by 12% owing to imposed cutbacks, so that many working centers had to close down partly or completely. No less conclusive is the fact that imports fell by almost 38%, markedly reducing the availability of inputs. The entire economy suffered fromthe scarcity of fuel, and only one half of the areas sown to sugarcane could be fertilized.

The *exports of goods* dropped by 21.4% in vale due to low prices for nickel, Cuba's leading export, weak markets for tobacco and rum and limited supplies of other gods. Since sugar is virtually unavailable, the opportunity was lost to take advantage of the high world prices for that product in 2009.

The announced growth of 4.5% in the *agricultural sector* seems unlikely, given the remarkable scarcity of many farm products throughout the year. Moreover, the reported expansion stands in contradiction with the 7.7% drop through the close in August in the volume of agricultural production (excluding sugar cane, and production in backyards and small plots) according to information published in October by the National Statistics Office. The reduction in non-cane harvests was 4.7% as of the date mentioned, while animal husbandry fell by 11%. Sugar output reached 1.38 million tons, 2.4% less than in the previous sugar harvest, with an industrial yield of only 10%--that is 22% below the average for the 10 years prior to 1959.

With regard to the *manufacturing industry* as a whole, the Physical Volume Index based on the origin of the products shows that less than half of the level reached in 1989 was attained; a 46.1% drop compared to 2008. By value, and excluding the sugar industry, a 0.1% decline from the previous year was announced.

Electric power generation rose only 0.2% in 2009, while losses reached 14.3% of the total—lower than the 15.9% reported for 2008, but still high. Oil and natural gas production fell by 9.1% and 0.5%, respectively. Data on nickel production and exports were not provided, for the second year in a row.

Growth rates reported for other sectors are truly debatable, including a a rise of 2.5% in tra*nsport, warehousing and communications* in spite of a severe shortage of fuel, and a 10% increase in *hotels and restaurants* even though earnings from tourism dropped by 10.3 % even though the number of foreign visitors rose 3.5% Equally strange is the increase in *construction* (0.6%), contrasting with a plunge in investment (16.0%) and in housing completions, which went from 44,775 units in 2008 to 35,085 units in 2009. In *domestic trade* even the minute growth that was announced (0.1%), was virtually impossible taking into account the acute scarcity of all types of articles that was observed even in the foreign-currency stores.

The same doubts arise regarding the increases reported for various services, in particular *science and technological innovation* (10.7%), education (1.5%) and *public health* and *social assistance* (3.4%), already intrinsically overvalued by a methodology that differs from that established by international organizations. These sectors must have been hard hit by the lack of energy resources and other inputs, especially raw materials for the manufacture of medical drugs, and in education by the new policy of drastically reducing boarding schools in the countryside.

Other overall indicators also lack credibility. The *Consumer Price Index*, which refers only to the market in national currency fell by 0.1%. Yet, because of scarcities, prices have shot up markedly, particularly in the black market (which accounts for a significant share of all transactions), and in agricultural markets, where supply fell appreciably in the early part of the year because of the effects of three hurricanes in the second half of 2008. Even the prices of goods subject to rationing, such as potatoes and peas, rose sharply. Prices for tubers increased from 40 cents to one peso per pound and for legumes from 20 cents to 3.50 pesos per pound.

In the external sector, total *trade in goods* dropped by 44.1%, with exports falling by 21.4% and imports by 37.4%. This triggered a noticeable reduction in the availability of inputs and had a decisive influence in the previously noted 25% drop in total investment in real terms, the huge liquidation of inventories, and the 18%drop in gross fixed capital formation, at constant prices. Thus, after some recovery in 2007-2008, there was a return to the de-capitalization of the early 1990s, with the ratio of gross fixed capital formation to GDP falling to 11, undoubtedly the lowest in the region, with the resulting adverse implications for the nation's development.

Exports of services increased 4.6%, at constant prices, which helped to offset the huge deficit on merchandise trade and contributed to a shift in the balance on goods and services to a surplus of 1.2 billion pesos in 2009. As is well known, exports of qualified labor to Venezuela, mainly physicians, paramedical staff and teachers, explain most of the rise in services exports in recent years, but they could vanish anytime in view of the delicate political situation in that country.

Another figure that offers little credibility is that for the unemployment rate which was reported at 1.7%. In April of the previous year, President Raúl Castro had announced that there were more than one million redundant workers in the state sector—more than 20% of a labor force of 5.1 million.

The government has taken some measures to repair the *fiscal situation*, such as reducing social assistance and expenditure in other budgeted areas. However, the money supply–which includes currency in circulation and time and savings deposits denominated in pesos—remains high at just over 25 billion pesos.

ONE has not published data for the *balance of payments*. Nevertheless, it is evident that the external financial situation is extremely serious. In 2009 Cuba froze back the assets of foreign concerns deposited in national banks, complicating relations with companies operating in the country. In fact, according to information published in September 2009, the number of firms with foreign capital declined from 314 to 258 at the end of 2008. Everything indicates that this trend has not been reversed. With regard to the *foreign debt*, prestigious publications such as *The Economist* place it in the neighborhood of 20 billion dollars. However, an item by the EFE news agency at the in May of this year ranked Cuba in the second spot on the list of Paris Club debtors, with a debt of 30.4 billion dollars.

After three years of consecutive decline, Cuba's *population* rose by 6529 persons in 2009, but demographic projections indicate that the decline will resume in 2010 and continue over the following 10 years. Among the factors that allowed the small demographic increase in 2009 was the birth rate which reached 11.6 births/1,000 inhabitants in 2009, compared with 10.9 in 2008. The mortality rate remained at 7.7 per 1,000 inhabitants, while child mortality edged up from 4.7 to 4.8 per thousand 1,000 live births.

At the end of 2009, 17.5% of the population was older than 60 years of age. *ONE* foresees that the trend toward aging will continue and that in 2020 more than a fifth of the population will be in its senior years. This will require a considerable increase in the resources dedicated to hospitals, nursing homes and other facilities. It will also increase the burden on the economically active population in a country where productivity levels are extremely low – a serious problem recognized by the authorities.

The continued rapid increase in pension liabilities has exceeded for some time the rise in workers' contribution to social security and this constitutes a disturbing problem. This increase occurred despite the fact that the average monthly pension at the end of 2009 was only 240.70 pesos, equivalent to 12 dollars. Faced with the worrisome demographic outlook, the government raised the retirement age for men to 65 years and that for women to 60 years – an economic palliative, but not a solution. The true solution would reside in creating the conditions for achieving a rise in productivity levels and freeing the citizenry's creativity, which is currently stifled by the lack of labor incentives, especially the low wages.

The *labor force* was of 5,159 thousand persons at the end of 2009, of whom 5,072 thousand \ were employed. This translated into an unemployment rate of 1.7%, one of the lowest in the world. As noted above, President Raúl Castro stated that there were more than a million redundant workers. An official study carried out at hospitals and polyclinics, which employ 70.4% of all workers in the health sector, concluded that more than 22,000 were not needed. Another study indicated that 7,000 unnecessary workers had to be relocated from the tobacco sector. The situation is similar in the sugar sector. The number of employees in the Basic Units of Cooperative Production (UBPCs) is considered to be excessively high; in some of them, security staff represented more than 10% of the workforce, while there was a shortage of agricultural workers.

The truth is that the rationalization of the workforce in Cuba is an imperative need. To reorganize the work centers and make them profitable with the existing large surplus of personnel is unthinkable. In order to raise the prevailing low rates of productivity–which dropped 1.1% in 2009–the first task should be to retain the workers who are really needed. This would also help to raise the existing low wages, which in 2009 averaged 429 pesos per month, equivalent to 21.45 US dollars.

Nevertheless, it is impossible to carry out this plan, without undertaking the economic reforms that would allow the surplus workers to move to sectors in urgent need of labor. Incentives and proper conditions need to be created, including decent wages. To create employment for the redundant workers the government should issue a broad authorization for self-employment, create small and medium-sized private enterprises, and provide for private ownership of land without the current prohibitions and hindrances. In addition, small stores and other small production units–individual or cooperative–as well as commercial and service centers, which are virtually impossible to control centrally, should be privatized. This would, in a first stage, facilitate the organization and resizing of the large state enterprises (a task that cannot be carried out now owing to excess staff) as well as the restructuring of the government's administrative system to make it considerably smaller, more effective and flexible, and less costly.

The restructuring of the workforce could also be a decisive element in the fight against corruption, which is rooted in a system that does not allow citizens to earn a decent living from honest work, while hindering their creativity and interest in their jobs. The evil of corruption also has its origin in the lack of control prevailing in the country, which creates ideal conditions for pilferage and speculation. In 2009, corruption reached high levels with the intensification of product shortages. Theft is no longer limited to warehouses, enterprises and budgetary units; there is stealing in electrical power towers, where profiles are pilfered with the danger of bringing them down; railroad ties and rails; benches and other items at bus stops; and non-payment of bus fares. Major scandals have involved high spheres of government, as happened recently with the Río Zaza enterprise, about which the government has yet to provide an explanation.

Labor indiscipline has reached striking levels, reflected in very high absenteeism, decamping during working hours, lack of interest in the work, and the shoddiness present in most sectors. All this leads to inefficiency and low productivity rates.

As regards the budget for 2009, the deficit is expected to narrow to 4.8% of GDP, down from 6.9% in the previous year. This would result from a reduction of expenditure, including cuts in a whole range of programs such boarding schools in the countryside and social assistance. Overall, there are elements of rationality this policy, but could reduce benefits accruing to the population without at the same time creating possibilities for citizens to earn income through an independent and honest job. If the cutbacks in social expenditure continue and measures are not taken to allow the population to defend itself economically, this could turn into another factor of dissatisfaction.

The Outlook for 2010

If there was a serious worsening of the economy in 2009, the outlook for 2010 is even worse. As Minister Marino Murillo Jorge himself acknowledged, even the meager GDP growth of 1.9% that is envisaged, is not consistent with the projected inflow of external resources. The Minister admitted that "... the volume of expenditure in foreign currency envisaged (in the Plan) falls short of the income which the country is expected to receive." This means that the financial underpinning for next year's plan is missing.

Although the authorities have not provided concrete data on the performance of the economy, available information indicates that the difficulties experienced in 2009 have continued in the first half of 2010. The shortage of foreign currency is evident and there continues to be a lack of liquidity to repay the frozen deposits of foreign companies with Cuban banks and to complying with other financial commitments. It may even be argued that circumstances are now worse, than last year because reserves shrank considerably during 2009.

The volume of farm output dropped in the first quarter of 2010 relative to the same period in 2009; there was a 13% reduction non-cane land cultivation and a 3.1% decline in animal husbandry. It should be recalled that the first quarter of 2009 was marked by the disastrous effects of the three devastating hurricanes that ravaged large areas of Cuba since September 2008. The drop in production has also reflected the generalized lack of inputs and fuel, particularly to satisfy the requirements of the tomato and potato crops, which were very poor.

The 10th Congress of the National Association of Small Farmers (ANAP) took place in May. In its conclusions, Minister Marino Murillo reported that 920,000 acres of land had been handed out in usufruct, in accordance with Decree-Law 259, but that around one half remain idle or insufficiently exploited. He threatened to take the land away from those farmers who keep the land unproductive, and to reassign the land to others, without taking into consideration the difficulties faced by the new producers who lack adequate resources, face many bureaucratic hurdles, and must deal with a land infested by weeds. In view of these difficulties, the failure of Decree-Law 259, which two years ago established the handover of idle lands to farmers, should not come as a surprise.

At the congress, the minister also stressed that the need for compliance with the contracts signed with the peasants: "... what is agreed must be sown, harvested and marketed, and should not be sold on the markets of supply and demand without proper certification that they constitute surpluses resulting from over-compliance with contracts, or that they are not subject to contractual obligations." From this it is inferred that pressure continues to be exerted on farmers to sow what is centrally deemed convenient, and to deliver the harvests according to the conditions and prices determined by the State—otherwise they will not be authorized to participate in the markets of supply and demand, where better prices are available for their products. At this event it was also announced that tax policy as a whole would be reviewed, and that this will affect the farm sector. If the inflexible current conditions under which the peasants work are also loaded with high taxes, without greater freedom to work and to sell their products, this policy could further affect the already depressed agricultural output, with even more disastrous results for the people's nutrition.

As regards cane production, although there is no data on the size of the harvest, existing estimates indicate that it may barely have exceeded one million tons. The Cuban press points out that on this occasion the yield per hectare averaged 27 tons of cane and that 59% of the enterprises had reached less than 30 tons/hectare, which means that the yield of cane per unit of surface is around one third of the international average, according to the Food and Agriculture Organization. In the period 2003-2008 the international yield was

67 tons/hectare, with countries like Brazil, the world's largest producer, reaching 77.6 tons/hectare.

In the case of tourism, by the end of May 1,225,717 visitors had arrived, 1.2% more than in the same period of the preceding year. Arrivals from Europe declined markedly so that the small increase with regard to 2009 was probably due to a rise in trips by Cubans traveling from the United States. Although figures on earnings from tourism have not been released, it is estimated that they were below the levels of last year owing largely to the depreciation of the euro, which makes Cuba more expensive for Europeans. Also playing a negative role is the unfavorable economic situation in the Old World, with the high unemployment levels current prevailing, especially in Spain. These factors ought to continue impinging unfavorably on the sector for the rest of the year, particularly if Cuba doesn't provide more competitive touristic offerings and keeps the exchange rate for the convertible peso unchanged.

In the other sectors of the economy, although precise data are unavailable, it is known that the scarcity of inputs and replacement parts is causing rising difficulties. This is reflected in lower activity in transport, as officially recognized. In the commercial area, the lack of supplies extends to basic products such as rice, beans, edible oil, medical drugs and even sugar, items that on occasion are hard to find even in the stores that sell in convertible pesos.

As regards the lack of economic control, the situation is not improving. In the second quarter, the General Comptroller of the Republic performed the "5th National Overview of Internal Control" on 20.0% of enterprises and budgetary units. Although not all the results have been published, it has been reported that 41% of enterprises audited were classified of "deficient" or "bad", including 19% of those listed under the hyped Enterprise Optimization. Accounting analysts who have been consulted have stated doubts about the quality of the auditing, adducing that many of the participating auditors lack the necessary qualifications for such a major undertaking. According to these criteria, the share of enterprises showing deficient or bad conditions is much higher, and that more than half of the enterprises and budgeted units in the country have untrustworthy accounting systems.

Added to all these problems, there is considerable uncertainty regarding the situation in Venezuela, shrouded in serious economic and political difficulties which could have negative effects on the strategic bilateral cooperation on which the Cuban economy depends.

The Budget for 2010, calls for reductions in both revenue and expenditure in relation to 2009 of 1.2% and 2.9%, respectively. This would translate into a deficit of 3.5% of projected GDP for the year, compared with 4.9% in 2009. Achievement of these goals, will require the following fundamental steps:

- the conversion of a group of budgeted units into enterprises,
- a 3.5% reduction in budgeted current expenditure,
- a cut in subsidies for enterprise losses,
- the government's refusal to finance some material investments, which must now be funded through bank credits.

This plan means the continuation of the policy of reducing social expenditure, including through the continued elimination of boarding schools in the countryside, a major rationalization of personnel, a cut in outlays for social assistance, and the closing down of workers' dining rooms and possibly of ministries. These steps might have a degree of economic rationality, but at the same time they reduce the standard of living of certain sectors of the population, without compensating options for those affected.

The first half of the year still did not see the structural and conceptual reforms promised three years ago by General Raúl Castro. The measures applied, while encouraging and perhaps the prelude to future changes, are often limited to cosmetic matters. As an example there is handing out under lease of barbershops and hairdressers' to individuals, or the reopening of the licenses to provide private transport. New, easier conditions have also been provided for the construction of dwellings with builders' own resources, and some establishments have been allowed to sell construction materials to the population. However, supply and transportation continue to be seriously deficient.

It has been recognized that other measures, like labor compensation based on results and *pluriemployment*, have yielded very limited results because, although in principle they are sensible and break with obsolete schemes, they do not work in the existing economic and social context. As regards the first of these measures, it is very hard to put it into practice at working centers with large labor surpluses, uncertainty about the supply of resources, and a suffocating bureaucratic environment. The miserable wages paid in a currency that isn't accepted by the majority of the government's own stores are another obstacle to payment for results, because it doesn't stimulate work effort; the same situation affects *pluriemployment*.

According to official figures, 97% of the people who have accepted an additional job have done so in education. Important measures have been adopted to attempt to reverse its continuous deterioration of this sector and increase the quality of teaching. The training of emerging teachers and of comprehensive high-school teachers have been suppressed, the former discreetly and the latter gradually, doing away with these noxious practices which harmed the quality of education. Additionally, university entrance exams have been established to raise the demand for knowledge, and more positions were made available to medium-level technicians and qualified workers—two categories that have been neglected even though they are in short supply. There is a certain rationality in the measures adopted to repair the considerable damage inflicted on the educational sector, including wage increases and improvements in the working conditions of educators at various levels. But many difficulties remain, such as the generalized scarcity of material resources and the persisting damaging effects of a dogmatic and politicized education.

At the same time, absurd programs such as the so-called Battle of Ideas, the 'social workers' and other aberrations have been discreetly disappearing. The violation of human rights persists and the first half of the year has seen brutal events such as the death of prisoner of conscience Orlando Zapata Tamayo and violent rallies of repudiation against peaceful women. It is nonetheless true that the level of debate on the problems of society has been expanded. This can be appreciated on Fridays in the Granma newspaper, where issues are being addressed that for many years were only raised by dissidents. Well-known intellectuals and artists, who for many years kept silent and in some cases unconditionally backed the regime, nowadays criticize fundamental aspects of policy and pronounce themselves in favor of changes.

2

THE GROWTH OF THE CUBAN ECONOMY IN THE FIRST DECADE OF THE XXI CENTURY: IS IT SUSTAINABLE?

Ernesto Hernández-Catá[2]

O fficial statistics indicate that the Cuban economy expanded at an exceptionally rapid pace during the first decade of the XXI century. The expansion was strong by international standards and very strong in comparison with Cuba's own performance in the previous decade. This paper seeks to understand the factors that accounted for Cuba's recent economic expansion and asks questions about its credibility and its sustainability.[3]

[2] I would like to thank Pavel Vidal, Lorenzo Pérez, Rolando Castañeda and Luis R. Luis for their valuable comments on previous drafts of this paper.

[3] This paper uses mostly data published by Cuba's National Statistical Office (*Oficina Nacional de Estadísticas*, or *ONE*). In its annual publication, the *Anuario Estadístico de Cuba*, ONE publishes a large number of statistical series on all aspects of the Cuban economy. However,

Characteristics of the Recent Expansion

Real GDP in Cuba rose at an average annual rate of 5.3 percent during the period 2000–2010 (Table 1, line 1). This was well above the growth of GDP in the world as a whole (3.7 percent), in the advanced countries (1.8 percent), and in Latin America and the Caribbean (3.5 percent), although it fell short of growth in the developing and emerging market economies (6.2 percent).[4] Real GDP growth in Cuba was quite variable during this period, partly because of sizeable year-to-year movements in the terms of trade. It was less strongly correlated with world output growth than was the case for major country groups — not surprisingly since Cuba is a relatively closed economy. Population growth during the decade was very small, and therefore real GDP per capita increased at approximately the same rate as absolute GDP.

Growth in Cuba was also exceptionally high by historical standards. As illustrated in Figure 1, the level of real GDP during the first decade of the XXI century[5] was always higher than in the corresponding year of the previous decade except for the first two years of each decade. Real GDP in the early 1990s had been severely affected by the end of Soviet assistance to Cuba, and it was only in 2005 that output exceeded its peak level of 1989.

---

certain sectors are insufficiently covered, such as the balance sheets of the Central Bank and the banking system, and some information has not been published for several years, notably on the balance of payments. Most importantly, the methodology used in deriving some of the statistics reported by ONE does not conform to international standards. This is particularly the case for the data on GDP originating in the social services sectors of the economy.

[4] Numbers for international groupings are from the International Monetary Fund's *World Economic Outlook.*

[5] References to the "first decade" of the XXI century relate to the 11–year period 2000–2010.

Table 1: Cuba: Key Economic Indicators

		2000	2001	2002	2003	2004	2005	2006	2007	2008	2009	2010
		Indicators of Economic Activity (percentage changes, unless otherwise noted)										
1	Real GDP	5.9	3.2	1.4	3.8	5.8	11.2	12.1	7.3	4.1	1.4	2.4
2	Real domestic purchases	4.0	3.9	0.4	4.7	4.7	6.8	16.5	4.1	2.9	-2.3	4.9
3	Total employment	0.5	2.9	1.2	1.1	0.8	1.7	0.7	2.4	2.4	2.5	-1.7
4	Participation rate	-0.4	1.1	0.3	0.0	0.1	1.5	0.0	2.2	1.4	0.9	-0.7
5	Unemployment rate (a)	5.4	4.1	3.3	2.3	1.9	1.9	1.9	1.8	1.6	1.7	2.5
6	Labor productivity	5.4	0.3	0.2	2.7	5.0	9.5	11.4	4.9	4.1	-1.1	4.1
	Fixed capital formation											
7	(% of GDP)	12.6	11.9	10.6	9.6	9.7	10.5	13.5	12.9	13.4	11.9	11.3
8	Capital stock, net	8.8	8.4	8.6	7.3	5.5	4.3	4.5	5.7	9.7	8.8	8.7
9	Utilization rate	1.4	10.0	4.2	3.6	2.4	5.6	0.2	9.0	5.9	3.0	-5.9
		Indicators of macroeconomic stability (percentage changes unless otherwise noted)										
10	Consumer prices	-3.0	-1.4	7.3	-3.8	-2.9	1.7	0.7	2.4	1.7	2.5	1.6
11	GDP deflator	1.8	0.5	4.5	3.0	0.6	0.3	10.4	3.6	-0.3	0.6	1.2
12	Consumption deflator	3.4	-0.5	0.1	0.7	-1.4	7.0	9.8	1.4	0.2	-0.8	0.5
13	Money (M2)	5.9	17.6	10.4	-0.6	7.3	34.7	2.7	7.5	16.9	1.7	1.7
14	Budget deficit (% of GDP)	-2.2	-2.3	-3.0	-3.0	-3.7	-4.6	-3.2	-3.2	-6.9	-4.9	-3.6
		Indicators of efficiency (percent of total)										
	Non-state sector shares of:											
15	Monetary earnings	12.1	12.8	12.7	14.1	12.7	15.6	13.2	12.1	15.6	17.1	20.5
16	Consumer purchases	28.6	28.3	28.0	28.1	25.1	22.9	18.9	19.2	19.3	19.6	20.6
17	Employment	21.8	28.8	18.0	18.3	20.4	19.6	18.2	17.1	16.9	16.2	16.1
18	Housing completions	51.9	52.0	28.5	53.1	46.0	63.5	73.3	57.1	58.2	44.6	36.0
		(percent of GDP)										
19	Government subsidies	10.4	8.5	9.2	9.7	9.6	10.1	9.6	10.5	15.0	12.0	10.1
	For enterprise losses	1.9	1.2	2.4	3.3	3.1	3.2	2.0	1.3	1.7	1.2	3.2
20	For price differentials	7.3	6.0	5.7	5.5	4.8	3.5	2.6	2.8	4.5	5.7	3.5
	Other	1.2	1.2	1.1	0.9	1.6	3.4	5.0	6.4	8.8	5.1	3.4

Sources and methods: see Annex.

Figure 1. Cuba: Real GDP in Current and Previous Decades
(in billions of pesos)

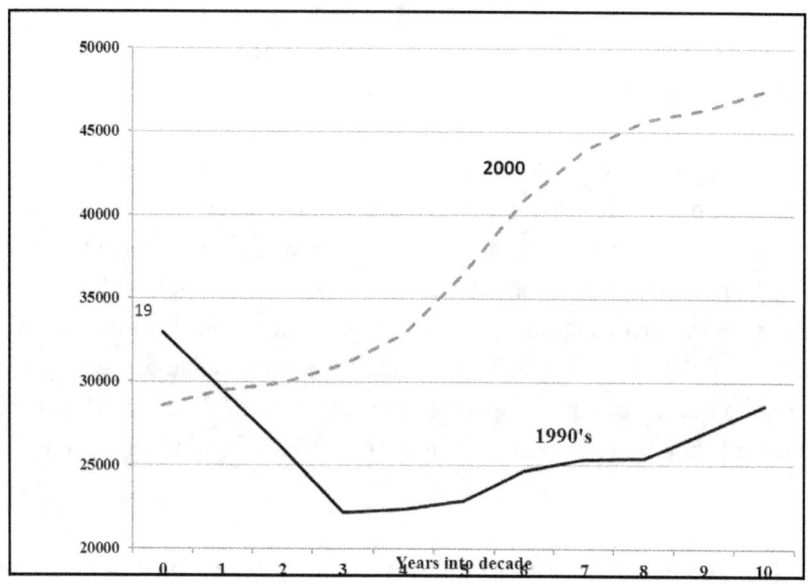

Figure 2. Cuba: Growth of Real GDP and Gross Domestic Purchases
(percentage changes)

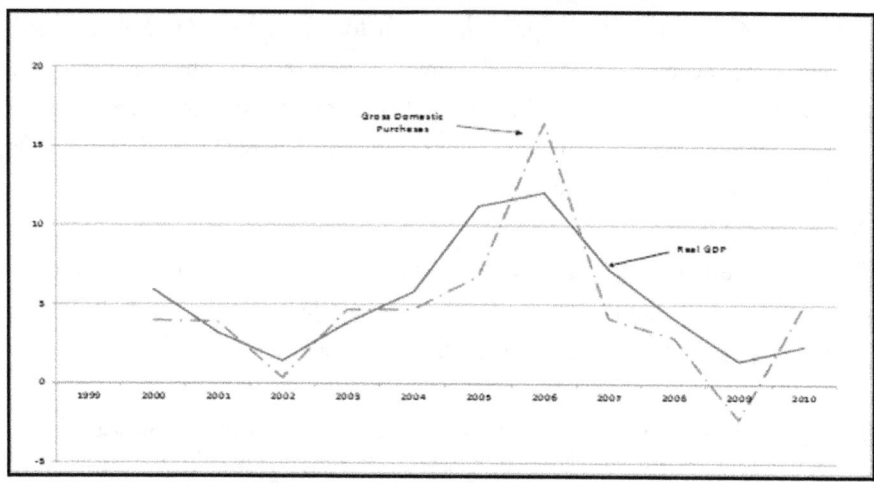

The evolution of growth from 2000 to 2010 features three distinct sub-periods: a moderate slowdown in 2000–02, a sharp acceleration in 2003–06, and a pronounced slowdown in 2007–10 (see Figure 2). As explained more fully below, these sub-periods were associated with large changes in government spending, investment, and exports of services to Venezuela.

Growth in 2000–10 was concentrated in the services sectors. Output fell in agriculture and in the sugar sector, while industry and construction jointly accounted for only 15 percent of the total increase in GDP. Among the tertiary sectors, transportation and communications, commerce, hotels and restaurants, and financial intermediation together accounted for almost 30 percent of the rise in real GDP. Other services combined for a remarkable 55 percent of the total rise in output: culture & sports (8 percent), administration and defense (6 percent); education (9 percent); and public health (a whopping 38 percent).

Real GDP in the public health sector increased at an unbelievable average annual rate of 21 percent from 2004 to 2010 — unbelievable, that is, until you learn that it reflected the activities of Cuban doctors and medical personnel in Venezuela and a few other Latin American countries (more on this in the following sections). But there is more to the story. In 2005, the government announced that it would value social services at a much higher price than is customary in the United Nation's system of national accounts. The most dramatic manifestation of this change was an 80 percent increase in real GDP in the health and social assistance sector in 2005! Nothing, not even the rise in the output of Cuban medical personnel in Venezuela, could possibly justify such a massive increase.

The average annual growth of **employment** in the period 2000–10 was 1.7 percent (line 3 of Table 1) — a relatively high number considering Cuba's stagnating population.[6] It resulted from an increase in the participation rate,

---

[6] Population increased by 1/2 of one percent (annual rate) in 2000–2010, remained virtually unchanged during the second half of the decade, and actually fell in 2010. The population of working age rose by even less (1/3 of 1 percent); it also fell in 2010, as did employment and the labor force.

which in turn reflected a transfer of redundant employees (particularly in the sugar sector) to study programs, where they were counted as employed. The rate of unemployment declined from to 5.4 percent in 2000 to 2.5 percent in 2010. This is a remarkably low rate by international standards, but it is really not much to write home about: President Raúl Castro himself recognized that there is a huge rate of hidden unemployment in the public sector. Nevertheless, the decline in unemployment is an indication of the rapid absorption of economic slack during the period.

Real gross fixed capital formation averaged 11.6 percent of GDP in 2000–2010 (line 7). This was low by the standards of other developing and transition economies but well above Cuba's average in the 1990s. (Investment plunged in 1989–1994 following the end of Soviet assistance, although it recovered during the rest of the decade.) The ratio of fixed investment to GDP declined in the first four years of the XXI century, but surged in 2004–08, resulting in rapid growth in the net capital stock (line 8). Moreover, the rate of utilization of capital is estimated to have increased substantially during the decade (line 9).

The **annual rate of increase in the official Consumer Price Index (CPI)** averaged ½ of one percent in 2000–2010. Except for a spike in 2002, consumer price increases were low or negative throughout the period, significantly lower on average than in the emerging market, developing countries, and the Latin American groups in the IMF's *World Economic Outlook* classification. As Oscar Espinosa Chepe (2000) observed, the basket used in constructing the official CPI includes only items sold in national currency markets, where many products remain subject to price controls. However, Vidal (2010) has pointed out that the CPI basket does include uncontrolled prices sold in informal and self-employment markets, with a combined weight of 30 percent. Therefore, what is missing from the CPI basket, are those items sold in convertible peso (CUC) markets. Those prices are government controlled, but they are occasionally raised by considerable amounts — Espinosa-Chepe mentions increases in diesel fuel and gasoline prices of 33 percent and 20 percent, respectively, in 2008. It should be noted that the deflators for GDP and household consumption increased somewhat faster than the CPI during the decade, although movements in the three price variables were correlated (lines 10 through 12). The behavior of prices in the context of Cuba's monetary policy is examined below.

Can Cuba's Recent Growth be Accounted for?

The collapse of investment and the steep deterioration of the terms of trade associated with the cessation of Soviet aid explains part of the massive contraction of Cuba's real GDP in the period 1989–1993. However, these factors account only for a small fraction of the subsequent recovery and expansion in 1994–99. Therefore, explanations for that period have focused on the macroeconomic stabilization and structural reform measures adopted around 1993–94, which were thought to have boosted total factor productivity, and therefore output growth.[7] In particular, a remarkably strong fiscal adjustment brought down sharply the budget deficit and the level of state subsidies from the record levels observed during the 1990–92 recession. Furthermore, various structural measures resulted in a significant rise in the participation of the private and cooperative sectors in the economy, and the de-criminalization of the use of the U.S. dollar helped to boost remittances from Cubans residing abroad.

A Neo-Classical Approach

The situation in the first decade of the XXI century was quite different. First, as indicated in the previous section, the growth of capital and employment was fairly strong and is estimated to have made substantial contributions to GDP growth (Table 2). It should be noted that the estimated contribution of employment is probably overstated for two reasons: (i) students are now considered employees in the Cuban statistics rather than members of the inactive population; and (ii) an unknown but significant share of state

---

[7] See Hernández-Catá (2000).

employment has virtually zero productivity and is therefore inactive for all practical purposes. In addition to the brisk expansion of the capital stock, the rise in capacity utilization (a variable intended to capture the extent to which the capital stock is actually utilized), also made a substantial contribution to growth.

Large terms of trade effects occurred from year to year, but they were relatively small for periods of 3–4 years. (The Annex explains how this variable was calculated.) For, example, there was a huge negative effect in 2008 due mostly to the collapse of world nickel prices and a rise in the price of oil, but this was partly offset by a sizeable terms of trade improvement in 2010 when both nickel and sugar prices rose. However, residual growth (i.e., the growth of output that remains unexplained after taking into account the growth of inputs) is still large and volatile—which is not surprising in view of the mysteries of Cuban data and the limitations of the growth accounting framework. Much of the large positive residual shown for the period 2003–06 in Table 2 probably reflects the overstatement of output growth in the health sector that was referred to above.

Table 2. Cuba: Accounting for the Growth of Real GDP
(percentage changes at annual rates)

	2000–02	2003–06	2007–10	2000–10
Real GDP growth	3.5	8.2	3.8	5.3
Contributions to GDP				
growth of changes in:				
employment	2.6	0.7	1.0	0.8
capital	2.6	1.6	2.5	2.2
capacity utilization	1.6	0.9	0.9	1.1
terms of trade	-0.6	0.2	-0.4	-0.3
residual	-2.6	4.8	-0.1	1.6

Sources and methods: see Annex.

A Keynesian Approach

The exercise presented in the previous sub-section sought to account for the growth of output from the supply side. This section raises a different question: can the growth of production also be explained in terms of the expansion of the "exogenous" components of aggregate demand? Table 3 seeks to answer this question using a highly simplified Keynesian framework. In this framework, investment, exports of goods and services, and government current expenditures are considered exogenous (i.e., independent of national income), while private consumption and imports are endogenously related to income through fixed marginal propensities. For simplicity, the Keynesian multiplier is assumed to be one.[8]

It is clear from the table that the sharp rise in current government spending during the middle years of the decade (which affected all major categories of expenditure) was the main source of growth in aggregate demand. It was followed by the growth of exports and investment. As explained more fully below, the rising contribution of exports reflected mostly increasing exports of services to Venezuela.

---

[8] These are, of course, highly simplified assumptions. In particular, imports are determined not only by national income, but also by administrative controls; and both exports and imports depend upon relative prices.

Table 3. Cuba: Growth of Real GDP and the Exogenous Components of Aggregate Demand

(Percentage contributions to GDP growth, annual rates)

	2000–02	2003–06	2007–10	2000–10
Growth of real GDP	3.5	8.22	3.8	5.33
Resulting from changes in:				
1. Exogenous components of demand	2.28	7.86	3.64	4.68
Investment	0.47	1.76	0.05	0.66
Current government expenditure	0.91	4.30	1.07	2.20
Exports of goods and services	0.91	1.80	2.50	1.81
2. Terms of trade	-0.60	0.19	-0.35	-0.30
3. Residual	1.82	0.18	0.51	0.94

The Role of Policies

Macroeconomic Policies

In attempting to explain residual growth (i.e., that part of GDP growth not explained by input growth or terms of trade effects) we ask whether economic policies may have been at work. Beginning with macro-stabilization policies, the **fiscal deficit** of the central and local governments widened in relation to GDP from 2.2 % in 2000 to 6.9 % in 2008, before narrowing to 3.6 percent in 2010 (Line 14 of Table 1). The deficit averaged 3¾ percent of GDP for the decade as a whole, and never came close to the alarming levels recorded early in the previous decade. This is partly because much of the surge in state expenditure was accompanied by an increase in Venezuelan oil subsidies and payments for services provided by Cuban professionals. In sum, from the standpoint of macro-stabilization, fiscal policy was expansionary through 2008, and restrictive in 2009–10, i.e., since President Raúl Castro took control of economic policy.

Government subsidies (an indicator of both macro-stability and efficiency) rose in relation to GDP by two percentage points from 2000 to 2010. The government did a creditable job in keeping subsidies for enterprise losses under control, and there was a decline in subsidies associated with price differentials (which reflect mostly the gap between import and domestic sales prices for food and medicines). However, a mysterious category of "other subsidies" surged, reflecting probably Venezuelan subsidies on Cuban oil imports. Figure 3 shows how the major types of subsidies evolved over the past two decades.

Has **monetary policy** played a role in stabilization? There is no perceptible correlation between inflation and money growth in the short run (see table 1, lines 10 through 13). In the long-run, however, there is a significant correlation between currency and prices, and also between M2A and prices.[9] It is likely that monetary policy has restrained the growth of non-controlled prices so far in the XXI century. But inasmuch as 70 percent of the prices in the local currency sector are still controlled (and to the extent that they are not adjusted), changes in the money supply can translate into changes in the monetary overhang rather than inflation, thus limiting, but not suppressing, the efficacy of monetary policy (see Hernández-Catá, 2011).

In sum, **inflation** remained subdued in 2000–10 partly because of price controls and partly because a restrained monetary policy kept the expansion of aggregate demand from outpacing the rise in potential output in spite of the surge in government expenditure. An additional restraining factor was the rigidity of nominal wages, which are not indexed to inflation and in fact have risen slowly during the decade. Finally, the interpretation of monetary policy is complicated by the fact that the published monetary aggregates include only assets denominated in non-convertible pesos (CUPs), thus excluding those denominated in CUCs. Accordingly, the point made by Espinosa Chepe with respect to consumer prices is also relevant here.[10]

---

[9] M2A is currency plus time and saving deposits denominated in non-convertible pesos.

[10] This is an area where secrecy complicates analysis. A price index constructed as a weighted average of prices in national currency and in CUCs would help the analysis of monetary policy, as would information on the evolving share of prices subject to state control.

The current account of the **balance of payments** remained under control through 2007, but it came under substantial pressure in 2008. The value of Cuba's merchandise exports weakened owing to the slowdown in world economic activity, and actually fell in 2009 as national income dropped in Cuba's major trading partners, including Venezuela and Western Europe. Receipts from tourism also fell in 2009, while interest payments on the country's external debt surged. Against this background, and with import demand increasing rapidly, the central bank defended the exchange rate of the peso through intervention in the foreign exchange market, administrative restrictions on imports, foreign exchange rationing and, most dramatically, a freeze on CUC-denominated bank accounts held by foreign concerns.

As Vidal (2010) convincingly argued, the central bank must have intervened heavily in both 2008 and 2009 to sterilize the effects of unusually large fiscal deficits on the money supply and maintain price stability. Whatever the short-run effects of that policy on domestic prices, it evidently helped to keep the **exchange rate** fixed. However, Vidal is right in that intervention is a costly way to maintain internal and external stability and that it would have been better to let the peso depreciate, thus changing relative prices and providing the incentives needed to improve the external balance. It is also important for the central bank to remember the heavy price paid by many countries that insisted on defending an overvalued exchange rate since the Mexican crisis of 1994, including Russia, Turkey Indonesia, Korea, and Argentina. Finally, while there is no doubt that a depreciation of the peso will help to improve the current account balance, the improvement will materialize only if domestic expenditure is reduced relative to domestic output. In that fundamental sense, the tightening of fiscal policy under the Raúl Castro administration was entirely appropriate, if not indispensable.

Structural Policies

We now turn to micro-policies and ask whether the **private sector** was allowed to play a more important role in the economy. Data on the private share of GDP are not available in Cuba, but there are a number of indirect proxies for the importance of the private sector, and they show a mixed picture (lines 15 to 18 in Table 1). For example:

- The monetary earnings of the non-state sector (particularly its non-agricultural component) increased rapidly during 2000–2010, and the non-state share of total monetary earnings surged from 12 percent of GDP in 1990 to over 20 percent in 2010. These earnings reflect only payments received from state organizations and exclude payments among entities in the non-state sector.
- The share of household consumption supplied by markets in the non-state sector fell from 29 percent in 2000 to 21 percent in 2010.
- Most disappointingly, the share of the non-state sector in total employment fell during the decade from 22 percent to 16 percent.
- The proportion of agricultural land operated by the non-state sector increased from 64 percent in 2007 to 83 percent in 2011, in spite of a drop on the share of UBPCs — the Basic Units of Cooperative Production that were created in 2004 and have been struggling since then. Most of the increase came from private farms and the Cooperatives of Credit and Services (CCS). However, as pointed out by Nova González (2012), the conditions of land tenure remain fraught with uncertainties that discourage producers, and the prevalence of non-market prices squeezes farm profits and constitutes a major disincentive to producers.
- Finally, the private share of housing completions fell from 52 percent to 36 percent. This indicator is unreliable, however, because the series is extremely volatile.

In sum, it is difficult to infer from these indicators that the relative importance of the private sector has increased or that this sector has contributed appreciably to output or productivity growth in the first decade of the XXI century.

Has the economy become more open to **foreign trade**? The ratio of total merchandise trade (exports *plus* imports) to GDP did rise from about 23 percent in 1990 to 32 percent in 2010. However, almost 60 percent of that increase reflected transactions with Venezuela, much of it in oil — hardly a sign of improved competitiveness. Cuban imports in general remain highly sensitive to changes in national income; Vidal (2008) has estimated the income elasticity of imports at 3.

Was there evidence of **fiscal decentralization**? None that is very persuasive. The share of total government expenditure executed by local jurisdictions has oscillated between 30 percent and 34 percent in recent years, without exhibiting any discernible trend. The share of investment carried out by the central government rose from 46 percent in 2000 to almost 82 percent in 2007, but then dropped to an annual average of 62 percent in 2008–10. Local governments are still barred from undertaking capital projects.[11]

To sum up, it is hard to find evidence that structural measures helped to improve economic performance in the first decade of the XXI century. This was to be expected given the policy changes introduced in the middle of the decade that amounted to a wholesale backtracking from the market liberalization measures adopted in1993–94. These changes included the harassment and over-taxation of the small private services sector, the prohibition of several self-employment activities, and various measures that reduced sharply the autonomy of state enterprises, culminating in the obligation to deposit all hard currency earnings in a single account (*cuenta única*) at the central bank.

Another repressive measure adopted in 2003–04 was the re-prohibition of the U.S. dollar, effectively ending the period of dollarization that had started in 1994. The old system was replaced by an abstruse **multiple exchange rate system** that introduced numerous distortions and discriminates against export-oriented enterprises while subsidizing import-intensive lines of production.[12] The evolution of the exchange system is summarized in Table 4.

But things have changed since then. Indeed, some of the recently-adopted or announced measures could have a significant effect on productivity.

First, implementation of a plan to fire as many as half a million employees from the public sector (roughly one tenth of the work force) has started. ONE

---

[11] The numbers for non-government investment (corresponding mostly to state enterprises) were obtained by subtracting government investment (budget basis) from total investment (national accounts basis). They must be interpreted with caution because of methodological differences between the two series.

[12] For a clear analysis of the problems involved see Vidal (2009 and 2012).

has recently reported that private employment jumped from 589 thousand at the end of 2010 to 929 thousand at end-2011, reflecting largely a surge in self-employment. As a result, the share of non-state employment rose during 2011 from 16 percent to almost 23 percent. A further substantial transfer of employees from the public to the private sector — provided the latter is ready to absorb them — would help to reduce disguised unemployment and greatly increase the average productivity of the national labor force.

Second, sales and purchases of homes and cars by residents have been authorized.

Third, the list of private employment categories authorized to operate legally was expanded, although it remains short, and prohibition in the absence of explicit authorization remains the rule. Moreover, categories such as engineers, accountants, economists, doctors and nurses, professional athletes and educators, remain confined to the state sector. Yet they could make a substantial contribution to economic activity and welfare if allowed to operate privately.[13]

Fourth, a legal framework that would authorize access to bank credit by the self-employed, microenterprises, and private farmers was published in 2011 (Vidal, 2012, provides a full description). The framework also considers the possibility of (i) allowing households to access bank credit to purchase houses and cars; and (ii) authorizing the private sector to use bank deposits to make payments. This could have implications for the conduct of monetary policy since the private sector so far has been restricted to use currency for payments, complicating its relations with state enterprises that operate almost exclusively with bank accounts.

Fifth, sales of various consumer goods (including computers and DVDs) have been authorized.

---

[13] In the case of health practitioners and educators, permission to operate privately could help to avoid unemployment if and when those now working abroad were to return home.

Table 4. Cuba: Evolution of the Multiple Exchange Rate System

	1994	2000	2001	2003	2004	2005	2011
U.S. dollar	Legalized	--------------------->replaced by			ceases to be		
	<-----------dollarization period------------> CUC				legal tender		
Cuban peso[14]	<--------------------Fixed against US $ throughout the period------------------->						
CUC[15]	Introduced <---------- currency board----------------->					revalued vs. US $	devalued vs. US $
Exchange rates							
Peso/U.S. $							
Official	1.0	1.0	1.0	1.0	1.0	1.0	1.0
Exchange houses[16]	95	21	24.2	24.2	24.2	22.3	22.3
Pesos/CUC[17]	21	21	26–27	26–27	26–27	24–25	24–25
CUC's/U.S.$[18]	1.0	1.0	0.93	0.93	0.93	0.93	1.00

Source: Sources and methods: see Annex.

Finally, the permission given to Cuban citizens to visit hotels heretofore reserved for foreign tourists eliminates an unjust and unnecessary form of discrimination.

As promising as they are, however, these measures are very recent, and they could not have influenced economic performance in the period under review in this paper. Moreover, these measures still have to be implemented in full. Even if they are, serious distortions would remain in many sectors of the economy, including controls on imports and foreign exchange, limitations on the legality and size of private firms and on the autonomy of state enterprises, interest rate controls, and an absurd multiple exchange rate system. Last but not least the system of price controls continues to distort resource allocation and interfere with the effectiveness of

---

[14] Currently used in inter-enterprise transactions and for official accounting.

[15] Peso Cubano Convertible.

[16] Implicit exchange rate based on the peso/CUC and CUC/dollar rates.

[17] In exchange houses (CADECA); applies to household transactions.

[18] A 10 % tax on conversion of dollars into CUCs applies since 2005.

macroeconomic policies. A particularly sad example of the damage caused by this system is the exploitation of Cuban farmers through the imposition of high input prices and low sales prices by the bureaucratic empire of *Acopio*.

Dependency and Sustainability

In several periods of its independent history, Cuba has relied on various forms of assistance granted by foreign nations. For a long time in pre-revolutionary days, Cuba benefited from a preferential sugar quota granted by the United States. In the 1980s, Cuba received massive amounts of aid from the Soviet Union, mostly in the form of subsidies on oil imports and on nickel and sugar exports. Now Cuba receives subsidies on imports of Venezuelan oil and large payments for the services rendered in Venezuela (and other "friendly" Western Hemisphere countries like Bolivia and Nicaragua) by Cuban doctors, teachers, and military and security personnel. These payments have exceeded by a substantial margin the value of salaries that would have been paid under usual international practice (Castañeda, 2011).

Table 5 shows two rough proxies for Venezuelan payments to Cuba. For comparison, it also shows Soviet assistance flows in the 1980s, which were very large until they suddenly vanished in 1990 because the Soviet Union disappeared and Russia could not afford, and did not wish, to continue carrying the burden. Precise information on Venezuelan aid to Cuba is not available from the countries involved, but two indicators based on data published by ONE and presented in Table 5 can help to gauge its magnitude. These indicators suggest that, in relation to Cuba's GDP, inflows of Venezuelan aid in recent years have been large, albeit lower than the peak values of Soviet aid in the period 1985-88. Cuba's dependence on Venezuelan payments is reflected in both the balance of payments and the fiscal accounts.

Table 5 presents the two indicators: for the relevant periods. Venezuela's total contribution to Cuba's budgetary revenue (the "budget proxy"); and the value of services provided by Cuban personnel abroad (the "BOP proxy").

Table 5. Cuba: Estimated Foreign Assistance Inflows in the 1980's and the 2000's

Flows from the Soviet Union in the 1980s	1985	1986	1987	1988	1989	1990
Billions of dollars	4.5	4.5	4.5	4.5	2.2	0
Percent of GDP	*22.3*	*22.9*	*23.3*	*22.2*	*10.7*	*0*

Flows from Venezuela in the 2000s	2005	2006	2007	2008	2009	2010
Budget proxy						
Billions of dollars	3.0	2.5	4.7	8.3	11.5	16.6
Percent of GDP	*7.1*	*4.7*	*8.1*	*13.7*	*18.5*	*16.6*
BOP proxy						
Billions of dollars	4.1	4.4	5.7	6.2	5.7	7.2
Percent of GDP	*9.7*	*8.4*	*9.8*	*10.2*	*9.2*	*11.3*

Source: Sources and methods: see Annex.

➤ The **"budget proxy"** is equal to non-tax government revenue net of state enterprise contributions and subsidies to "other enterprises". The latter, which corresponds broadly to subsidies associated with purchase of Venezuelan oil, must be be netted out to avoid double counting.[19]

➤ The **"BOP "proxy",** which is expected to capture payments associated with Cuba's exports of professional services to Venezuela, is equal to

---

[19] This is because, in essence, oil imports are bartered against Cuban exports of professional services. In theory, Cuban oil purchases are debt-financed. But with an interest rate of 1 percent and a grace period of 10 years, Cuba right now is paying very little for its oil imports. If all transactions with Venezuela were eliminated, oil imports presumably would remain roughly unchanged in the near term (except that Cuba would have to contract with other suppliers and pay for oil with cash or short-term debt). At the same time, however, exports of professional services and non-oil transfers from Venezuela would disappear, and this would constitute the net effect on the current account of the Cuba's balance of payments.

Cuban exports of services minus receipts from tourism and transportation. The numbers are close to those reported, typically for a single year, by other authors. For example, Castañeda (2011) cites estimates of $4.5 billion for 2006, $5.2 billion for 2007 and $6.4 billion for 2008, while Lopez (2012) reports an annual average of $5.1 billion for 2007–10.

➢ The difference between the "budget" and the "BOP" proxies becomes very large in 2008-2010, owing probably to transfers and investments from BANDEC (the *Banco de Desarrollo Económico y Social*) and other Venezuelan state agencies.[20] Of course the difference could also result from the inclusion in both proxies of items unrelated to transactions with Venezuela, and from other errors and omissions.[21]

A large part of the revenue from Venezuelan aid is offset in the budget accounts by matching expenditures on exports of health and education, by the pass-through to Cuban enterprises of Venezuelan oil import subsidies, and by government investments. In the end, the effects on the fiscal deficit of discontinuing Venezuelan payments to Cuba probably would not be very large. Unfortunately, this cannot be said about the effect on economic activity. I recently estimated the impact of ending Venezuelan payments (including the net effect of the doctors/teachers/soldiers and spies program) would be, using 2011 as a baseline, in the range of 7 to 10 percent of GDP.[22]

---

[20] Lopez (2012) estimates these subsidies at roughly 4 billion a years in in 2007-2010.

[21] Because it is derived from balance of payments statements, the estimates in Table 5 do not include "below the line" items such as loans which, in principle, should be recorded in the capital account of the balance of payments.

[22] See Hernández-Catá (2012).

How will Cuba Finance Food Imports and Service its' External Debt?

Surplus on Services and Deficit on Trade

Since 2004, the Cuban balance of payments has shown a rising trend in two important items: (i) the merchandise trade deficit; and (ii) interest payments on Cuba's external debt.[23] The trade deficit reflects large and growing fuel and food imports (about one-half of total imports in recent years) as well as the depressed level of exports. The twenty-year period can be broken down into three sub-periods.

From 1989 to 1993 the trade deficit narrowed as the disappearance of Soviet assistance forced a sharp contraction of imports.

From 1994 to 2003 the combined negative items rose and then stabilized at a high level, as the trade balance deteriorated. However, this was compensated by a strong rise in tourism. Later, the de-criminalization of the U.S. dollar in 1993–94 encouraged a rapid increase in remittances received by Cuban residents from their relatives abroad.

After 2004, interest payments and net imports surged while foreign remittances declined following the restrictions imposed in 2005, and tourism ran out of steam around the turn of the century. However, these changes were offset by a large increase in receipts from the state-sponsored activities of Cuban personnel stationed mostly in Venezuela. Considering Cuba's inability to sustain a massive increase in borrowing from world markets, this "Venezuelan miracle" avoided the need to slash imports or interest payments, both of which would have been problematic in Cuba's circumstances.

---

[23] For a comprehensive analysis of external developments, see Pérez-López (2011), and Pérez (2009).

The miraculous advent of the new "special transactions" prevented the Cuban balance of payments from crashing. Whether or not these transactions represent economic value is a matter of taste. What is clear is that if these transactions were to disappear, or to fall substantially, Cuba could face a severe balance of payments crisis.[24]

What Should Be the Policy Response?

In 1989–1990, the Cuban government reacted to the disappearance of Soviet aid by providing massive subsidies to state enterprises from its own budget. The resulting fiscal deficits were financed by monetary expansion and, with most prices rigidly controlled, this led to a huge monetary overhang and to forced saving on households. It was all a big mistake, and a steep contraction of investment and production could not be avoided. After this short and disastrous attempt to deal with the crisis by brute force, in 1993–94 the Cuban government launched a far-reaching stabilization plan involving a sharp across-the-board reduction in government expenditure and structural measures that fostered economic recovery from the supply side. The economic history of that period provides invaluable lessons that should not be forgotten.

Now, the interruption of Venezuelan aid could result in a contraction of real GDP—not as dramatic as the one stemming from the cessation of Soviet aid in 1989–90, but still involving serious consequences for the standard of living of the population. Clearly, it would not be wise to hope that this will never happen, to wait until it happens, or to wait for another "miracle" to occur. Extending the doctors' and teachers' program to Angola and Algeria will not be a permanent

---

[24] The Cuban authorities may be able to delay the adjustment by dipping on their foreign exchange reserve if there are any left after several years of large-scale intervention to defend the peso. Cuba has not published capital account data for several years now. However, Luis Luis (2010) has estimated, using Bank for International Settlements (BIS) data, that Cuba accumulated assets in BIS-area banks to the tune of US$4 billion during the period 2005–2009. The part of that increase corresponding to the Central Bank of Cuba is unknown, but from analytical standpoint this is relatively unimportant because Cuban banks are generally under government control,

solution. Waiting for oil to flow out of the Caribbean wells would be risky and could take too much time. The only way out is an audacious program of structural actions to remove those controls that stifle the country's capacity to produce, to invest, and to export. This program should include:

Figure 3. Cuba: State Subsidies
(In percent of nominal GDP)

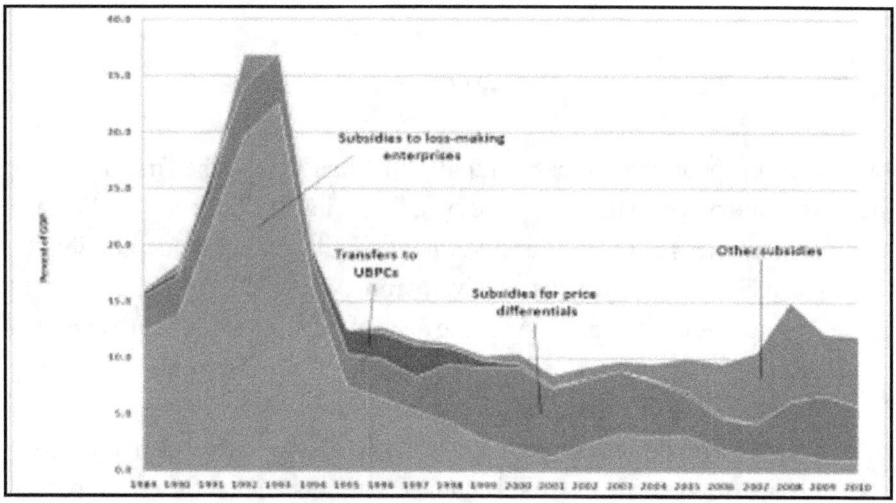

- the elimination price controls;
- the unification of the exchange rate system with a market-determined value for the Cuban peso;
- an aggressive plan to increase the number of employment categories opened to the private sector;
- continued efforts to reduce public sector employment and increase the flexibility of wages;
- and intensification of the ongoing efforts to reform the banking system and expand the availability of credit to the non-state sector, particularly in agriculture.

These actions should be coupled with restrained monetary and fiscal policies aimed at avoiding the large budget deficits high inflation that could otherwise result in the hopefully growing, non-regulated sector, particularly during the period following a devaluation of the peso. Finally, a gradual restructuring of the budget should be started. It would involve a shift in expenditure from budgetary subsidies and from the education and health sectors (which could happen automatically with the ending of Venezuelan programs), to infrastructure, social security (a sector in financial difficulty because of the aging of the population), and social assistance, and the creation of a system of unemployment insurance.

Conclusion

Income and production increased rapidly in Cuba during the first decade of the XXI century. Growth was fueled by a surge in government spending and a boom in services exports and investment — all of them made possible by the rapid increase in payments received from Venezuela. The expansion of domestic and foreign demand during the decade did not visibly result in higher inflation or in a large deterioration of the country's external position, partly because some of the recorded growth reflected statistical fabrication and partly because potential output also increased rapidly owing to the relatively strong performance of investment. (In this connection, it is a good thing that part of the Venezuelan money was used to finance capital formation rather than consumption.) However, capacity utilization also increased markedly, and the gap between actual and potential GDP must have dwindled considerably, leaving little room for supply to respond to additional demand pressures.

While there was no explosion in the current account of the balance of payments for most of the decade, severe pressures did emerge in 2008 and the authorities had to restrict imports, ration foreign exchange, and take measures that damaged the nation's reputation in world financial markets. The Central Bank also intervened on a large scale to keep the exchange value of the Cuban peso fixed — a policy that cannot continue forever.

The large size of Cuba's dependence on Venezuelan aid makes the country hostage to fortune. A sudden interruption in such aid would trigger a deep recession and put the balance of payments in a critical position. Therefore, the structural measures that were taken or announced in 2009 and 2010 should now be extended and pursued much more aggressively.

This will not be easy. But, as Russia's former Finance Minister Boris Fedorov once said, dependence on foreign largesse is a luxury that a free country cannot afford.[25]

References

Castañeda, Rolando (2011). "El insostenible apoyo económico de Venezuela a Cuba y sus Implicaciones." *Cuba in Transition — Volume 20.* ASCE. Miami, Florida.

CEPAL (2011). "Cuba: Evolución Económica Durante 2010 y Perspectivas para 2011." Naciones Unidas, Comisión Económica para América Latina y el Caribe.

CEPAL (2012). "Balance preliminar de las economías de América Latina y el Caribe, 2011." Naciones Unidas, Comisión Económica para América Latina y el Caribe.

Espinosa Chepe, Oscar (2009). "Crisis Sobre Crisis: La Difícil Situación Ecónomica, Social y Política Cubana. Probabilidades de su Agravamiento." *Cuba in Transition — Volume 19.* ASCE, Miami, Florida.

Espinosa Chepe, Oscar (2010). "La Economía Cubana. Tiempos de Esperanza?." *Cuba in Transition — Volume 20.* ASCE, Miami, Florida. Reproduced as Chapter 1 in this book.

---

[25] At the Conference on *Russia's Economic Reform* held in Stockholm in June 1994. In response to an injunction by Jeffrey Sachs to suppress hyperinflation by fixing the value of the Ruble and borrowing massive amounts from abroad.

Hernández-Catá, Ernesto (2000). *The Fall and Recovery of the Cuban Economy*. IMF Working Paper WP/01/48. International Monetary Fund: Washington, D.C.

Hernández-Catá, Ernesto (2012). "Cuba, the Soviet Union, and Venezuela. A Tale of Dependence and Shock". *Cuba in Transition — Volume 23*. ASCE, Miami, Florida.

Hernández-Catá, Ernesto (2011). "Macroeconomic Effects of Exchange Rate and Price Distortions: The Cuban Case." *Cuba in Transition — Volume 21*. ASCE, Miami, Florida.

Lopez, Vanesa (2012). "Venezuelan Assistance to Cuba." *Cuba Focus*, Issue 155, January 10. Institute for Cuban and Cuban-American Studies. University of Miami.

Madrid-Aris, Manuel (1998). "Economic Policies, Growth, Human Capital and Technological Change in a Centrally Planned Economy. Evidence from Cuba." ASCE, Miami, Florida.

Luis, Luis (2010). "Crisis Management of Cuban International Liquidity." *Cuba in Transition — Volume 20*. ASCE, Miami, Florida.

Nova González, Armando (2012). "La agricultura cubana y el actual proceso de transformaciones económicas." *Desde la Isla,* Cuba Study Group. Havana (April).

Pérez, Lorenzo (2009). "The Impact of the Global Financial and Economic Crisis on Cuba." *Cuba in Transition, Volume 19,* ASCE, Miami, Florida.

Perez-López, Jorge. "Cuba's External Sector and the VI Party Congress." *Cuba in Transition — Volume 21*. ASCE. Miami, Florida.

U.S. Department of Commerce. *Survey of Current Business*. Washington, D.C.

Vidal Alejandro, Pavel (2010). "Cuban Economic Policy under the Raul Castro Government." Institute of Developing Economies, Japan External Trade Organization.

Vidal Alejandro, Pavel (2012). "Monetary and Exchange Rate Reform in Cuba: Lessons from Vietnam." Institute of Developing Economies. Japan External Trade Organization, No. 473 (February).

Vidal Alejandro, Pavel (2012). "Pasos hacia la bancarización del sector no estatal cubano." *Desde la Isla,* Cuba Study Group. Havana (February).

Annex: Sources and methods

NOTE: References to the *Anuario Estadístico de Cuba* of the Cuban Statistical Office (Oficina Nacional de Estadísticas e Información, or ONE) are to various, issues of the publication. References to table numbers are to the 2010 issue. The same applies to the reports on Cuba of the Economic Commission for Latin America and the Caribbean (CEPAL).

Table 1

Line 1. Real GDP at constant 1977 prices. From *Anuario Estadístico de Cuba,* Cuadro 5.1. Figures before 1996 were converted from base 1981 to base 1997 by applying to the first observation of the base-1997 series the corresponding percentage changes of the base-1981 series and then extrapolating backwards to extend the levels of the 1997–based series.

Line 2. Real Gross domestic purchases. Real GDP minus net exports of goods and services. From ONE, Cuadro 5.

Lines 3 to 5. Total employment, the participation rate and the unemployment rate are from ONE, Cuadro 7.1.

Line 7. <u>Gross fixed capital formation</u> (in constant 1997 prices) as percent of real GDP. From ONE, Cuadro 5.15.

Line 8. The net <u>capital stock</u> series was derived by using the perpetual inventory equation:

$$K_t = (1-\delta)\ (K_{t-1} + I_t) \tag{1}$$

Where K is the capital stock net of depreciation. The starting level of the net capital stock K_0 was calculated by using the formula proposed by Madrid Aris (1998): $K_0 = I_0/(\delta + g_{Y0})$, where I is gross fixed capital formation in constant 1997 prices, δ is the rate of depreciation, g_Y is the growth rate of output. The subscript **0** indicates the benchmark year, which was chosen to be 1989 when output was probably not far from potential. Following Madrid-Aris, δ was set equal to 4.5 percent, which may be on the low side for Cuba.

Line 10, <u>Consumer prices,</u> percentage changes from CEPAL.

Lines 11 and 12. <u>GDP and private consumption deflators.</u> From ONE, Cuadros 5.4 and 5.16.

Line 13. <u>Money supply (M2A).</u> Currency plus peso time and saving deposits. From ONE, Cuadro 6.3 and CEPAL.

Line 14. <u>Budget deficit</u>, central and local governments, from ONE, Cuadro 6.2.

Line 15. <u>Non-state share of monetary earnings</u>. From ONE, Cuadro 6.1. These are payments received by the non-state sector from the state sector and exclude intra-sector payments. The non-state sector includes the private non-farm sector, the agricultural cooperatives, and private farmers.

Line 16. <u>Non-state share of consumer purchases</u>. Share of household purchases supplied by non-state markets. From ONE, Cuadro 5.13.

Line 17. <u>Non-state share of total employment.</u> From ONE, Cuadro 7.2.

Line 18. <u>Non-state share of housing completions.</u> From ONE, Cuadro 12.1.

Line 19. <u>Subsidies to enterprises.</u> From ONE, Cuadro 6.2.

Table 2

The estimated factor contributions were derived from the linear homogeneous Cobb-Douglas production function:

$$g_Y = (1 - \alpha)\, g_L + \alpha\, g_K + \alpha\, g_\rho + g_A \tag{2}$$

where α is assumed to be to 0.3, g is the percentage change operator, Y, L and K stand for output, employment and the capital stock respectively; g_A is residual growth (which includes total factor productivity growth and a terms-of trade effect); and ρ is the unobservable rate of utilization of the capital stock. There is no easy way to estimate ρ, but one possibility is to assume

$$\rho = E^\varphi = (L/N)^\varphi$$

where E is the labor utilization rate (proxied by L/N, the ratio of employment to population of working age) and φ is a positive constant. Plugging into equation (2) yields:

$$g_Y = (1 - \alpha)\, g_L + \alpha\, g_K + \alpha\, \varphi\, g_{E} + g_A \tag{3}$$

In order to estimate the value of φ we define the growth of potential GDP as:

$$g_{Y*} = (1 - \alpha)\, g_N + \alpha\, g_K + {}_+ g_A \tag{4}$$

Subtracting equation (3) from equation (2) and taking into account the definition of ρ, the percentage change in the capital utilization rate can be expressed as a weighted average of capacity utilization rates for labor and output. Using

1989 values for g_Y and g_E, and assuming the growth of potential GDP was negligible in that year, the value of φ can be calculated as follows:

$$\varphi \approx g_Y / \alpha \, g_E + [(1-\alpha)/\alpha]$$

Following the methodology used by the U.S. Department of Commerce, the **terms of trade effect** was calculated as the difference between actual GDP and command GDP (see U.S. Department of Commerce, Survey of Current Business, Table 1.8.6). This can be expressed as:

$$T = x \, (p_x/p - 1) - m \, (p_m/p - 1)$$

where T is the terms of trade effect, x and m are export and import volumes respectively; p_x and p_m are export and import prices; and p is the deflator for gross domestic purchases. The variable used in the table was defined as the change in T divided by GDP in the previous period.

Table 3

GDP, investment, government expenditure, and exports of goods and services, all in constant 1977 prices, are from ONE, Cuadro 6.3. The contribution of each variable is calculated by taking first differences and dividing by GDP in the previous period. The terms of trade effect is calculated as in Table 2.

Table 5

Manuel Madrid-Aris provided the data on **Soviet aid** to the author (except for the 1989 observation which came from conversations with Russian officials).

The **"budget proxy"** is the line labeled *"otros ingresos no tributaries"* ("other non-tax revenue") in the budget for the state government minus *"transferencias al sector empresasarial, otros"* ("other transfers to enterprises"). Both ONE, Cuadro 6.4. ONE notes that "other non-tax revenue" consists of "external payments" and "price differentials from foreign trade." It is therefore likely that it includes most payments from Venezuela, although it may also include other items, which could be the source of errors in the estimates.

The **"BOP proxy"** for **Venezuelan aid** is the difference between exports of services and earnings from tourism and transportation. From ONE, Cuadros 5.1, 5.2, and 5.11; and CEPAL, 2012.

3

RAÚL CASTRO'S DILEMMA: HOW TO FIX THE CUBAN ECONOMY WITHOUT RISKING POLITICAL POWER

Jorge A. Sanguinetty

Looking at it from different angles, everything indicates that Cuba's purportedly socialist (or centrally planned) economy stands today at the end of a very long line. The Cuban government has reached a point at which it will have to get serious about the country's economy once and for all. In the last few years the severity of the economic situation has been frequently recognized by Raúl Castro, indicating explicitly that without a significant improvement of the economy's productive capacity the socialist revolution will no longer be sustainable. One cannot help but think that the spectrum of the collapse of the Soviet Union and the entire socialist bloc probably has been haunting him since its occurrence, but now more than ever.

The crisis was reflected, though not in detail, in the recently-held VI Congress of the Cuban Communist Party (CCP) and its economic guidelines or *Lineamientos* (2011). Cuba's chronic dependence on external subsidies suggests that its economy is insolvent but the causes of such straits are not thoroughly appreciated by many observers of Cuban affairs, and even less by the general public, inside and outside the island. Yet it is not possible to fully understand the country's economic crisis (in fact, a 50–year old crisis) ignoring the string of events that have affected all and every single aspect of the Cuban economy during the last five decades. To understand it, it is necessary to examine the economy not only at the macro or aggregate level, but also through a microscope, i.e., at the level of the socialist enterprise in all sectors of economic activity. In the Cuban case, macroeconomic analysis, even when performed with faulty and unreliable data, does show the economic regression of the country under Fidel Castro's rule, although it does not explain the wide range of causes of the economic debacle.

As I posit in this paper, some critical causes lie on the partial or total disintegration of the country's productive enterprises, an evolutionary result of Fidel Castro's policy of having a political (not necessarily ideological) agenda that took the enterprises' productive capacities and requirements for granted after the expropriations of the early sixties. His agenda carried a macroeconomic policy by default, as the revolutionary government implicitly but erroneously assumed that under the new regime nationalized (now socialist) enterprises would continue producing with the same or similar levels of efficiency and productivity to what they had reached under capitalism. The government also ignored the complexities and consequences of replacing the United States as Cuba's main trading partner with the Soviet Union.[26]

---

[26] Fidel Castro expressed his disappointment (and I believe his misunderstanding) about the economic capabilities of the Soviet Union, especially regarding its agriculture, in a rare string of unpublicized and bizarre personal appearances on the steps of the University of Havana, late at night during the tensest moments of the October 1962 Missiles Crisis. I was among the few dozen students that heard his complaints, never understanding to this day what Castro's real intentions were. These appearances were not reported in the government-controlled media and Castro never expressed such views in public.

Cuba's economic crisis is not a case of systematic mismanagement by an incompetent government that was supposed to be concerned with the economic health of the country. Rather, it is a result of policies by a government that neglected economic affairs, profoundly disrupting and irreversibly damaging an economic system that evolved for four and a half centuries and had reached a certain capacity and level of efficiency in 1959. The available quantitative data from government sources are neither sufficient nor reliable enough to describe the depth and extent of this disruption, as discussed by Sanguinetty (2009). But even if sufficient quantitative data were available and reliable, a careful qualitative or institutional analysis would be indispensable to produce an accurate assessment of an economy that has suffered an avalanche of incoherent structural changes inflicted primarily by government decisions. In this paper I try to provide some elements of such assessment hoping to contribute to a better understanding of the causes of the current crisis and the dilemmas a government faces, now that it seems committed to improve the current conditions while avoiding the concomitant political risks and costs.

The Origins of Insolvency

The roots of Cuba's current crisis were planted at the very beginning of the revolutionary process, as political considerations consistently took precedence over economic ones. Such roots developed in the name of socialism. In reality, they were intended to serve an economically unsustainable political agenda that was never made explicit by Fidel Castro after 1959 when he became in charge of virtually everything in the Cuban government. Since then, the public record repeatedly shows how Fidel Castro's attention appears to have been focused on political issues in order to: (1) consolidate his personal grip on power in Cuba; (2) project his influence to other countries; and (3) become a renowned world leader by playing the card of anti-Americanism. He greatly succeeded on points 1 and 3, while making significant yet incomplete gains on point 2. The evidence that neither the Cuban economy nor its development was a priority in Castro's agenda is abundant, albeit fragmented, scattered, and badly documented. Unfortunately, most analysts have failed to recognize such an unusual condition despite the extensive research efforts that have been carried out for half a century.

The first serious signal of neglect of economic issues became apparent during Castro's unofficial visit to the United States in April 1959. At the time, Castro's entourage included a team of prestigious and competent Cuban economists that was supposed to hold a series of meetings in Washington, D.C., with officials of the International Monetary Fund, the World Bank, the International Finance Corporation, the Export-Import Bank of the United States, and the U.S. Treasury Department. Surprisingly, Castro himself gave orders to cancel all the meetings before the plane landed in the United States territory, leaving the members of his delegation with nothing to do during the trip, as reported by López-Fresquet (1966). The original objective of the meetings was to start negotiations with the named organizations to find ways to alleviate the critical financial situation of the country, as its international reserves had been depleted by the previous government and Cuba needed some loans to stabilize its balance of payments. In fact, the Cuban peso was already overvalued at the time as the central bank artificially kept it pegged to the U.S. dollar under a newly-implemented exchange control regime.

But at some point during the trip, Castro thought that he did not want to appear as the traditional Latin American leader coming to the United States to ask for economic aid.[27] It was an early signal that political considerations would be lexicographically preferred to economic factors. There would be no trade-offs between political and economic variables. The performance of Castro's administration would quickly demonstrate that there would be no trade-offs between the needs of the Cuban economy and its people's aspirations, and the political and international goals of the new leader. The promises about new economic prosperity during the brief honeymoon of early 1959 would be utterly forgotten.

Many other instances of the economy's subordinate role may be cited. The sweeping expropriations of the mid-1960s, for example, destroyed the economic base of those individuals who were perceived by Castro as his future

---

[27] Carlos Quijano, a member of the mission, provided me with some of these details.

enemies, regardless of the economic consequences for the country, while the frequent mass mobilizations disrupted all forms of economic activity. Mass mobilizations (militia, literacy campaigns, public rallies) were well-conceived political exercises to organize Cubans around a central government command which monopolized virtually all forms of organization in the country. Civil society, already weak, quickly disappeared and so did the private sector within the economy, the independent judiciary, the free media, and all political parties.[28] With regard to the three-week nation-wide militia mobilization involving millions of workers launched on December 31st of 1960 (the day chosen to preclude any spontaneous and independent celebration of the New Year 1961), even Ernesto Guevara publicly complained about the enormous cost to the Cuban economy of such lengthy campaign, but his rare and apparently insubordinate utterance was unnoticed and ineffective. Guevara was showing at that time to be more concerned with the Cuban economy than Fidel Castro. I believe that this was subtle but significant evidence that both men had different views and expectations about what kind of socialism would prevail in the country.

Perhaps the most significant yet unrecognized instance of the little regard Fidel Castro had for the economy became evident (but not widely known) in 1961 when the Cuban government de facto abandoned — without any official announcement or explanation — the Quadrennial Economic Plan (*Plan Cuatrienal*) 1962–1965 even before its formal launching, scheduled for January 1, 1962. That plan had been formulated and coordinated by the Central Planning Board (*Junta Central de Planificación* or *JUCEPLAN*), with technical assistance from economists loaned to Cuba by Central European socialist countries and by Latin American economists hired by the Cuban government as consultants or advisors. That year had been officially declared with much fanfare "The Year of Planning," and considered an essential step towards building a socialist economy based on central planning. Yet the Cuban government did not show much concern about the many requirements for a coherent formulation of the Plan, among them a sound statistical data base, and sufficient knowledge

---

[28] Even the old Cuban communist party, the *Partido Socialista Popular* (PSP), was absorbed by Castro's embryonic party, *Organizaciones Revolucionarias Integradas* (ORI), the precursor of a future formally established Cuban Communist Party under Castro's absolute control.

about central planning. There was no central statistical base, especially regarding the private economy and its performance previous to 1959. The productive memory of enterprises, developed when they were private, was erased by the expropriations of 1960s and the replacement of the old managers — many of whom had left the country and gone into exile — by generally incompetent revolutionary loyalists. The country was not prepared for central planning and the top government officials were not aware of these insufficiencies or simply underestimated its consequences.

Nevertheless, the formulation of the Plan was undertaken, but it had to be abandoned after completion and before it was launched because the figures generated by the state enterprises, partially consolidated by the corresponding ministries, and finally aggregated by JUCEPLAN, were not reliable and showed glaring incompatibilities. The figures reflected volumes of production, investment and consumption; levels of employment; imports and exports, etc., that were unrealistic and internally inconsistent. The weak statistical base caused a few comical instances of incoherence, such as the case when a single government agency "planned" an annual total demand of toilet paper that surpassed the total production for the entire country. It had become apparent that the Plan's targets were not simply unrealistic but utterly inadequate and unsustainable, forcing the economic authorities to forfeit a development plan that could not be executed.

The massive expropriations of enterprises in the mid-sixties forced a newly hypertrophied state sector to improvise management systems and practices aimed at avoiding at all costs the collapse of the Cuban productive system. The first measure was to shift all workers left unemployed by closed enterprises into those which remained open. An example of efforts to cope with the new changes was in 1963 when the Ministry of Industry was forced to conduct surveys to gather household data about garment and shoe sizes to guide manufacturing plans by enterprises the government had confiscated. But despite the efforts to avoid a complete collapse of the enterprises' economic activity, the transfer of private to socialist ownership was so dominated by political and security concerns, that efficiency and productivity considerations were always secondary. It was the beginning of the managerial disintegration of Cuban enterprises, a condition that was never taken into account explicitly by the planning authorities.

To make things worse, Ernesto Guevara, appointed President of the Cuban National Bank in November 1959, did away with the rudimentary national accounts system that the Cuban National Bank developed and published annually from 1950 to 1959. This happened in early in 1960, when Guevara refused to accept that the preliminary estimates of growth of Cuban national income for 1959 showed a meager growth of only one percent.[29] The Cuban government did not publish national account data again until the 1970s. One can only wonder what kind of government, especially a highly centralized one, could operate effectively for such a long period of time without the most basic statistical information about its economy, and what kind of economic decisions could have been made with almost zero visibility.

In this regard it must be noted that for decades, Fidel Castro could go on talking for hours in his famously lengthy speeches without ever referring to the Cuban Gross Domestic Product or some of its basic aggregates such as consumption, investment or the level of employment or prices. His public references to the Cuban economy were focused on specific sectors, never on the economy at large, based on physical measurements — tons of sugar produced or hectares of land planted — and never in monetary terms. These are additional symptoms that the country's economic performance was not a top concern for Fidel Castro. Moreover, Castro's reluctance to mention values in money terms were in my view an indication of his misunderstanding of Marxian economics, and his fear that recognizing what he considered capitalist or "bourgeois" concepts would send the wrong message to the public and to the world regarding his rhetorical commitment to build a socialist society in Cuba.

Despite the existence of *JUCEPLAN* since 1960 and the fact that the agency was directly managed by President Osvaldo Dorticós from 1964, acting

---

[29] For more details about this bizarre incident see Sanguinetty (1999).

simultaneously as Minister of Economy, which empowered it in theory to allocate all consumption and investment goods, there never was an attempt to reformulate the four-year plan and early on the country's economy started suffering from a lack of coherent direction. Instead of the typically socialist central planning agency, *JUCEPLAN* operated with annual plans that were in fact attempts to keep some order in the economy through the budget by allowing the state enterprises to remain open while letting their workers continue receiving salaries regardless of profitability, levels of production or productivity. This started a process of organic and managerial decomposition of virtually all enterprises which remained in operation after the nationalization wave of 1960. As they lost their corporate governance and financial management systems, along with functions like human resources administration, inventory and asset management, etc., in line with losing all of their autonomy to deal with suppliers and labor and capital markets, enterprises were gradually transformed into rudimentary shops, presumably receiving guidelines ("directivas") from their corresponding ministries. In the process, these enterprises lost another element of their productive and managerial memory: their ability to deal with a price system ruled by demand and supply forces in product and factor markets. Prices and salaries were arbitrarily fixed by bureaucrats, sometimes even by Castro himself, and besides losing the capability to read market signals, Cuban enterprises lost their capabilities to make autonomous decisions and operate efficiently. Such reductions in capabilities were further accentuated by the advent of a new cohort of managers most of whom had very little experience, if any, to perform their duties properly. Political allegiance to Fidel Castro was the main qualification for the job.

Meanwhile, the economy at large suffered under an already overwhelmed government administration loaded with innumerable state enterprises, managed by incompetent executives (or just care-takers of government assets and workers), that evolved progressively into forms of economic organization that became increasingly dysfunctional and inefficient, while losing installed capacities for lack of maintenance, skilled labor, spare parts and supplies.

Also at Guevara's initiative, and with the tacit blessing of Fidel Castro, the state enterprises were subjected to an accounting and cash management regime that eliminated all profit centers. Under the new system, called "centralized budgeting" — with an explicit Stalinist tone — all revenues from the enterprises would flow into the National Bank which would serve as the central source of funds for all the enterprises. The bank would fund the operational costs of enterprises, regardless of their ability to generate enough revenues. In what was a phenomenal misunderstanding of Marxian economics, Guevara justified his actions — opposed by many within the government that defended a more decentralized management system, especially old communists — on the notion that accounting systems were dedicated to measure profit, a capitalistic or bourgeois concept unacceptable in a communist society. Guevara, with no education as an economist and with the arrogance that comes with unchecked political power, did not understand that profit was a measure of productive efficiency, or surplus value in Marxist terms, and was not inconsistent with the need to measure efficiency even in a socialist economy that was presumably to be grown and developed to improve the living conditions in the country.[30] Unknowingly, Guevara was contributing to install an economic system that not only carried the deficiencies typical of socialism but went beyond to make it even less manageable. After decades of operating under such conditions, managers of Cuban enterprises became adapted to a work ethic devoid of the concept of efficiency, and a concomitant result was the absolute lack of incentives to operate with competitive levels of productivity.[31]

Since enterprises lost all visibility of profits (or loses) as a measure of economic efficiency, most became insolvent, forcing the National Bank to subsidize them.[32]

---

[30] Socialist economies and socialist monopolies are intrinsically inefficient. These measures not only added considerably to that inefficiency but also made it impossible to measure efficiency and monitor it at any level. As a result, efficiency started drifting downwards steadily in almost every enterprise owned exclusively by the Cuban state.

[31] For a recent review of the many factors that determine productivity levels and their measurement see Syverson (2011).

[32] Accounting systems and the elaboration of financial statements became worthless, a process that culminated in 1968 when Cuban accounting schools were closed as money was deemed unnecessary in the communist society Cuba was building. The country has yet to recover from

As aggregate demand for goods and services consistently exceeded aggregate supply, the Bank had to print money to cover costs, debasing the Cuban peso and in so doing reducing the purchasing power of workers' salaries and deepening the lack of incentives for managers and workers to work hard and efficiently.[33] This cumulative process rapidly advanced like the metastasis in a cancer and rendered the country insolvent as a whole, thus requiring for the economy to be heavily subsidized externally, although this was not sufficient to stop the gradual sinking of the productive system inherited by the revolution. The most massive and dramatic evidence of this process is the quasi-disappearance of the internationally relevant Cuban sugar industry.

Over the years, Cuba's authorities developed an addiction to external subsidies and loans, which were mainly extended by the Soviet Union until 1989. From the early 1960s *JUCEPLAN* was already estimating Cuba's gap between aggregate demand and aggregate supply a year in advance, to provide the country's top authorities with a base on which to negotiate the level of external aid needed in the following year. This process continued every year until the collapse of the Soviet Union, only to be replaced by new subsidies from the Venezuelan government under the presidency of Hugo Chávez at the end of the 1990s, and other forms of subsidies as, for example, the dollar remittances of Cubans living abroad.

Fidel Castro's economic policy has not only been incoherent but haphazard and wildly improvised. A study of his speeches would lead anyone to conclude that his stated policies were basically irrational if we assume that the official strategy was focused on the economy. I think, however, that the actual policies, when taken as a whole, were not precisely irrational if we believe that Fidel Castro's goals were essentially political, for which he needed to: (1) use whatever resources he could extract from the economy he had de facto "privatized," and then (2) use external resources to fill the gap between what his political agenda required (e.g., funding guerrillas in Latin America and

---

the loss of the accounting profession and discipline, as evidenced by a recent interview with Lina Pedraza, Minister of Finances and Prices, cited by Rendón (2011).

[33] For an analysis of Cuban financial system see Castillo (2011).

a military presence in Africa) and what Cubans could produce. Granted, Castro's disorganized, unexpected and out-of-plan interventions in the economy that he started treating as his own can be seen as irrational if considered under strict economic criteria. As I stated before, Fidel Castro seems to have taken the economy for granted, perhaps his major mistake as head of government, assuming that the newly socialized enterprises would keep operating as if nothing happened, unaware that the enormous trauma they suffered would irreversibly damage their productive capacity.

The Expansion of Redundant Labor

Let us return to what happened after the Four-year Plan was silently abandoned. Following the massive socialization of large enterprises, national and foreign, of 1960, plus the same treatment of medium and small enterprises, mostly Cuban, in 1961 and 1962, the government faced the problem of how to avoid a dangerous increase in unemployment. As a result of the expropriations and the insertion of badly understood Marxist principles in the society entire sectors of economic activity were eliminated. Typical examples were the financial sector (banks, insurance companies, etc.), most service industries (law offices, advertising, publicists, media, etc.), the commerce sector (retail, wholesale, distribution and transportation systems, etc.), among others. All those employees who became redundant and did not migrate were re-employed in existing enterprises, thus swelling payrolls with unnecessary workers and accelerating the growth of redundant labor. This nurtured the illusion of full employment, though in effect it was disguised unemployment. Payrolls continued swelling as population growth expanded the supply of labor.

It is important to point out that for Castro, unemployment was not an economic or social problem as much as a political one. An unemployed worker is free to engage in political activities against the government, particularly in a context of increased dissatisfaction with the revolution. Providing employment, even if fictitious, is a way for the government (now a monopsonistic employer) to know where every worker is and what he/she is doing. This is how the problem of redundant labor started and developed, compounded by a fall in the levels of production that caused widespread scarcity of traditional goods and services in 1961, presumably forcing the government to institute a rationing regime in March 1962.[34]

In 1962, the main objective of the official economic policy appeared to be the industrialization of the country, breaking the heavy dependence on the sugar industry by promoting an import substitution strategy. The champion of this process was Ernesto Guevara. In 1963, Cuba obtained the lowest sugar harvest in many years. But the country was taken aback in 1964 when Fidel Castro shifted 180 degrees and announced that a new goal for the Cuban economy was to produce a record sugar harvest of 10 million tons in 1970. This announcement took everyone by surprise at JUCEPLAN and other government agencies, as there had not been any previous preparation or feasibility study to analyze the costs and benefits of such an ambitious goal. Politically incorrect expressions of disapproval by members of the Communist Youth were heard in the University of Havana, disappointed about Cuba returning to the old trilogy of sugar, coffee and tobacco instead of industrialization. Castro's marching orders came virtually overnight. The economic or even political rationale of this radical policy change is still open to debate.

Meanwhile, the industrialization plans championed by Guevara and inspired in the traditional Stalinist preference for the development of heavy industry at the expense of light industry (mainly consumption goods) were also surreptitiously abandoned, despite the fact that Cuba had already purchased — mostly on credit — scores of turn-key manufacturing plants valued at hundreds of millions of dollars. Only a few seemed to have prospered or even survived. Many of these plants purchased by Guevara were never installed, and the few that did operated at low levels of efficiency.

---

[34] It can be argued that the government installed the rationing system as a control instrument of the citizens, as the government required households and their members to be registered in given retail establishments. Regardless whether this was a premeditated reason, the rationing represented ex post facto an effective means of citizen control by the state.

But several developments were taking place simultaneously in the Cuban economy. After the massive expropriations of 1960 and 1961, enterprises lost most of their management and technical personnel through heavy migration flows. Such skilled personnel were mostly replaced with unqualified individuals, especially at the management level but also at the level of technicians and operators. This became apparent by the collapse of production and productivity levels in many industries and farms, compounding the problem of scarcity. Productivity levels, either labor productivity or total factor productivity, decreased significantly. Along with the loss of qualified personnel, enterprises suffered from lack of spare parts and supplies, not to mention a sense of direction within what was supposed to be a centrally planned economic system. Another grave complication was the lack of coordination or synchronization of supplies that plagued every enterprise in the country. The inter-sectoral (input-output) relations of the economy collapsed; enterprises had considerable trouble receiving supplies on time, in the required amounts and with the required specifications, a situation that caused long periods of low production or no production at all. These deficiencies working together reduced further the levels of production and productivity, as workers continued to be paid regardless whether their factories or farms were idle or not producing at full capacity.

Meanwhile low production levels reduced the investment capacity of the country making it insufficient to create new employment. At the same time, the rise in the years of schooling available to Cuban youth delayed their entry into the labor force. After all, it is easier and less expensive to educate than to create jobs, but sooner or later the new graduates had to be "employed" to maintain the official promise that the revolution eliminated unemployment, but under the vigilant eye of the state, while keeping them artificially busy and out of trouble, politically and otherwise. Obviously, after fifty years, elementary economics helps us conclude that this systematic swelling of payrolls would eventually lead to: (1) the debasement of the level of salaries and wages, as (2) the levels of productivity fell continuously, causing (3) lower levels of production, lowering (4) the levels of personal consumption, which (5) lowered further the standard of living of the population.

The Problem

To a great extent by omission, but also by commission, Fidel Castro created a distorted economic system whose main purpose was to serve his political agenda. As a result, the economy that Raúl Castro inherited from his brother is overwhelmed by a network of interlocking distortions and anomalies that even if he and his colleagues in the Cuban Communist Party could understand, they would have considerable trouble in transforming into a more efficient productive system. Among the most critical distortions of the economy are those affecting the prices of all goods and services, including the prices of the factors of production, labor, capital, and land, in the corresponding forms of salaries and wages, interest, and rent. Price distortions appear when a major force intervenes in competitive markets, not allowing prices to freely reach levels of equilibrium generally determined by supply (representing production capabilities) and demand (mostly representing consumer preferences and investment decisions).

Such distortions started with the nationalization of private enterprises and continued with the freeze of consumer and investment goods prices, but were consolidated by the introduction of a central planning system that fixed all prices as required by the annual budgets. The problem was that all those prices had resulted from supply-demand equilibrium conditions generated by relatively free competitive markets. Nevertheless, as a result of the upheaval created by the rapid avalanche of political measures such as the nationalizations, severe import restrictions, and the exodus of significant proportions of the stock of human capital, the supply of practically all goods and services contracted, while their demand expanded rapidly while there was no price flexibility mechanism to reach equilibrium. The old absolute and relative prices were already obsolete.

In a normal market economy, where sellers and buyers are free to establish the prices of goods and services based on their personal interests and capabilities, prices are signals that indicate to the economic actors what and how much to produce and to purchase. In any economy, shortly after prices are fixed by government decree, imbalances between supply and demand appear overnight, a phenomenon that quickly becomes apparent in the widespread development of black markets, where transactions take place generally at much higher price levels than the previously predominant ones. This is exactly what happened in Cuba starting in 1961, becoming more acute in 1962 and continuing until recently, when some partial market instruments have been allowed by the government in an urgent search for stable equilibrium. This is one of the roots of the many problems Raúl Castro faces: the challenge of how to transform a monstrously disfigured and bankrupt economy into a solvent one, which will not require continuous injections of foreign aid and can develop a minimum capacity to grow in a sustainable way so it could satisfy the basic needs of the population. With the uncertainty around the Venezuelan economy and the latest news about Hugo Chávez's health, the quest for economic independence has grown more urgent.

After the disappearance of the Soviet subsidies in the 1990s, the Cuban government was forced to rapidly open the door to foreign investment, international tourism, and dollar remittances from Cubans living abroad. All this required the creation of new enterprises that would operate with foreign exchange and could not afford the shoddy management styles of the typical state enterprise in Cuba. Such enterprises were managed by military personnel who appeared to be among the very few qualified to manage them with a certain level of organization and discipline. After all, military and security affairs were always taken very seriously by Fidel Castro and the crisis that followed the collapse of the Soviet Union forced him to reluctantly take economic issues seriously too, even if merely for survival reasons. These enterprises in fact created a degree of solvency although only for a significant yet relatively small sector of the economy.

Cuba needs to become solvent now and for this Raúl Castro needs to increase the number of solvent enterprises even if he has to implement reforms that are not palatable to either Fidel Castro or to other CCP hardliners. Those reform measures are: (1) allow the emergence of small private enterprises to absorb the redundant labor of the state sector; and (2) introduce reforms at the state enterprise level that will make them produce at higher levels of productivity. These are in fact the general objectives of the *Lineamientos* recently issued by Cuba's only legally allowed party.

Raúl's Dilemma

Cuba's macroeconomic solvency requires that its enterprises be solvent, for which productive efficiency is a *sine qua non*. But in the Cuban case, macroeconomic policy cannot achieve overall solvency by decree. The role of macroeconomic policy is to raise the degrees of freedom under which the enterprises can operate at higher levels of productivity by lifting the multiple constrains binding the management of productive activities, and allowing the enterprises to create worker incentives necessary to become efficient. Total Factor Productivity depends on many factors, especially workers' attitudes and motivation, together with their qualifications.[35] Machinery and other physical assets in a production process can function automatically, but workers do not. The intensity of workers' incentives depends on the degrees of freedom they have as workers in the production front, but also as consumers, to choose where and how to produce, what to consume, how much they earn, where to live, etc.

And here precisely is where Raúl Castro's dilemma lies: in the trade-off between efficiency and control: efficiency requires workers' and citizens' freedom to choose as an incentive to work hard and be efficient, while political control to avoid political instability requires constraining workers' and consumers' behavior. It is safe to assume that neither Raúl Castro, nor the hardliners within the CCP, will promote or support radical reforms. That is why a reading of the *Lineamientos* signals how cautiously they are approaching reforms, with all kinds of caveats and restrictions, afraid of losing political control at any step. But they know that the current economic situation of the country is precarious and probably not sustainable for much longer, requiring gains in production and productivity (as long as they cannot count on indefinite external subsidies or a miracle).

Thus a compromise policy of minimalist reforms will probably be the most acceptable to the different factions within the government to solve their conundrum: obtain sufficient gains in efficiency to reach solvency by

---

[35] See Syverson (2011).

creating a subsistence economy. Such an economy is, by definition, less vulnerable to external shocks and can become stable, but does not grow. Raúl Castro can buy some political stability but at the price of secular economic stagnation. Under a subsistence economy, Cubans will be too busy making ends meet to have enough time to dedicate to political activities, at least for a while. Once this new equilibrium is reached, and Cubans learn how to operate within this economy, new aspirations may eventually arise and by that time more profound economic reforms may become politically feasible, perhaps under a more promising post-Castro era. But will it work? Can that strategy benefit enough Cubans in time to avoid political unrest before the Castro era is closed? Will Cubans demand something more significant than marginal or subsistence economic benefits, such as political freedoms and a more promising future?

Concluding Remarks

Raúl Castro's dilemma can be conceptualized as a non-cooperative game of strategy between two major players: the Cuban government and the Cuban population. In a static framework, the government is trying to minimize the increase in the degrees of freedom granted to the people. This is implemented by strictly fine-tuning shifts in the economic and political constraints. The Cuban people, on the other hand, can be expected to maximize what they can do with their newly enlarged, yet still constrained, choice sets as workers, entrepreneurs, and consumers. This combination of forces is similar to a Prisoners' Dilemma and makes one think of a possible Nash equilibrium if a stable solution can be reached.[36] Nevertheless, the Cuban people at large might not behave as only one player, but as at least two — those who think they can benefit from the newly-relaxed constraints and those who either do not see its advantages or believe that the new degrees of freedom granted by the government should go farther and be more comprehensive.

---

[36] For a reference see Dasgupta and Mäller (1995), pp. 2439–2441.

As we write, the stream of popular protests taking place in Cuba suggests that we might be facing a more complex and evolutionary game, whose most likely path is impossible to predict. Under such circumstances one thing that can be predicted with a reasonable degree of certainty is that the Cuban society as a whole has reached a point at which the secular stagnation, at the current level of production, is no longer tenable.

References

Castillo, Miguel A., "El sistema financiero y la banca cubana: Características fundamentales desde el establecimiento del régimen socialista," Capítulo XIII, in

Córdova, Efrén, (ed.), *El Ocaso del Régimen que Destruyó a Cuba*, InterAmerican

Institute for Democracy, Miami, Florida, 2011.

Dasgupta, Partha and Mäller, Karl-Göran, "Poverty, Institutions, and the Environmental

Resource-Base," in Behrman, J. and Srinivasan, T.N. (eds.) *Handbook of Development*

Economics, Volume III, Elsevier Science, Amsterdam, 1995.

López-Fresquet, Rufo, *My Fourteen Months with Castro*, The World Publishing Company, Cleveland and New York, 1966.

Partido Comunista de Cuba, *Lineamientos de la Política Económica y Social del Partido y la Revolución*, VI Congreso, La Habana, 2011.

Rendón, Fidel, "Ratifican necesidad de resolver problemas de la contabilidad," *Granma,* July 19, 2011.

Sanguinetty, Jorge A., "La Transfiguración de la Economía," Capítulo III, in Córdova, Efrén (ed.), *50 Años de Revolución en Cuba*, Ediciones Universal, Miami, Florida, 2009.

Sanguinetty, Jorge A., "La Industria," Capítulo III, in Córdova, Efrén (ed.), *40 Años de Revolución en Cuba*, Ediciones Universal, Miami, Florida, 1999.

Syverson, Chad, "What Determines Productivity?" *Journal of Economic Literature*, 49.2, 326–365, 2011.

4

PESOS, POVERTY, AND PERVERSIONS: WHAT'S WRONG WITH CUBA'S MONEY AND HOW TO FIX IT

Ed Canler

S tudents of recent Cuban economic history will be familiar with the crisis the country underwent after the collapse of the Soviet Union and of the system of economic relationships between socialist countries known as COMECON (Canler, 2001). Almost overnight, Cuba lost the international economic relationships that underpinned its domestic economy. Among the resulting painful consequences was the steep depreciation of the Cuban peso (CP) versus the dollar and its loss of purchasing power in the domestic market. The government found it prudent in 1993 to legalize the U.S. dollar for domestic transactions. Three currencies were suddenly legal tender in the country: the U.S. dollar, the depreciated Cuban peso, and a "convertible" peso (CUC) that could be exchanged for one U.S. dollar. Subsequent fiscal prudence by central bank authorities allowed the Cuban peso to appreciate from over 100 to the dollar to around 20, but it has never appreciated further. Moreover, the exchange rate between the "convertible" peso and the Cuban peso, and thus between the peso and the dollar, was only for the purposes of personal transactions. For commercial transactions between enterprises, transactions between government and enterprises, and in foreign trade, the Cuban peso was deemed to be at par with the U.S. dollar, until 2006.

In 2003 a new wave of monetary reform started, geared toward centralizing foreign exchange transactions via the central bank, taking the U.S. dollar out of circulation, and fixing the rate between the Cuban peso and the CUC at 25 to 1 (González-Corzo, 2007). In 2006, the exchange rate between the CP and CUC was modified to CUC$1.08 per CP. In other words, the "convertible" peso and Cuban peso were both appreciated against the dollar. The current status is that US$1.08 will fetch one CUC, and 25 CP will fetch one CUC. The implied rate between the dollar and the CP is CP=US$0.0432. The large gulf in exchange rates between 1.08 and 0.0432 should suggest a giant misallocation of resources at the national level that pinches on the economy's growth potential.

However, the specific purposes of this paper will focus on three other themes: (1) to show that the economic unit that bears the brunt of the dual exchange rate system is the household; (2) to show that the consequent powerfully perverse incentives that are created will greatly limit the salutary effects that future economic reforms might have; and (3) to suggest a mechanism for unifying the exchange rate that may be painful to some, but which will probably improve equity in the society and allow the benefits of other reforms be fully gleaned.

Cuba's Double Exchange Rate System

For the stated purposes of the paper, it is a useful simplification to assume that the CUC does not exist, and as long as it remains fixed to the dollar, the results are identical regardless of whether the CUC or the CP is analyzed. So the exchange rate of the peso (CP) is framed in what could be called a classical approach, whereby the price of the dollar in pesos is determined by the intersection of a demand and a supply curve for dollars. The Cuban market for U.S. dollars can be depicted as in Figure 1. There is a typical negatively sloped demand for dollars in terms of pesos (D). The supply of dollars (S_1), however, is discontinuous in Cuba. The government makes available at a price p_0 (CP0.926=US$1.00 or, conversely, US$1.08=CP1.00) a limited amount of dollars (q_0) to official importers. Beyond that quantity there may be further sales by the government at CP23.15=US$1.00 levels plus additional sales at the same price by households receiving family remittances from abroad and/ or have other sources of dollar income. (For simplicity, exchange fees, which in Cuba are different for exchanging U.S. dollar versus other currencies, are not considered.) Ostensibly the government will sell any amount of dollars (in actual practice, CUC) at 23.15 to 1. The relative sizes of the market for non-personal transactions (q_0) and the so-called "free" market (q_1—q_0) is not public knowledge. Under this schematic the "free" market is at equilibrium at d, with price p_1, currently established at 23.15.

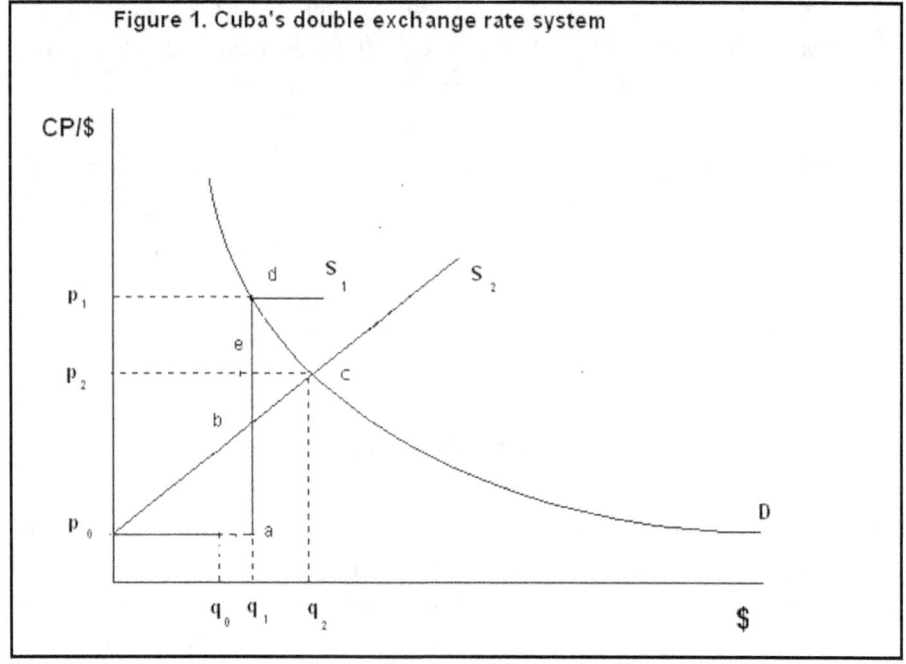

Figure 1. Cuba's double exchange rate system

If the imposition of the CP0.926 = US$1.00 ($p_0$) exchange were eliminated from official dollar earners, it is reasonable to suppose that its supply curve would assume a more typical continuous positive slope, as in S_2. The logic is that if dollar holders could make more than 0.925 CP on the first dollar sold or exchanged, they should be willing to earn less than today's "free" market rate on the last dollar earned. In this scenario the equilibrium exchange rate would be at c, with price p_2 and quantity q_2. The slope of this continuous supply curve is unknown, especially at points beyond q_1, but it is reasonable to assume that in a free market the exchange rate p_2 would be lower than today's "free" exchange rate at p_1. It would also be closer to a true exchange rate in that economic agents are free to transact as they choose. Thus, p_1 will henceforth be described as "free" only in quotation marks to signify that it is free in name more than in deed.

In this schematic, the area circumscribed by the triangle P_0ab represents a loss in producer surplus, i.e., a loss to foreign exchange earners forced to exchange at CP0.926=US$1.00 ($p_0$). The area circumscribed by the polygon p_1dcp_2 represents a loss in consumer surplus, i.e., by buyers of the "free" exchange rate. This loss is mitigated by government transfers to consumers from the garnishments in P_0ab. The area circumscribed by the triangle ecb represents a deadweight loss, i.e., losses from which neither consumers nor producers benefit.

This analysis also suggests that the common practice of translating Cuban salaries into dollars using the "free" exchange rate is as misleading as using the official exchange rate for non-personal transactions. The economic reality is that a salary of CP400 is worth less than the US$432 suggested by the official exchange rate, but also more than the US$17.28 suggested by the CUC exchange rate.

Winners and Losers

The difference in exchange rates between the current system and what would prevail under a free market (p_1—p_2) implies that there are winners and losers, as the market is distorted away from a free equilibrium. The winners are those who can buy at the preferential rate p_0 (below the free equilibrium price) and those who can sell at p_1 (above the free equilibrium price). The losers are their counterparties, i.e., those who have to sell at p_0 and buy at p_1 when they could be selling higher or buying lower (at p_2).

The Cuban government, with few exceptions, owns the country's productive infrastructure. Thus the delineation of buyers and sellers is less distinct in Cuba than in other economies, and so is the distinction between losers and winners. However, in this framework it helps to differentiate between government enterprises and the government itself, the latter being the institution that legislates and executes laws. Whereas one can assume there will always be a government, the incidence of government in enterprise can be variable, and has been variable in Cuba over time. For example, many formerly 100% government-owned enterprises are now joint ventures with foreign partners. In agriculture there are also private farmers and the cooperative production units, which are ostensibly no longer in the state sector and have at least an organizational distinctiveness from other state agricultural entities. Least fuzzy is the delineation of households, which remain distinct and apart from the government and which figure prominently among the winners and losers.

The Winners

The first group of winners is made up of those who are able purchase or procure dollars at p_0. These include the importers of basic commodities, including food, medicine, and energy. By extension the consumers of these commodities also benefit. These will be the households that purchase food from the ration book (almost all of them), households that receive free healthcare (almost all of them), and households connected to the energy grid (almost all of them).

The second group of winners is composed by those who sell foreign exchange at p_1. These include government entities that may have some discretionary sales of dollars through exchange houses, and households that receive remittances from abroad or receive some dollar income. Other beneficiaries are local producers whose competitors have to buy at p_1. These would include light industrial goods manufacturers such as footwear and some parts of non-export agriculture. A Cuban consumer can either go to the store where only CUC are accepted (called "shoppings") and purchase food at the p_1 exchange rate or go to the local farmers' market. The "shopping" and the farmers' market are competitors. Similarly, a Cuban shoe manufacturer might be able to sell part or all of its production at a store where the alternatives are shoes priced on the basis of a p_1 exchange rate.

The Losers

The first groups of losers are those sectors which have to sell foreign exchange at p_0. These include the state exporters such as the tourism sector, export agriculture, mining, and biotech.

Foreign investors figure among the losers too. Their investment funds are valued at p_0 and/or their local purchases are valued at p_1. Thus the cost of their share ownership is high as well as the cost of local inputs. This probably acts as inhibitor to foreign direct investment, but this is a subject worthy of its own paper and is only mentioned here.

Additional losers include the local producers whose competitors buy at p_0. This group may include non-export agriculture, which may have to compete with some commodities produced in government units such as farms operated by the army with access to dollars at p_0. It would stand to reason that private farmers (as opposed to the Basic Units of Agricultural Production, which may not have much latitude) would choose products or market timing so as not to compete head on with these state institutions, but the competition may not be altogether avoidable. Thus non-export agriculture stands to both win and lose from the double exchange rate, depending on what they produce and when they produce it.

The domestic oil producer who may compete against imported oil priced at p_0 also stands to lose. It is reported that Cuba's oil production is almost entirely destined to the generation of electricity (Piñón Cervera, 2005). Thus the exchange system serves to penalize production of oil in favor of consumption, both in industry and households.

The Big Losers

It can be argued that the biggest losers, outside of the economy as a whole, are the households. Cubans overwhelmingly work for state enterprises that sell or price at p_0. These entities will obviously have a derived factor demand function based on p_0 as well. Moreover, government regulations, in the pursuit of equity, prohibit wages based on p_1 or paid in foreign exchange, except for tips and some bonus packages. The households receiving these tips and bonuses (dollar income) are still a small minority of total households. Thus for most Cuban households every single purchase that they make of goods priced on the basis of a p_1 exchange rate leads to a loss in welfare.

The households' situation can be represented as in Figure 2. Households have demand D for household goods. Let us say, for the sake of argument, that at one time peso stores (those selling at p_0) met all the demand, at $q_{f(p0)}$. However, as offerings at the peso stores have shrunk, the households have had to resort to the "shoppings," farmers' markets, and/or the black market, which are a function of p_1. Thus the households face a kinked supply curve, with a new equilibrium at $q_{f(p1)}$. If the quantity of goods offered at the peso stores keeps shrinking then a new equilibrium may be at $q_{f(p1')}$. Alternatively, if the offerings at peso stores stay the same, but the peso appreciates against the dollar as it did in 2006, then the slope of the supply past the kink becomes less vertical (as in the dashed portion), and there would be a higher equilibrium level of Q. This higher level of consumption for households was probably the rationale for the government's decision to revalue the CP. But as can be seen by the shift from $S_{f(p1)}$ to $S_{f(p1')}$, any reduction of offerings in the peso (CP) stores can easily neutralize any benefit of a revaluation. It is clear that *any* purchase based on a p_1 exchange rate in a household whose income is based on p_0 represents a loss in economic welfare. With p_1 being over twenty times the value of p_0, it is easy to surmise that the double exchange rate system represents a large welfare loss for the Cuban household with access only to CP.

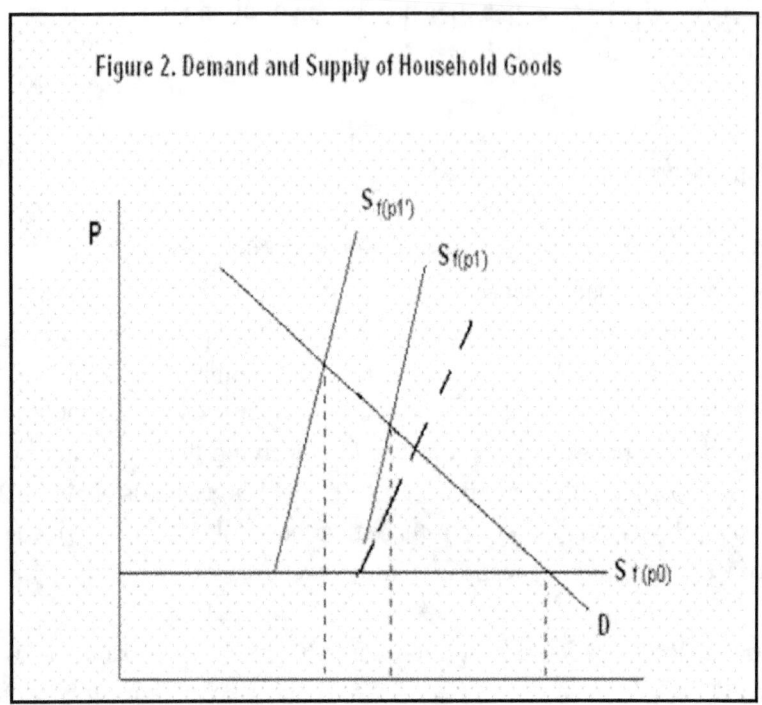

Figure 2. Demand and Supply of Household Goods

Remedial Perversion

What can householders do about their shrinking fortunes? They can supply goods and services on the basis of a p_1 exchange rate. This can be accomplished through legally registered self-employment or through the private production of goods, such as in private farming. Households can also provide black market goods and services. Since the state is basically the sole owner of all the means of production, the goods perforce have to be illicitly acquired from the state's stock.

As more goods and services are offered at price levels above the government set ones, the effect is to flatten the supply curve at quantities beyond the kink in Figure 2. Also the "disappearance" of goods from state stocks has the effect of moving the kink to the left (reducing the availability of goods at government set prices). The net effect is that the householders' efforts to subsist

create a smoother, less kinked supply curve as S_2 in Figure 3. The new equilibrium level may be at a lower price and larger quantity, but, as presented in
the last section, if the kink caused by the disappearance of state goods shifts
sufficiently to the left because of reduced offerings at the peso stores, With
the CUC set at nearly 25 times the value of the CP, and many essential goods
and services available only in CUC, it behooves the householder to supply
those CUC-earning goods and services regardless of their intrinsic value to
the economy as a whole. Economic activity no longer is allocated according
to its intrinsic value in the economy. Economic perversions occur such as
"engineers operating restaurants, psychiatrists working as car rental agents,
and doctors moonlighting in taxis" (Peters, 2002). These perverse incentives
can attract resources away from sectors that could ostensibly lead to higher
economic growth, e.g., education the net gain may be close to nil. In either
case, wildly perverse incentives are created.

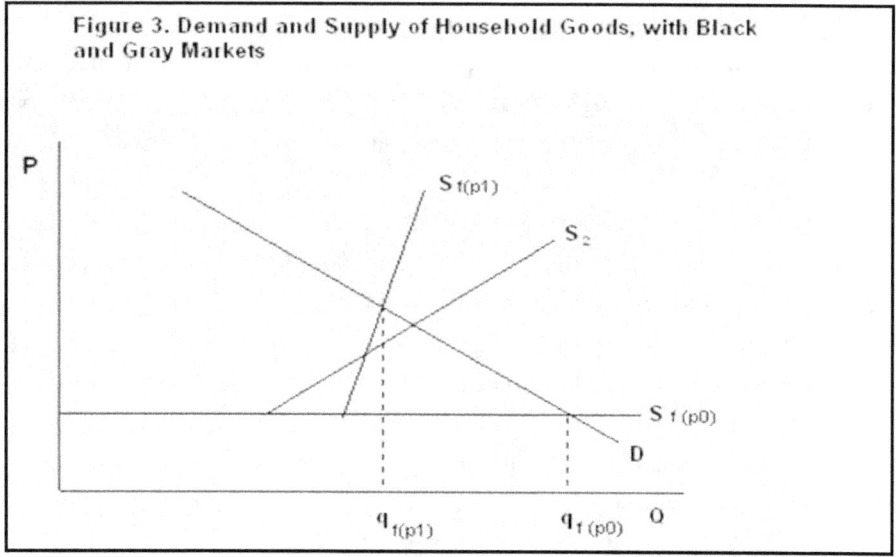

Figure 3. Demand and Supply of Household Goods, with Black and Gray Markets

Perhaps more importantly, they will also reduce the effectiveness of any
future market opening measures. For example, if restrictions on agriculture were relaxed, and farmers were allowed more freedom to grow and
sell whatever they wished at whatever prices they could fetch, the supply

response would be reduced if tip money at a nearby tourism facility could still represent many times the average wage. If that option were not available, more labor would stay or return to the farm to produce the goods made more remunerative by the market reform measures. However, if the government liberalized the restrictions on self-employment, perhaps too many resources would be drawn to that sector because it would price at p_1 and leave other important sectors such as healthcare and construction economically bereft. It is thus prudent, if not imperative, that exchange rate reform be a prerequisite to other market-opening measures. The double exchange rate system not only penalizes the householder, it can also vitiate the effectiveness of otherwise sensible reforms.

A Suggestion for Exchange Rate Reform

Cuba has four basic approaches available for its exchange rate regime: (1) do nothing, keeping dual exchange rates; (2) strive for a closer alignment between the CP and the CUC through careful monetary policy; (3) achieve unification through a sudden float; or (4) achieve unification at a new fixed rate.

Government policymakers officially acknowledge the need to unify the currencies. Indeed eliminating the dollar as legal tender for domestic transactions was seen as an interim measure toward unification (EIU, 2006). The Cuban government has publicly opted for (2), keeping inflation in check and avoiding the rapid currency movements experienced in the 1990s. However, the differential between the CP and the CUC has hardly budged in ten years, effectively making (1) the unofficial government approach, with the prolonged detrimental effects on householders and the economy in general discussed above. Alternative (4) could be workable in theory, but the government probably lacks the credibility and reserves to establish an exchange rate that is both convertible and fixed. (Foreign reserves would be necessary to counteract any run on the currency and its new parity value.) However, alternative (3) can prove workable in practice, and finally rid the country of its dual exchange rates and the resultant household poverty and economic perversions.

Since the CUC is largely an artifice of the economic crisis of the 1990s, and since wages and settlement of accounts still take place overwhelmingly in CP, it is proposed that the CUC be entirely eliminated from circulation. (Some might argue that the sordid history of the CP would make it the better candidate for elimination, but the choice of currency is not intrinsically important.) The government could announce that the CUC would cease to be legal tender on a given date, similar to the elimination of the national currencies when the Euro became the legal tender in many European countries. Holders of CUC would have a known number of days to exchange their notes for CP.

The central bank of Cuba knows the amount of CUC in circulation. In preparation for the reform, it can print new CP notes at a fraction of the nominal value of the CUC in circulation. The value of this fraction would depend on several factors, including the relative stock of bills currently in circulation of CP versus CUC and the desired range of final value that is desired for the CP relative to foreign currencies. The amount of new CP bills will depend on whether authorities want the CP to be close to parity in relation to, say, the Euro or if it desires a future exchange rate of, say, ten CP per Euro.

The central bank can then divide the stock of new bills to be exchanged into lots of equal size and equal in number to the trading days before the CUC is no longer legal tender. The exchange houses can then bid for the day's stock of CP with the CUC they have in hand. The central bank will auction off the day's lot according to the highest bids received. The highest bid on the last day will determine the final value and thus the value of the CP relative to foreign currencies. For example, if the final value of the CP is CUC0.10 and the CUC was being exchanged at €0.70, then the new value of the Euro in relation to the CP would be $1/(0.1)*(0.7)=14.29$.

As a way of maintaining the CP as a store of value, interest-bearing Euro accounts should be made available to households and legal entities. (The American economic sanctions program would make the dollar a difficult substitute.) By making possible a flight to the Euro by individuals and economic entities, the Cuban central bank would be motivated to keep the monetary base in check and to influence total money supply via differentials in interest rates between CP and Euro accounts. A flight to Euros could be staunched by a rise in interest rates in CP accounts, taking CP out of circulation. With prudent management over time, confidence in the CP would increase and interest differentials could decline.

As with the current situation, this exchange rate reform would create winners and losers. The reform will have the effect of pushing p_0 and p_1 together. The losers will be all those individuals and entities that are holding CUC at the beginning of the reform who had originally exchanged foreign currency at the p_1 exchange rate. Among the losers will also be those who are holding inventory in CUC. Losers will also be any entities that are able to exploit the differential between p_0 and p_1 that will cease to exist, such as government employment agencies that pay in CP but charge foreign entities in CUC. However, the winners will be the overwhelming majority of Cuban households which receive wages denominated in CP. At least equally as important, the overall Cuban economy will also be the winner, as it sheds the perverse incentives caused by the current system and add to the effectiveness of any future market-oriented reforms.

Moving to a unified managed float is not a panacea. Difficulties, both techni-cal and political, will arise. For example, mechanisms will have to be put in place to prevent possible manipulation by powerful players in the exchange market. Also, the losers will surely exert powerful political pressure to keep the status quo: mere lip service about moving toward a unified exchange rate. But the economic welfare of the vast majority of Cuban households and the sustainable future economic growth of the country are at stake. Cuba's central bankers and politicians can ignore these factors only at their long-term peril.

References

Piñón Cervera, Jorge R. "Cuba's Energy Challenge: A Second Look." *Cuba in Transition—Volume 15* (2005).

Economist Intelligence Unit (EIU), *Cuba Country Report*. August 2006, p. 7.

Canler, Ed. "The Miracle of the Cuban Economy in the 1990s." *Cuba in Transition—Volume 11* (2001).

González-Corzo, Mario A. "◇Cuban Monetary Reforms and their Relationship with Policies to Attract Remittances During the Special Period." *Cuba in Transition—Volume 17* (2007).

Peters, Philip. *Survival Story: Cuba's Economy in the Post-Soviet Decade.* Lexington Institute, May 2002.

http://www.jornada.unam.mx/ultimas/2008/02/24/discurso-de-raul-castro-texto-integro

5

CUBA. ECONOMIC GROWTH, AGEING, AND LONG-TERM FISCAL SUSTAINABILITY

Gabriel Di Bella, Rafael Romeu,

Andy Wolfe [37]

1. Introduction

Social security is at the center of the economic debate in most of the world. The intense population aging occurring in many advanced countries of Europe and Asia is causing social security finances to be under severe pressure, threatening fiscal sustainability. In Latin America and the Caribbean, the presence of relative young populations has shaped the debate around the type of social

[37] The views in this paper are those of the authors and do not represent the views of IMF's Management or its Executive Board. The corresponding author is Gabriel Di Bella (gdibella@imf.org). We thank Marcello Estevao for comments on an earlier draft and participants at the 2012 ASCE Annual Conference, including Sergio Diaz-Briquets, Jorge Dominguez and Silvia Pedraza for comments and suggestions. The usual disclaimer applies.

security system (with the discussion focusing on the advantages or disadvantages of pure pay-as-you-go, pure capitalization, or a mixed social security systems), rather than on the imminent problems associated with population aging. Cuba, however, constitutes an exception in this regard: while the policy discussions in the island have included elements associated with how to manage and finance social security, the core of the debate appears to be around on how to cope with the consequences of population aging.

With sustained increases in life expectancy, net negative migration flows, and low birth rates, the Cuban population has begun to decline, while the working-age population is projected to fall during the next 15 years. As a consequence, the share of people 65 years or older is expected to grow to about 1/3 of total population by 2050 (from less than 1/5 nowadays), turning Cuba in one of the 11 countries with the oldest population in the world (United Nations, 2011).

Recognizing this problem, the social security reform of 2008-09 increased the legal retirement age for both women and men by 5 years, avoiding what would otherwise had been a 2.9 percent annual increase in the number of social security beneficiaries during 2011-20. The reform also resulted in a significant decrease of the present value of future social security obligations.

In spite of the reform, however, current demographic projections still result in increasingly large social security spending, while there will be fewer workers contributing to the system. Concretely, the number of social security beneficiaries is expected to increase by 75 percent during the next 40 years to reach slightly less than 3 million by 2050, an increase of 1.4 percent per year. If long term GDP does not grow to offset the combined increase in the number of beneficiaries and the average pension, social security spending will increase as percentage of real GDP, threatening fiscal sustainability. Alternatively, higher long-term economic growth will result in larger social security contributions and will reduce the net present value of future social security spending flows. Thus, an accurate assessment of factors contributing to long-term growth is essential for evaluating the solvency of entitlement programs, and more generally, the sustainability of fiscal policy (Gordon, 2003).

This paper analyzes the interaction between population aging, long-term economic growth, and fiscal sustainability in Cuba. Although the problem of social security in Cuba has been analyzed in the literature (Mesa Lago 2008), this paper constitutes a first effort in quantifying the impact of its future imbalances on fiscal sustainability. After this introduction, Section II describes Cuban demographic trends and their implications for labor supply and social security spending. Section III calibrates a simple general equilibrium model using macroeconomic data for the last 40 years together with population and labor market projections, with a view to assess Cuba's sources of long-term economic growth and the challenges that population aging brings about. In turn, Section IV assesses Cuba's social security spending trends and evaluates long-term fiscal sustainability for a number of scenarios that consider alternative long-term economic growth rates; levels of social security benefits in real terms; levels of foreign transfers; and, tax rates. The results presented in this section allow arguing that the process of economic reforms recently launched (including the recent social security reform), is likely related to the need to increase long-term productivity and output growth, save government resources, and improve long-term fiscal dynamics in the context of an intense population aging, and still large, dependence on foreign transfers. The last section concludes.

Cuban Demographic Trends[38]

Cuba witnessed a continuous decrease in fecundity rates during the last 60 years. The number of daughters per woman decreased below the key value

---

[38] The analysis in this section is based on the projections published by the United Nations (World Population Prospects 2011), and the Cuban National Statistics Office (ONE, 2009), both of which are similar in spite of some level differences (e.g. the share of people 65 years and older as of 2010 is higher in ONE, 2009). Although ONE (2009) acknowledges that Cuban population will start decreasing faster than previously envisaged, the absolute decrease that is projected is a bit lower than that in United Nations (2011). The lower population decrease is the result of assuming a slight increase in total children per women and a decrease in net negative migration. United Nations (2011) includes three population projections, a "high" variant, a "medium" variant, and a "low" variant, each associated with different assumptions regarding the net birth rate. The one used in this paper corresponds to the "medium" variant.

[39] Population aged between 0 and 14 years old, peaked at 3.5 million in the mid-1970s, decreased to about 2 million by 2010, and is projected to continue decreasing before stabilizing at about 1.1 million by the end of the century.

of one (consistent with a zero growth population) by the mid-1980s, it is projected to reach a minimum of less than 0.7 by 2020, and to slowly return to one thereafter, in a process that would take decades. Against this backdrop, the Cuban population has begun to deline, and aging pressures are expected to accelerate during the current decade. The lower fecundity rate is being reflected in cohorts of newborns that are of a lower size than those than preceded them.[39]

Together with the lower fecundity rates, the median age of the Cuban population is increasing. It went from less than 25 years in the 1950s to about 40 years by 2010, and it is projected to reach 50 years by 2040. Contributing to this increase, the life expectancy at birth rose from less than 60 years in the 1950s, to 78 in 2010, and is projected to reach 81 years by 2030. In particular, the life expectancy of those reaching 65 years of age is also increasing, and this\ has a direct bearing on social security expenses.[40] Reflecting population aging, the country's age structure is changing (Figure 1). The number of people 65 years or older are projected to increase from about 1.4 million in 2010 (12 percent of population), to 2.5 million by 2030, and to more than 3 million by 2050 (30 percent of population). This intense population aging would turn Cuba in one of the 11 countries with the oldest populations by 2050, and with the oldest population in Latin America and the Caribbean (United Nations, 2011).

---

[40] See Peñate and Gutiérrez (2000), and United Nations (2011).

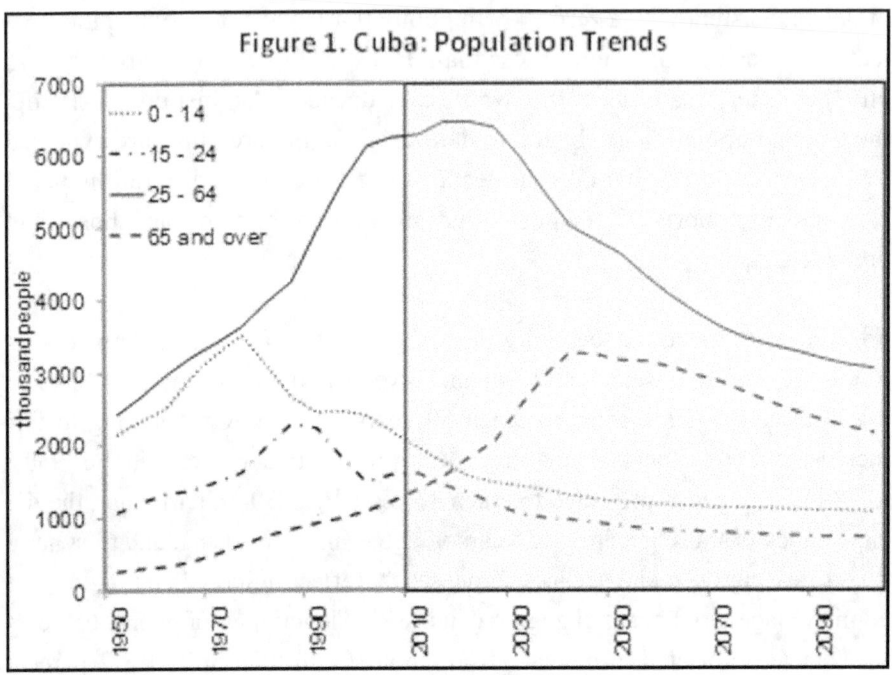

Figure 1. Cuba: Population Trends

Population aging will also affect labor supply, as the (legal) working-age population is projected to peak sometime during 2020-25.[41] In particular, people between 25 and 64 years old are projected to decrease from about 8 million in 2010, to about 7 million in 2030, and further to 5.5 million by 2050. Assuming people continue to retire at legal ages, and barring a further increase in the legal retirement age, the decrease in the working-age population (and thus of the number of people contributing to social security) will occur simultaneously with the increase in social security beneficiaries.

Net negative migration rates have contributed both to the increase in the median age of the population and to a lower growth rate of the labor force. United Nations (2011) estimates suggest that net migration rates have been above the world median (among immigrant sending countries) for the most

---

[41] The (legal) working-age population would have peaked before 2020, if not for the increase in the legal retirement age by 5 years for both men and women approved in 2008. Working-age population includes people aged 15-64 years.

part of the last 50 years, and is projected to remain negative (but decreasing) during the next few decades.[42] While migration during the first few years after 1959 included a significant number of elderly people, migrants during the last 20-30 years are mostly of working age (Lopez, 1986; Orozco, 2009).

The expected changes in the age structure will create policy challenges and demand difficult decisions. In particular, population aging will change the composition of the typical household and the functions within the family; produce an increase in the dependency ratio; put pressure on health and social security systems; require an increase in the supply of geriatric services, and a strengthening of health services aimed at the elderly; demand an adaptation of the working environment to allow for the working elderly; decrease the labor supply; and demand an analysis of the incentives behind the low fecundity rate (ONE 2009).[43]

2. Assessing Trend Growth Using a Simple General Equilibrium Model

Assessing long-term growth is essential to analyze the sustainability of fiscal accounts, and in particular, of social security entitlements. Economic growth feeds into the value of marginal pension benefits, which together with the number of beneficiaries determine social security spending; the value of tax receipts and contributions that finance social security spending; and the (net) present value of future flows of social security obligations.

With that in mind, this section calibrates a general equilibrium model with Cuban macroeconomic and demographic data, in order to assess long-term economic growth; such assessment will be later used to evaluate the sustainability of fiscal and social security policies.

---

[42] United Nations (2011) projects that net negative migration in Cuba will slowly decrease in the coming decades, similarly to what is assumed to Puerto Rico. Net negative migration flows for Jamaica and the Dominican Republic are projected to be negative for a longer period of time.

[43] The dependency ratio expresses inactive population as percent of working population. According to ONE (2009), it will increase swiftly beginning in 2020.

The Model

The economy is deterministic and is populated by a representative household, a representative firm and a government, and is composed by two planners. The economy is open in the sense that external trade in goods in services is allowed, though the size of any trade deficit $(-TB_t)$ is bound by the sum of exogenous and known levels of foreign transfers (FT_t) and, zero-interest, real external public debt net flows (B_t), which are centrally managed by the first planner, so that $-TB_t = FT_t + B_t$. The first planner also defines the level of government spending (G_t), and given the exogenously determined path for foreign transfers and real external public debt net flows, it defines the average (net) tax rate (τ_t) on total aggregate output (Y_t), so the following condition holds, $G_t = \tau_t \cdot Y_t + FT_t + B_t$.[44] Inflows from foreign transfers need to be spent during the period they are received, as there is no technology to convert them into savings.

The second planner, taking the decisions of the first planner as given, maximizes the household's (discounted) utility derived from consumption of goods and basic services:

$$\sum_{t=0}^{\infty} \beta^t \, N_t \cdot U(\frac{C_t}{N_t}) \qquad (1)$$

For computational purposes, it will be assumed that the utility function $U(\cdot)$ is of the form, $U(x) = x^{1-\sigma}/_{1-\sigma}$, with $\lim_{\sigma \to 1}$, so $U(x) = lx(x)$. Aggregate consumption is denoted by C_t, $0 < \beta' \leq 1$ is the discount factor, and N_t denotes, the exogenous and known, non-sleeping hours of the (working age) population. This formulation implies that aggregate utility depends on the utility of consumption per available hour for the representative agent times the number of

---

[44] Taxes are understood to be net of domestic transfers, and to include all forms used by the government to extract resources from productive activities to finance public spending. Although the model is non-monetary, taxation is meant to capture, e.g., the real transfers from the "inflation tax". The two-planner model is based on a model by R. Manuelli (Chapter 14, Ljunqvist and Sargent, 2004).

available hours of the population. The economy has access to a constant return to scale Cobb-Douglas technology:

$$Y_t = z_t \cdot F(u_{k,t} K_t, H_t L_t) = z_t \cdot (u_k K_t)^\alpha (H_t L_t)^{1-\alpha} \qquad (2)$$

where, z_t is a measure of total-factor, or neutral, productivity and α is a production function parameter that in a competitive equilibrium denotes the gross share of output allocated to capital, with $0 < \alpha < 1$. Aggregate labor effort (in hours) is denoted by $L_t = N_t \cdot \eta_t \cdot (1-\mu_t) \cdot h_t$, where η_t is the (exogenous and known) labor participation rate, μ_t is the (exogenous and known) unemployment rate, and h_t denotes the (exogenous and known) hours worked per year for the average worker as a ratio of available non-sleeping hours.[45] There are two types of capital, physical capital, K_t, whose (exogenous and known) utilization rate is denoted by $u_{k,t}$, and human capital, H_t, which is assumed to linearly augment labor input. Effective working hours are thus defined as $H_t \cdot L_t$. Without loss of generality, it is assumed that $Z_t = \gamma_z^t$, $H_t = \gamma_H^t$, $N_t = \gamma_N^t$, where γ_z denotes the (gross) growth rate of neutral productivity, γ_H, the (gross) growth rate of human capital, and γ_N, the (gross) growth rate of the working-age population.

Disposable income (which by construction is equivalent to output of goods and basic services), $Y_t^D = (1-\tau_t) \cdot Y_t$, can be used for either consumption or (gross, non-housing) investment, I_t:

$$Y_t^D = C_t + I_t \qquad (3)$$

The stock of physical capital evolves according to,

$$K_{t+1} = K_t (1-\delta_t) + I_t \qquad (4)$$

where δ_t is the depreciation rate. The second planner's problem then involves picking paths for consumption and investment so that (1) is maximized,

---

[45] It is assumed 16 hours per day are non-sleeping.

subject to (3) and (4) and the usual non-negativity constraints, which in the current model are satisfied by the assumed functional forms. All labor force variables are exogenous. To complete the model, the following trans-versality condition (TVC) must be satisfied for the saddle path equilibrium, $\lim_{T\to\infty} \beta^T \lambda_{I_t} K_{T+1} = 0$, where $\beta^T \lambda_{I_t}$ denotes the Lagrange multiplier for the feasibility constraint (3), at time $t = T$.

Balanced Growth Path Conditions

Through an appropriate change of variables, the problem in (1) - (4) can be transformed into one in which all endogenous variables are stationary in steady state. This can be done by applying the transformation $\tilde{x}_t = X_t / \gamma_y^t$ to $X_t = \{C_t, I_t, K_t, Y_t\}$, where $\gamma_Y = \gamma_Z^{1/(1-\alpha)} \gamma_{H,N}$ is the (gross) rate of output growth, and $\gamma_{H,N} = \gamma_H \cdot \gamma_N$.[46] Moreover, the production function (2) implies that output per effective hour will grow, along a balanced growth path (BGP), at a (gross) rate equal to:

$$\gamma_y = \gamma_z^{1/(1-\alpha)} \tag{5}$$

In turn, if one is interested in output per hour, equation (5) should be modified to incorporate the rate of growth of human capital, as follows:

$$\overline{\gamma}_y = \gamma_z^{1/(1-\alpha)} \gamma_H \tag{6}$$

Applying the change of variables to problem (1) - (4), finding the Steady State from the Kuhn-Tucker conditions, and dividing by y, results in the following Balanced Growth Path (BGP) conditions:

$$1 = (\beta / \gamma_Y)[(1-\tau) \cdot \alpha \cdot (\tilde{k} / \tilde{y})^{-1} + (1-\delta)] \tag{7}$$

---

[46] This transformation is similar to that in Greenwood, Hercowitz, and Krusell (1997).

$$\tilde{i} / \tilde{y} = \tilde{k} / \tilde{y} \left[\gamma_Y - (1-\delta) \right] \tag{8}$$

$$\tilde{c} / \tilde{y} + \tilde{i} / \tilde{y} = (1-\tau) \tag{9}$$

In (7) - (9) above, $\tilde{c}/\tilde{y}$ denotes the steady-state private consumption ratio, $\tilde{i}/\tilde{y}$ is the steady-state investment ratio, and $\tilde{k}/\tilde{y}$, is the steady state value for the non-housing capital stock as percent output.

Data and Calibration

The calibration of the model presents some challenges. A first challenge is related with the quality of Cuban historical data, including for the sample period used in this paper (1970-2010). National accounts data through 1985 corresponds to estimates produced and published by the United Nations, as official Cuban data was compiled using the "Material Product System" (MPS), a technique developed in the former Soviet Union and used by most centrally planned economies (Mesa Lago and Perez Lopez, 1985). From 1985 onwards, national accounts compiled following the United Nations' National Accounts Manual are available from a variety of sources (the United Nations Economic Commission for Latin America –ECLAC-, and the Cuban National Statistics Office –ONE-). However, even for the period post-1985 a number of methodological breaks introduce some noise to the time series (Perez Lopez and Mesa Lago, 2009). The dual monetary and exchange rate system that is in place since the second half of the 1990s creates some additional problems. In particular, the use of official exchange rates in the compilation of official national accounts may be biasing upwards the share of wages in national income and downwards the share corresponding to the remuneration of capital (Di Bella and Wolfe, 2008). Annex I describes the data series used for calibration and their definitions.

A second challenge is that Cuba is in the middle of a population transition. The growth rates of the work force have steadily decreased during the last 60 years, are projected to continue decreasing during the next 15 years, and to turn negative thereafter during a number of decades before reaching a non-growth steady state (United Nations, 2011). This implies that calibrating the steady state value of γ_N so it coincides with its observed average value during the historical sample period (as in Kydland and Prescott, 1982) would be unwarranted, as it would not reflect actual population trends. This calls for a calibration procedure that incorporates expected population trends into the analysis.

A third challenge is to analyze potentially unsustainable fiscal dynamics within an optimizing general equilibrium model. To go around this problem, the maximization occurs only after the first planner has "picked" government spending and the tax rate, given exogenously determined paths for foreign transfers and real external public debt net flows. The model rules out the possibility for the second planner to optimally pick a path for consumption consistent with increasingly unsustainable private debt levels.

A fourth challenge is that the historical period considered includes the economic adjustment that followed the collapse of the Soviet Union. The calibration needs to take this into consideration. In this connection, Popov (1999, 2007) analyzes the experience of a large number of former socialist economies and finds that a significant part of the Soviet-era capital became effectively unusable during the transition; Izyumov and Vahaly (2008) argue that as much as 30 percent of the capital stock was destroyed.

A final challenge is related with the fact that the (unobserved) path for z_t depends on the assumed value for the initial capital stock, K_{1970}. This is important as γ_z, determines the long-term growth rate of output per effective hour along a BGP, as specified in (5).

Concretely, the BGP conditions (7) - (9) define a system that includes 8 unknowns γ_y, β, δ, α, τ, $\tilde{c}/\tilde{y}$, $\tilde{i}/\tilde{y}$, and $\tilde{k}/\tilde{y}$, so the solution requires calibrating 5 parameters. The parameters chosen for calibration are γ_y, β, δ, α, and τ, what allows obtaining $\tilde{k}/\tilde{y}$ from (7); $\tilde{i}/\tilde{y}$ from (8); and, $\tilde{c}/\tilde{y}$ from (9).

Calibration Period. To address the challenge caused by the ongoing population transition, the data used for calibration includes both historical data for
1970-2010, and going forward, United Nations (2011) population projections.
Historical data is "cleaned" of its short-term fluctuations to recover long-term
trends.[47] This approach implies that the macroeconomic dynamics post-2010
resulting from the model will be shaped by projected demographic trends. In
particular, for the period post-2010, it is assumed that the factors of production
are fully employed, as the endogenous variables (k/y, i/y and, c/y) converge
to their steady states, which occurs only after population stabilizes. In other
words, the historical time series for each variable is considered as part of a
longer-term path, where each such variable eventually reaches its steady state.

Output growth rate. The calibration of γ_Y is done in two stages. First, the
observed cumulated real output growth rate for 1970-2010, is decomposed into
its observed and unobserved components. To obtain the unobserved cumu-
lated growth rate for total neutral productivity ($\gamma_{z,1970-2010}$) it is assumed that the
unobserved cumulated growth rate for the capital stock is about equal to the
cumulated real output growth.[48] This allows recovering the initial capital stock
(K_{1970}) given the observed path for real investment rates and the calibrated
path for depreciation rates. In turn, K_{1970} allows recovering the initial level
for total neutral productivity, given the observed output levels, labor market
data, and human capital, whose gross growth rate is assumed to be equivalent
to that of the years of education of the average worker. The cumulated rate
$\gamma_{z,1970-2010}$ allows obtaining the (average) annual gross growth rate γ_z. Second, the
average annual productivity growth rate for 1970-2010 is assumed to remain
unchanged post-2010. The same is assumed for the growth rate of human capital. The working force's growth rates post-2010 are taken from United Nations
(2011), which slowly converge to $\gamma_N = 1$. These allow us to obtain $\gamma_Y = \gamma_Z^{1/(1-\alpha)}\gamma_{H,N}$.

---

[47] The capital stock utilization rate was approximated by the ratio between observed electricity consumption by productive activities and its long-term trend; such trend was estimated by
filtering the original series with a Hodrick-Prescott filter ($\lambda=100$) as in Di Bella, Romeu and
Wolfe (2011). See Annex I for more details.

[48] The rate $\gamma_{K,1970-2010}$ is unobserved because it depends on K_{1970}, which is also unobserved.

Production function parameter. The value for α is chosen so it coincides with the average gross share of output allocated to capital observed during 1970-2010. This value is assumed to remain unchanged post-2010.

Depreciation Rate. There is no official information on depreciation rates. The calibration assumes that equipment depreciates in 11.25 years, while engineering works and structures depreciate in 50 years (as in Aguilar and Collinao, 2001). However, to account for the capital destruction after the collapse of the Soviet Union, it is assumed that depreciation rates increased by 0.15 above their "normal time" values during 1992-1993 (i.e., at the out-set of the "Special Period"), in line with the experience in other transition economies.

Table 1: Calibration Results

	Historical	γ_z=1.008	γ_z=1.015	γ_z=1.017
β	0.790	0.790	0.790	0.790
δ	0.048	0.048	0.048	0.048
τ	0.224	0.224	0.224	0.224
α	0.533	0.533	0.533	0.533
γ_γ	1.009	1.025	1.040	1.045
γ_z	1.001	1.008	1.015	1.017
γ_H	1.008	1.008	1.008	1.008
γ_N	1.000	1.000	1.000	1.000
K/Y	1.269	1.198	1.136	1.116
C/Y	0.703	0.689	0.677	0.673
I/Y	0.073	0.087	0.099	0.103

Source: Authors' calculations

Net effective tax rate, foreign transfers, and real external public debt net flows. The tax rates for 1970-2010 are approximated so $G_t = \tau_t . Y_t + FT + {}_t B_t$ holds, i.e., τ_t mirror the behavior of FT_t, as the real value of any external public debt net flows during this period was assumed to be *de facto* real foreign transfers.[49] In other words, when foreign transfers decline, the tax rate increases, given a level of government spending. For instance, after the collapse of the Soviet Union foreign transfers virtually disappeared, so effective tax rates increased in order to finance government spending (which decreased but a rate lower than that of GDP). In turn, the net effective tax rates decreased during the last few years with the increase of Venezuelan purchases of Cuban services (that the model treats as foreign transfers). For the period post-2010, the average tax rate is calibrated so it remains constant at its 2010 value. In turn, foreign transfers are assumed to remain constant in real Cuban pesos during the period post-2010, i.e., a gradual decrease as a percent of GDP. Any fiscal disequilibrium going forward is assumed to be financed by zero-interest, real external public debt net flows.

Utility discount rate. The discount rate β is chosen so the endogenously determined level for K_{2011} does not "jump too much" with respect to that of 2010. In other words, the endogenously determined growth rate for K in 2011 cannot be significantly different from the annual average growth rate observed for the period for which there is data available. The intuition behind this calibration procedure is that if β is too high, $\tilde{k}/\tilde{y}$ will also be too high, and thus, it would require a discrete jump in investment rates in 2011, and a non-smooth transition in the capital-output ratio. The opposite would happen if β is too low.

Calibration Results. Table 1 shows the calibration results. The calibrated long-term growth rates for neutral productivity (0.1 percent per year) and human capital (0.8 percent per year), determine the long-term output growth rate (0.9 percent per year).[50] The long-term growth rate of the working force is zero, consistent with population trends. The tax rate for post-2010 is cali-

---

[42] Much of the external debt contracted by Cuba previously to 1990 was never repaid, including debt with the former Soviet Union, former CMEA members, and other official bilateral debt.

[50] The growth rate in the years of education of the average worker during 1970-2010 is higher than those observed in, for instance, Canada, Chile or Costa Rica. However, among tertiary/university graduates, there is a predominance of non-technical degrees. This suggests that $\gamma_H=1.008$ might represent a higher bound.

brated at about 22.5 percent of GDP (i.e., its estimated value for 2010). The utility discount factor is calibrated at about 0.8, which reflects a clear preference for consumption in the present, as opposed to future consumption. The endogenously determined steady states for the private consumption rate is about 70 percent of GDP; for the non-housing investment rate is slightly below 7.5 percent GDP; and the non-housing capital stock is about 1.27 times the GDP level.

"Historical" and Alternative Output Growth Rates

The long-term output gross growth rate of γ_Y=1.009, is consistent with the historical data for 1970-2010, so it will be referred thereafter as the "historical" rate. The low output growth rate suggests that an important part of the headline growth observed since the 1970s was caused by the growth in the working age population, which averaged about 1.6 percent annually during 1970-2010. The low (and negative) net birth rates expected going forward suggest that this demographic bonus is already over.

As it was pointed out, one of the challenges of calibrating the model was that the value for neutral factor productivity growth depends on the value assumed for K_{1970}. To address this challenge, the model is calibrated for three alternative neutral factor productivity gross growth rates (γ_z=1.008, and γ_z=1.015, and γ_z=1.017), which result in long-term output gross growth rates of γ_Y=1.025, γ_Y=1.04, and γ_Y=1.045, respectively (Table 1). As a result, the endogenous steady state values for $\tilde{k}/\tilde{y}$, $\tilde{i}/\tilde{y}$, and $\tilde{c}/\tilde{y}$ all change (as well as the value for β, which is affected only marginally). The calibrated values for all other parameters (δ, α, and τ), remain unchanged. Figure 2 shows the forecast long-term dynamics for a number of selected variables. In the convergence to their steady states, the output growth rates are projected to be higher than steady state growth rates in the next few years, and then decrease below them, reflecting the shrinking working force. These four output growth rates (i.e., the historical and the three alternative rates) will be used to assess fiscal sustainability in what follows.

3. Social Security Trends, Long-Term Economic Growth and Fiscal Sustainability

This section presents social security spending projections that take into consideration the characteristics of the Cuban Social Security System. In turn, these projections are evaluated together with macroeconomic projections and demographic trends to make an assessment of long term fiscal sustainability.

Social Security beneficiaries in Cuba reached about 1.6 million in 2010 (from about 1.1 million in 1990); age-related pensioners represented 1 million while survivors' benefits and disability beneficiaries represented about 0.6 million. The large increase during the last 20 years is explained by population aging and by an increase in the number of people that apply for a pension at the minimum legal age (Izquierdo and Gutierrez, 2003). Social security expenditures represented about 10 percent of real GDP in 2010; about 65 percent of this corresponded to age-related pensions, 20 percent to survivors' benefits, and the rest to disability benefits. The average age-related pension was about equal to 1/3 of real output per worker in 2010 (a significant increase from the ratios observed at the beginning of the decade).[51]

Fiscal Sustainability for Alternative Long-term Growth Rates

The reform of the social security law of 2008-09 increased the legal retirement age from 55 to 60 years old for women and from 60 to 65 years old for men, reducing considerably the present value of social security obligations, and postponing to 2020 the increase in beneficiaries resulting from population aging. Indeed, absent such reform, the number of beneficiaries would have increased

---

[51] Disability benefits and survivors' benefits were about 90 percent and 85 percent of age-related pensions, respectively. Social Security expenses as percent of real GDP were larger in the mid-1990s than that at the beginning of that decade, as GDP decreased faster than social security spending during the "special period". The average monthly pension in 2010 was 248 Cuban pesos (183 Cuban pesos at 1997 prices), or about US$10 at "unofficial but legal" exchange rates. Pensions are mostly spent in the "rationed" system at below market prices. The marginal pension granted in 2010, at 1997 prices, was 223 Cuban pesos, what appeared to be lower than that established by law.

by about 35 percent by 2020 vis-à-vis 2010 (Figure 3). As a consequence of the reform, any increase in social security spending during this decade will only be the result of increases in the real value of social security benefits.

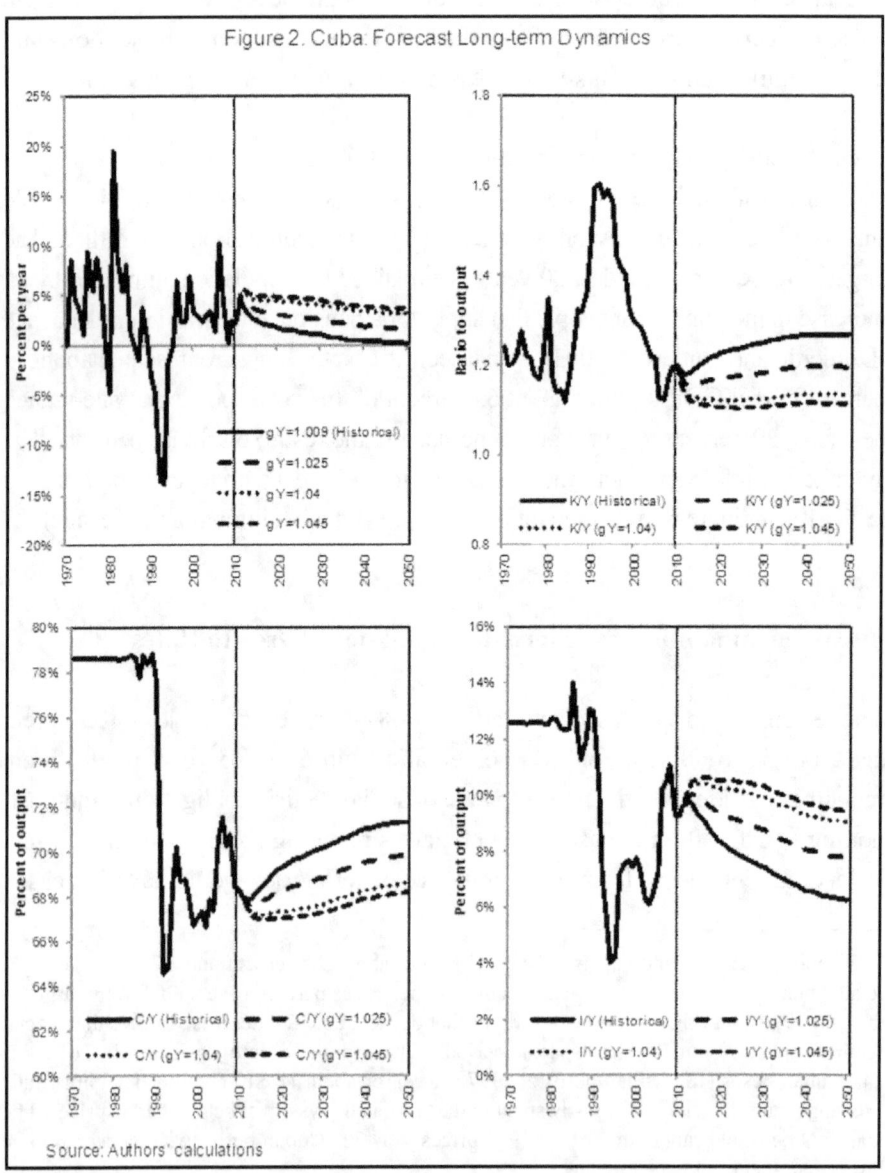

Figure 2. Cuba: Forecast Long-term Dynamics

Source: Authors' calculations

In spite of the reform, current demographic trends result nonetheless in a strong increase in social security beneficiaries in the medium and long-terms. Indeed, beneficiaries are projected to peak at about 2.9 million by 2050 (a 1.4 percent annual increase), as the result of both an increase in the number of people 65 years or older, and of their life expectancy.

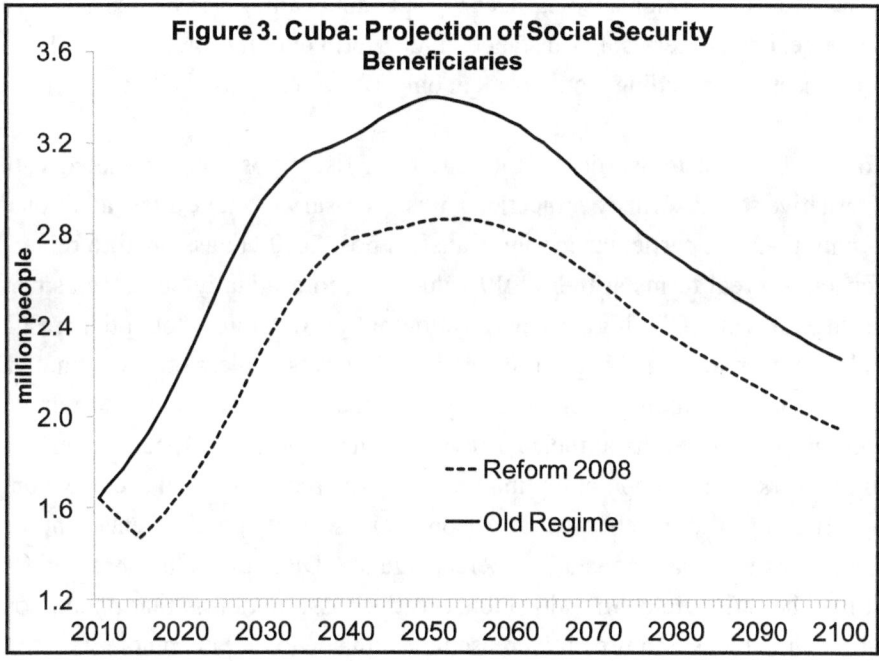

Figure 3. Cuba: Projection of Social Security Beneficiaries

In turn, the growth rate of social security (marginal) benefits will depend on the growth rate of real wages, which ultimately depend on real output growth. For instance, if long-term output growth was $\gamma_Y=1.009$, (and assuming that the ratio of observed to legal pensions remains constant at their 2010 value), the (average) marginal pension (in real terms) would increase by 1.4 percent annually during the next 40 years; if, in turn, output growth was $\gamma_Y=1.025$, the increase would be 2.7 percent annually. Clearly, the differences in the well-being of the marginal pensioners resulting from alternative output growth rates would be significant.[52]

---

[52] Social security benefits' projections are expressed in 1997 Cuban pesos. See Annex II.

The increase in both the number of beneficiaries and of real marginal benefits will result in an increase in social security spending as percentage of real GDP, if the long-term output growth rate is similar to that implied by historical trends (i.e. $\gamma_Y=1.009$). In such a case, social security spending would double, peaking at about 20 percent of GDP by the 2060s. If instead, long-term output growth rates were higher, social security spending would increase less, or even decrease, in GDP terms. For instance, if long-term output growth was $\gamma_Y=1.025$ social security spending would peak at only 12 percent of real GDP.

To assess the sustainability of the long-term fiscal position associated with alternative social security projections, it is necessary to make a few additional assumptions. In particular foreign transfers post-2010 are assumed to remain constant in real terms at their 2010 value, (i.e., to gradually decrease as percentage of real GDP); higher long-term output growth rates would thus result in larger decreases in foreign transfers in GDP terms. Unless otherwise noted, tax revenues, including social security contributions, are assumed to remain constant in GDP terms at their 2010 value (what given the expected decrease in the working age population, may imply an increase in social security contributions or in some other tax rate). Non-social security government spending is assumed to remain constant as percentage of GDP at the value observed for 2010. The rationale behind this (conservative) assumption is that population aging will at least require an increase in health spending per capita.

These assumptions would result in fiscal dynamics consistent with significant increases in public debt in the medium and long-term, in case output growth was $\gamma_Y=1.009$. Concretely, while fiscal deficits would remain manageable during the next few years, they will increase significantly afterwards, with cumulative deficits reaching 140 percent of GDP by 2040 and 250 percent by 2050. The fiscal picture would not be significantly affected in the next few years if output growth was higher, though in the long-term cumulated deficits in GDP terms would be lower for larger output growth rates (Table 2).[53]

---

[46] The cumulative fiscal disequilibrium is calculated as the sum of fiscal imbalances year after year. As pointed out above the solvency problem would be worse if financing would occur with interest-bearing debt. For instance, if $\gamma_Y=1.009$ and the real interest rate on debt

These results suggest that social security entitlements may not be sustainable if long-term growth stabilizes at a rate similar to that implied by historical data. In such a case, balancing the fiscal accounts would require that benefits grow at a lower rate, that social security contributions (or other taxes) increase, or that non-social security public spending decreases in GDP terms.[54]

Fiscal Sustainability for a Number of Alternative Scenarios

Fiscal sustainability can be affected by changes in policies or in the external environment. The analysis below presents a set of scenarios, each of which reflects an alternative calibration that includes a change in an exogenous or policy variable (Table 2). Each scenario results in 4 fiscal paths, as the change in the exogenous or policy variable is analyzed together with the four long-term output growth rates presented so far (γ_Y=1.009, γ_Y=1.025, γ_Y=1.04, and γ_Y=1.045).

Scenario 1. This scenario considers a linear increase in marginal social security benefits from a level equal to about 40 percent of real output per worker (as observed in 2010) to 50 percent in 2020, so as to bring them closer to that in the legal framework (i.e., 60 percent of output per worker). Such a policy change would result in an increase in the cumulated fiscal cost (at zero interest rates) of about 30 to 40 percentage points of GDP through 2050, depending on whether long-term output growth picks up or remains at that observed historically.

Scenario 2. This scenario considers a linear decrease in foreign transfers from 13 percent of real GDP (as estimated for 2010), to zero in 2020, in order to assess the vulnerability of fiscal accounts to a negative external shock. The resulting

---

was 1 percent, the cumulated cost through 2050 would be 30 percentage points of GDP; if the real interest rate was instead 2 percent, the cost would climb to more than 60 percent of GDP. Debt service charges could potentially create liquidity problems in addition to the solvency problem highlighted.

[54] As social security benefits are denominated in legal domestic currency, a devaluation of the Cuban peso (and the resulting inflation) would also result in a decrease in the real value of benefits in real terms.

fiscal dynamics are the worst of all the scenarios considered. Cumulated fiscal deficits (financed with zero-real interest debt) would reach about 70 percent of GDP by 2020 for all long-term growth rates, and would continue growing in what appears an unsustainable fashion going forward. Unsurprisingly, these results suggest that a sudden decrease in foreign transfers constitute the largest vulnerability of the Cuban economy. If this risk materialized, the resulting macroeconomic imbalances would require of strong compensatory policy measures.

Scenario 3. This scenario considers a linear decrease of foreign transfers to zero in 2020, with simultaneous offsetting increases in tax rates, in order to assess the impact on fiscal sustainability of a negative external shock that is compensated by active fiscal policy. Although fiscal dynamics in this case would be similar to those in Scenario 1, the underlying macroeconomic dynamics would be significantly different. In particular, the compensatory increases in tax rates would result in lower consumption and investment rates (both in the transition to their steady states, and in steady state), lower capital-output ratios, and lower output growth rates in the transition to steady state (i.e., a downward move for the real output path for every growth rate). In the very long-term, however, the debt to output ratios are lower than in Scenario 1, as the increase in tax rates is assumed to be permanent, while foreign transfers in such scenario were assumed to slowly decrease in GDP terms. For instance, in case long-term output growth was $\gamma_Y=1.009$, the increase in the tax rate needed to compensate the decrease in foreign transfers would be about 11 percentage points; steady state consumption rates (as percent of GDP) would decrease by about 10 percentage points, while steady state investment rates (as percent of GDP) would decrease by about 1 percentage point. In turn, real annual output growth post-2010 (and through 2050) would be (on average) about 2/3 that in Scenario 1 (Table 3).[55]

---

[55] The model only allows analyzing the effect of increases in income taxes. Future research could explore using a more refined model that allows for consumption taxes, and for the incorporation of leisure in the utility function.

Table 2. Cuba: Fiscal Sustainability under Alternative Scenarios (new debt as percent of real GDP)

	γY=1.009 (Historical)	γY=1.025	γY=1.04	γY=1.045	γY=1.009 (Historical)	γY=1.025	γY=1.04	γY=1.045
	Baseline: Sustainability under alternative long-term output growth rates				**Scenario 1:** Increase in benefits to 50 percent of real output per worker			
2015	2	2	3	3	3	3	3	3
2020	8	10	11	11	10	12	13	13
2025	22	25	28	28	27	30	32	33
2030	49	52	55	55	59	61	63	63
2040	137	133	130	129	161	154	148	146
2050	246	228	214	210	288	263	244	238
	Scenario 2: Decrease of foreign transfers to zero by 2020				**Scenario 3:** Decrease of foreign transfers to zero and increase in the tax rate by 2020			
2015	20	20	20	20	2	2	2	2
2020	69	66	65	64	7	9	10	11
2025	131	124	118	116	21	22	22	24
2030	236	188	175	171	61	42	40	41
2040	377	331	296	286	135	104	82	82
2050	568	477	413	395	246	169	121	117

Source: Authors' calculations

These results suggest that if a decrease in foreign transfers materialized, the downward scenario, where transfers are assumed to decrease gradually over a 10-year period.

Implications for Macroeconomic Policy

Cuba's external financing includes short-term trade and official bilateral financing; the country does not have access to voluntary credit markets. Most bilateral financing continues to be concentrated in a limited number of countries (the Soviet Union in the past, Venezuela currently), making Cuba vulnerable to changes in their policies or economic conditions. Domestic financing includes domestic credit from the Cuban Central Bank (BCC), and the domestic banking system, which is of insufficient depth.

Table 3: Impact of an external shock compensated by fiscal policy
(γ_Y=1.009)

	Scenario 1	Scenario 3
Tax rate (percent of output)	22.4	33.3
SS Consumption (percent of output)	70.4	60.5
SS Investment (percent of output)	7.2	6.2
Output Growth 2010-50 (percent per year)	1.2	0.8

Source: Authors' calculations

In this context (and barring structural changes in economic policies), any unsustainable financing gaps are bound to be dealt with further capital controls, exchange rate devaluations, further scarcity of goods in the rationed system, and decreases in the supply of tradable goods through the public services (e.g., medicines and complex procedures that require imported inputs by the health system), among other.[56] The unsustainable fiscal dynamics that may arise if entitlements remain unchanged and long-term growth does not pick up, will likely be dealt with a *de facto* reduction in the purchasing power of benefits (for instance through a devaluation of the legal tender), including those provided in the form of services.

4. Concluding Remarks

Low long-term growth and population aging are among the main policy challenges facing Cuba going forward. Historical data is consistent with very low productivity growth, high economic volatility, capital destruction (following the collapse of the Soviet Union), and significant external vulnerability. Moreover, while total population is estimated to be decreasing already,

---

[56] Given the dual exchange rate, dual currency system currently applied in Cuba, unsustainable domestic financing results in hard currency rationing, and potentially in exchange rate devaluations (of either domestic currency against reserve currencies, and of the exchange rate between both domestic currencies (the CUP and the Convertible Cuba Peso, CUC). The elimination of the dual currency system will be challenging in the presence of unsustainable fiscal dynamics.

working-age population is forecast to begin decreasing as early as next decade, and the number of pensioners is forecast to grow from about 1.6 million in 2010, to about 3 million during the next 40 years. This implies that the demographic bonus that fueled economic growth during the past few decades is already over. Higher than projected negative net migration rates of people of working age could worsen the situation further. Alternatively, the situation may improve if workers continue in the labor market beyond the legal retirement age.

Increasing long-term economic growth, decreasing government spending and employment, and increasing non-state employment are among the main objectives of economic policy in Cuba, as reflected in the "principles" announced after the conclusion of the sixth congress of the Communist Party (GoC, 2011). This suggests that policy makers are aware of the need to increase the dynamism of the economy; it also hints that the low productivity growth may be related to large increases in government employment, which explained most job creation during the last decade. In particular, with respect to social security, GoC (2011) establishes that the role of the government in the financing of social security benefits should decrease, and be gradually replaced by contributions of the non-state sector. The principles also recognize the economic policy challenges associated with population aging, in particular the increase in the number of pensioners.

This paper suggests that unless Cuba attains a higher long-term economic growth, social security entitlements may result in an unsustainable fiscal dynamics in the medium to long term. Fiscal accounts will be further compromised if marginal social security benefits are increased to align them with those established in the regulatory framework. Most importantly, the paper suggests that Cuba's vulnerability to a decrease in foreign transfers is very high, and that even a gradual decrease in transfers could cause fiscal dynamics to worsen very fast, even for long-term output growth rates that are many times as high as that observed historically. Tax increases to compensate for decreases in foreign transfers, would result in better fiscal dynamics during the next few years, but at a heavy cost in terms of output and private consumption losses, and would not alter significantly the fiscal picture in the long-term. This further stresses the need to increase productivity growth, including

through the incorporation of modern technology and better forms of organization of production. If higher productivity and long-term growth rates are not
attained, the alternatives to achieve sustainability are limited to an increase in
taxes and contributions, or a decrease in public expenditure growth rates (both
in social security and non-social security spending). Tax increases may be de
facto implemented through higher inflation rates.

References

Aguilar, X., and M. Collinao, 2001, "Calculo del Stock de Capital para Chile
    1985-2000",

Working Paper No. 133, Banco Central de Chile, Santiago.

Di Bella, G., and A. Wolfe, 2008, "A Primer on Currency Unification and
    Exchange Rate Policy in Cuba: Lessons from Exchange Rate Unification
    in Transition Economies," Cuba in Transition, Vol. 18.

Di Bella, G., R. Romeu, and A. Wolfe, 2011, "External Vulnerabilities and
    Economic Fluctuations: An Approximation to Cuba's Output Gap", mimeo.

Greenwood, J., Z. Hercowitz, and P. Krusell, 1997, "Long-Run Implications
    of Investment-

Specific Technological Change", American Economic Review, Vol. 87, No. 3,
    pp. 342–62.

Gordon, R., 2003, "Exploding Productivity Growth: Context, Causes and
    Implications,"

Brookings Papers on Economic Activity, Vol. 2003, No. 2, pp. 207–279.

Government of Cuba (GoC), 2008, Ley No. 105 de Seguridad Social, La
    Habana, Cuba.

Government of Cuba (GoC), 2009, Decreto No. 283 del Consejo de Ministros, La Habana, Cuba.

Government of Cuba (GoC), 2011, Lineamientos de la Política Económica y Social, La Habana, Cuba.

Izyumov, A., and J. Vahaly, 2008, "Old Capital vs. New Investment in Post-Soviet Economies: Conceptual Issues and Estimates," Comparative Economic Studies, Vol. 50, pp. 79-110.

Izquierdo, V., and Y. Gutierrez, 2003, "La Seguridad Social en Cuba en el Nuevo Milenio," mimeo, La Habana, Cuba.

Kydland, F., and E. Prescott, 1982, "Time to build and aggregate fluctuations",

Econometrica, Vol. 50, pp. 1345-1371.

Lopez, L., 1986, "Cubans in the United States", The American Academy of Political and Social Science, No. 487, September.

Ljunqvist, L., and T. Sargent, 2004, Recursive Macroeconomic Theory, Second Edition.

The MIT Press, Cambridge, Massachusetts.

Mesa Lago, C., 1985, "El Desarrollo de la Seguridad Social en America Latina," Revista de la CEPAL, No. 60.

Mesa Lago, C., 2008, "Envejecimiento y pensiones en Cuba: la carga creciente", Nueva Sociedad No.216, julio-agosto de 2008.

Mesa Lago, C., and J. Perez Lopez, 1985, "A study of Cuba's material product system, its conversion to the system of national accounts, and estimation of gross domestic product per capita and growth rates", World Bank.

Oficina Nacional de Estadística (ONE), 2009, "Proyecciones de la Población Cubana 2010-

2030", Publicaciones Ocasionales, La Habana, Cuba.

Oficina Nacional de Estadística (ONE), 2011, "Seguridad Social. Indicadores Seleccionados-

2030", Publicaciones Semestrales, La Habana, Cuba.

Orozco, M., 2009, "The Cuban Condition: Migration, Remittances and its Diaspora", mimeo, Inter-American Dialogue, Washington, DC.

Peñate Rivero, O., and L. Gutiérrez Urdaneta, 2000, La Reforma de los Sistemas de Pensiones en América Latina. La Alternativa Cubana, Ed. Ciencias Sociales, La Habana, Cuba.

Perez Lopez, J., and C. Mesa Lago (2009), "Cuban GDP statistics under the special period:

Discontinuities, Obfuscation, and Puzzles", Cuba in Transition, Vol. 19.

Popov, V., 2000, "Shock Therapy versus Gradualism Reconsidered: The End of the Debate (explaining the magnitude of the transformational recession)," Comparative Economic Studies, Vol. 42, pp. 1-57.

Popov, V., 2007, "Shock Therapy versus Gradualism Reconsidered: Lessons from Transition Economies after 15 Years of Reforms," Comparative Economic Studies, Vol. 49, pp. 1-31.

United Nations, 2011, World Population Prospects, the 2010 Revision, United Nations'

Department of Economic and Social Affairs, New York (http://esa.un.org/wpp/)

Annex I. Macroeconomic Data

This annex describes the data used in this paper, as well as their sources and definitions.

Gross Domestic Product (GDP). Growth rates for headline real GDP for the period 1971-1985 correspond to data published by UNDP at 2005 constant prices; growth rates for the period 1986 – 1996, correspond to data published by ECLAC at 1981 constant prices; data (in levels) for the period 1996 to 2010, correspond to that published by the National Statistical Office (ONE), in 1997 constant prices. The series for 1970-2010 in constant prices was obtained by chaining real growth rates. Headline GDP was first netted out of property income (assumed to be equal to 3 percent of GDP); the change in stocks (which also includes errors and omissions); and, beginning in 2000, the estimated value of Venezuela-related purchases of Cuban services (i.e., non-tourism service exports), that the model treats as foreign transfers. In order to obtain private disposable income the resulting GDP series is multiplied by the calibrated tax rate.

Gross Fixed Capital Formation (GFCF), Government Spending and Imports of Goods and Non-Factor Services. Growth rates for the period 1971-1985 correspond to data published by UNDP at 2005 constant prices; growth rates for the period 1986 – 1996, correspond to data published by ECLAC at 1981 constant prices; data (in levels) for the period 1996 to 2009, correspond that published by the National Statistical Office (ONE), in 1997 constant prices. Data for 2010 is estimated using information from ONE. The series for 1970-2010 in constant prices was assembled by chaining real growth rates.

Machinery and Equipment and Investment in Structures. Growth rates for the period 1971-1990 were assumed equal to that for GFCF; growth rates for the period 1990 – 1996, correspond to data published by ECLAC at 1981 constant prices; data (in levels) for the period 1996 to 2009, corresponds that published by the National Statistical Office (ONE), in 1997 constant prices. Data for 2010 is estimated using information from ONE. The series for 1970-2010 in constant prices was assembled by chaining real growth rates. In particular with respect to Structures, it was assumed that 65 percent of investment corresponds to housing structures, and the rest to non-housing construction.

Exports of Goods and Non-Factor Services. Growth rates for the period 1971-1985 correspond to data published by UNDP at 2005 constant prices; growth rates for the period 1986 – 1996, corresponds to data published by ECLAC at 1981 constant prices; data (in levels) for the period 1996 to 1999, corresponds that published by the National Statistical Office (ONE), in 1997 constant prices. Data for 2000-2010 results from netting out from the data published by ONE, the purchases of non-tourism services by Venezuela, estimated by subtracting exports and tourism receipts (in real terms) from the series of exports of goods and non-factor services. Purchases of non-tourism services by Venezuela are estimated by subtracting from the non-tourism services series, the average non-tourism exports for the period 1990-1999.

Labor and Population Statistics. Labor market statistics (hours worked per week, the labor participation rate and the open unemployment rate) were obtained from the National Statistical Office, and from the United Nations. Some data (including the unemployment rate) were estimated through simple econometric analysis, as there were years for which labor market data was unavailable. Historical population data was also obtained from ONE and the United Nations, as well as the years of education of the average worker. The long-term population forecast corresponds to the medium-variant published by the United Nations Population Division and available online.

Labor's share on output. Partial information for the period 1971-1985 corresponds to data published by UNDP at 2005 constant prices; partial information 1985-2010 corresponds to that published by the National Statistical Office (ONE), in 1997 constant prices.

Electricity Consumption. Data for electricity consumption is available annually online from 1957 onwards from the National Statistics Office. This data was used to approximate the utilization rate of the capital stock.

Exchange Rate System. The Available (official) fiscal statistics are compiled in current Cuban pesos (CUPs, the Cuban legal tender); income and expenditures denominated in currencies other than the CUP are converted into CUPs at legal exchange rates. Social security benefits are denominated and paid in CUPs, and spent in the "rationed" system. Goods sold in the rationed system include tradable goods, whose actual (market) prices are higher than the controlled prices for which they are sold. This implies that social security costs at market prices are higher than those reported by official statistics, and from the point of view of the pensioners, that the purchasing power of benefits is higher than their value in current US dollars.

Annex II. Social Security in Cuba and Forecasts

Cuba was among the first countries in Latin America to enact social security legislation, together with Argentina, Chile and Uruguay (Izquierdo and Gutierrez, 2003). Before 1958 there were a large number of autonomous pension schemes that served specific occupations both in the private and public sectors, each of which had its own legislation, administration, financing and benefits (Mesa Lago, 1985). After 1959, the different pension schemes were unified, and in 1963 the Social Security System was established, under the principle of universal coverage, and "pay as you go" financing (Izquierdo and Gutierrez, 2003). Social security financing is the responsibility of the state through the budget. Resources come from employers' contributions and from the state transfers to fill the gap between resources and expenditures. The social security system does not accumulate financial reserves or capital, and its expenses and income are treated as an independent budget within the state's budget.

In 1979 the system was reformed to formally separate the social security system from the social assistance system. In 1994, a new reform aimed at strengthening social security financing (Law 73, "Tax System Law") opened the possibility for workers to also contribute to the system; and increased employers' contribution from 12 to 14 percent in the case of firms with foreign capital participation, or privately managed cooperatives. Workers' contributions (established at 5 percent of gross wages), are only applied to a small number of firms. In 2003, the Social Security Institute was created to improve the management of social security's resources and provide a better service.

In 2008 a new Social Security Law (Law 105) is passed, that increases the retirement age by 5 years for both women and men (from 60 to 65 years for men, and from 55 to 60 years for women).[55] The law further establishes that to be eligible to receive a pension, a worker should have at least 30 years of service. Regular pensions are defined as the equivalent to 60 percent of the average of the 5 better wages received during the last 15 years of work. For each year in excess of 30 years of service, the pension is to be increased by 2 percentage points. Disability pensions are established in proportion of the years of service (50 percent of the average wage for those that worked at least 20 years, increasing by one percentage point for each year in excess of 20, and by two percentage point for each year of service in excess of 30). Survivors' benefits are calculated in relation to the dependents of the person that had received the original pension.[56] Social security benefits include, monetary benefits (i.e., paid in Cuban legal tender); service benefits (medical assistance); and, in-kind benefits (medicines and medical supplies provided free of charge).[57]

---

[50] A transitory regime through 2015 was established for the workers that turn 60 (men) or 55 (women), during the first 7 years after the approval of law (GoC 2008, 2009).

[51] In case of 1 dependent, the benefits are set at 70 percent of the original pension; in the case of two dependents, the benefits are set at 85 percent of the original pension; and for 3 or more dependents, the benefits are set to be equivalent to the original pension.

[52] Monetary pensions are classified into ordinary and extraordinary pensions. Ordinary are those granted for jobs not associated with any specific risks; extraordinary are granted for risky jobs. Monetary pensions are further divided between short and long-term; short-term are those granted only temporarily, for instance those granted to mothers right before and after giving birth (for a total of 18 months). Since 1986, short-term pensions are responsibility of the entities in which workers labor. There are special pension regimes for independent workers, the members of the armed forces, the employees of the ministry of interior, members of independent agricultural cooperatives and artists.

Social Security Beneficiaries Forecast

Beneficiaries as of 2010 and their life expectancy. The number of beneficiaries per type of benefit corresponds to those reported in ONE (2011); the age composition of beneficiaries is assumed to correspond to that of the general population, as reported by ONE (2009). Their life expectancy is line with that in United Nations (2011).

New beneficiaries each year (in gross terms) from 2011 onwards. Beyond the transition period (which ends in 2020), they are calculated as the sum of the annual net increase of men 65 years and older, and of women 60 years and older; annual cohorts of women and men through 2100 are interpolated from United Nations (2011), from original projections in 5-year cohorts. The number of social security beneficiaries (including regular pensioners and those receiving survivors' benefits) as percentage of people of legal retirement age is assumed to evolve with labor participation rates lagged 40 years. Disability beneficiaries are assumed to remain constant as a proportion of the working-age population for 2010, as reported by ONE (2009, and 2011). The forecast for the working-age population from 2010 onwards is that in United Nations (2011).

Social Security Compensation and Expenditure Forecasts

Compensation for the existing beneficiaries. It is assumed to be equal to the average benefit in real terms existing in 2010, per type of benefit. To obtain benefits in 1997 Cuban pesos, the benefits in nominal terms as reported in ONE (2011), are deflated by the GDP deflator.

Marginal compensation for new beneficiaries beginning in 2011. They are calculated as the average of the best 5 years of per capita GDP out of the last 15 years, as required by law (GoC, 2008, and 2009). The resulting average is multiplied by the ratio between the marginal benefit in real terms calculated from information in ONE (2011) and per capita GDP in 2010 (about 40 percent). Survivors' benefits and disability benefits are calculated from pensions, by keeping the ratios of the former and latter with respect to pensions observed as of 2010 (all in real terms), calculated from information in ONE (2011).

Social Security Expenditure. The forecast for each type of benefit is calculated as the sum of the product of existing beneficiaries and their respective annual compensation. The forecast for aggregate social security expenditures is the sum of the expenditures for each type of benefit. As benefits depend on the long-term GDP growth rate, social security expenditures (both in levels, and as percentage of GDP), will vary together with long-term GDP growth.

6

CUBA: EXTERNAL CASH FLOW, BARTER TRADE AND POTENTIAL SHOCKS

Luis R. Luis[60]

The external sector constrains Cuba's economic growth by failing to generate sufficient foreign exchange through exports and capital inflows to sustain a high level of investment. This paper examines Cuba's external sector by focusing on external cash flow in the light of convertible currency and barter trade sectors and international banking statistics. The paper also analyzes the adequacy of the nation's international liquidity and current policies in the face of potential external sector shocks, crucially the possibility of the sudden stop of the barter trade and finance from Venezuela.

---

[60] This paper benefitted from the thoughtful comments of Ernesto Hernández-Catá, Lorenzo Pérez and Roger Betancourt. All remaining errors are the entire responsibility of the author.

Cuba's external accounts show a sizable trade deficit offset by services exports, deriving mainly from tourism and income from Cuban health professionals in Venezuela. Though the Central Bank of Cuba has not released complete balance of payments statistics for 2009–2011, CEPAL reports that the current account is near balance in 2010 and 2011.[61]

But Cuban current account data differ markedly from actual cash flow, as payments do not accompany a large part of trade and services transactions. Consequently, the current account shows an incomplete picture of external sector balance. One key difficulty is the accounting of Cuban non-traditional exports of health and education services. These exports are part of a barter arrangement between Cuba and Venezuela which have been described in a number of articles and official publications.[62] Payment for Venezuelan crude oil and other petroleum products takes the form of services by Cuban personnel but prices and payment mechanisms are unclear. There is no transparent financing flow associated with these transactions, though it is evident that a sizable transfer of resources is taking place from Venezuela to Cuba.

A related problem applies to trade with a number of other countries. The bulk of Cuban imports that come from Angola, Brazil, Bolivia, China, Ecuador, Nicaragua, Russia and Vietnam are financed bilaterally by official banks and other state entities. As far as we know, there is no statistical information on the financing accompanying this trade. In this paper Venezuela and those eight other countries are treated as a group effectively engaged in barter trade that is self-financed bilaterally, and it is not feasible to match trade numbers with capital account transactions.

---

[61] CEPAL estimates the 2010 current account deficit at 0.3 percent of GDP and reports an improvement for 2011, CEPAL, *Balance Preliminar de Economias de America Latina y el Caribe*, 2010 and 2011.

[62] See for example Rolando H. Castañeda, "El Insostenible Apoyo de Venezuela a Cuba y sus Implicaciones," *Cuba in Transition — Volume 20*, ASCE, 2010, and Luis R. Luis, "Cuban External Finance and the Global Economic Crisis," *Cuba in Transition — Volume 19*, ASCE, 2009.

Figure 1. Cuban Assets and Liabilities in International Banks
(*in millions of US$*)

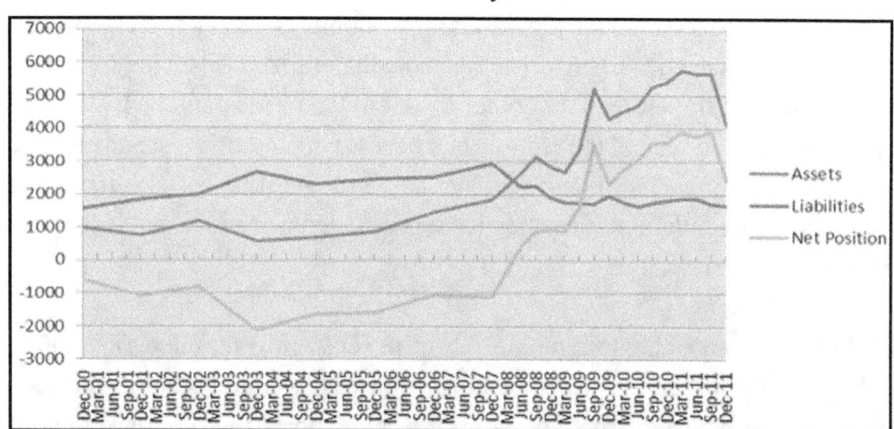

Source: Bank for International Settlements

Trade with other nations settles in convertible currencies and trade transactions match payments. In this paper, convertible trade is separated from barter trade.

International Liquidity and Cash Flow

The Central Bank of Cuba does not publish data on international reserves. One high quality source of data for Cuban international liquidity is up-to-date reporting on the assets and liabilities of Cuban banks, including the Central Bank, to international banks of 43 countries and financial centers reporting to the Bank for International Settlements. Cuban bank liabilities correspond to trade financing and other loans made to Cuban banks by most of the world's international banks. Cuban bank assets are deposits in the same international banks and constitute the bulk of the hard currency available to the Cuban government and state entities to meet short-term international financial and trade obligations.

Cuban bank assets reached $5649 million on September 2011, an increase of $368 million from September 2010 but unexpectedly fell to $4109 million by the end of December 2011. Nonetheless, in five years assets rose $2.7 billion, a significant sum for an economy with weak international credit, undergoing severe difficulties with traditional exports and needing to import much of its foodstuffs in adverse international markets. Some of the increase in Cuban assets abroad is needed to provide cash and collateralized financing for essential imports, as trade credit and other bank credits to the country have tightened. This can be seen in the red line of Chart 1, which shows a steady decline since 2007 of Cuban liabilities to foreign banks. A question posed below is the role of the accumulation of financial assets as a defensive mechanism against potential external shocks.

Table 1 shows an estimated summary external cash flow for the period 2008–2011. During this period, Cuba has been running a large deficit in the convertible trade balance largely because of weak exports and the weakening of Cuba's farm output, which requires the importation of the bulk of the island's foodstuffs. Austerity measures since 2008, a tightening of the allocation of foreign exchange to state companies and the recovery of nickel prices resulted in the halving of the trade shortfall by 2010. There are no official numbers for 2011, but an acceleration of growth and a loosening of the availability of foreign exchange to official importers suggest a somewhat larger trade deficit for 2011.

The convertible trade deficit is partially offset by a surplus on convertible services driven by Cuba's tourism receipts. Revenue from tourism averaged $2.2 billion per year in 2008–2010 according to official Cuban data, and it likely exceed that number in 2011 by around $200 million given a reported rise in the number of visitors.

Items C and D are small. Interest payments and royalties, C, is an estimate based on official Cuban balance of payments data for 2008. Item D, lending by BIS reporting banks to Cuba, is a hard data item. Item F, change in non-BIS external assets, is an educated guess based on the need for liquid assets in banks of barter trade countries to finance some trade operations such as transportation and imports from private entities in those countries. An unexpected and rapid shift out of BIS deposited assets in the last quarter of 2011 suggests a portfolio reallocation as well as a use of reserves to finance imports. This is partly shown as an estimated increase in non-BIS bank assets of US$0.5 billion in 2011.

Change in external assets at BIS banks, G, is hard data, enabling the calculation of a convertible currency residual, item E, "Investments, lending and transfers." This is a key line in the table, and it shows sizable cash flowing to Cuba, peaking in 2008 at US$7 billion, down to an average of US$3.6 billion per year in 2009–2011.

There are two key components of Item E: remittances from Cubans living abroad and investments, finance and transfers from Venezuela. Cash flowing from Venezuela includes investments in joint ventures, hard currency loans and grants.[63] Proceeds from the freezing of foreign accounts were also a sizable component in 2008. There is a wide range of estimates for remittances by various analysts and surveys such as Orozco and the Inter-American Development Bank.[64] These place annual remittances in the range of US$800 million to US$1200 million, and Cuban sources are attributed a somewhat higher estimate. Since 2010, remittances appear to be increasing given the higher number of Cubans visiting relatives.[65] However, it appears that much of the increased transfer takes place in the form of consumer products and tools used directly by relatives and friends and as merchandise and working capital for newly-established small businesses.

---

[63] Other countries engaged in barter trade with Cuba may provide cash transfers and finance. Nonetheless, the bulk of their financing and transfers are tied to barter trade transactions.

[64] Manuel Orozco, "On Remittances, Markets and the Law: The Cuban Experience in Recent Times," *Cuba in Transition — Volume 19*, ASCE, 2009; Mario A. González-Corzo, "ASCE's Contribution to the Literature on Remittances: 1991–2009," *Cuba in Transition — Volume 19*, ASCE, 2009; and Inter-American Development Bank, "Remittances to Cuba from the United States," Surveys, 2008 and 2009.

[65] CEPAL, op. cit., 2011

Barter Trade and Convertible Trade

Table 1. Cuba: Estimated External Cash Flow
(US$ billion)

	2008	2009	2010	2011e
A. Convertible Trade Balance	-4.4	-2.5	-2.1	-2.8
B. Convertible Non-financial Services Balance	0.8	0.6	0.8	0.9
C. Interest, Royalties/e	-1.0	-1.0	-1.1	-1.2
D. BIS Bank Lending**	-0.9	0.0	-0.1	-0.1
E. Transfers, Lending and Investment */e	7.0	4.4	4.0	2.5
F. Change in non-BIS External Assets/e	0.1	0.2	0.2	0.5
G. Change in External Assets at BIS ** a	1.4	1.3	1.3	-1.2
Memorandum				
Cuban Bank Assets at BIS Reporting Banks	2.8	4.3	5.4	4.1

Source: Estimated by the author with data from *Oficina Nacional de Estadísticas, Banco Central de Cuba* and Bank for International Settlements.
* Remittances and freezing of accounts are part of this residual
** Adjusted for foreign exchange rate changes e/ estimated

Cuba's international trade has undergone a significant shift since 2005. In that year barter trade represented a bit more than 40 percent of overall merchandise trade.[66] In 2010 barter represented almost 60 percent of all trade, underscoring the concentration and dependence on the oil barter trade with Venezuela.

---

[66] These figures refer only to merchandise trade. Including barter services would reinforce the point about the driving role of barter trade. Pricing and payments arrangements regarding Cuban services exports to Venezuela and other Latin American countries such as Nicaragua present difficulties in interpreting official statistics.

Table 2. Cuba's Barter and Convertible Trade[67]

(US$ million)

	2005	2006	2007	2008	2009	2010
Barter Exports	604	886	1538	1222	1246	2559
Barter Imports	3471	4586	4733	7364	4778	6480
Barter Balance	-2867	-3700	-3195	-6142	-3532	-3921
Convertible Exports	1556	2039	2147	2442	1617	2038
Convertible Imports	4133	4912	5346	6870	4128	4167
Convertible Balance	-2577	-2874	-3199	-4428	-2511	-2128
memorandum						
total barter trade	4075	5471	6271	8586	6023	9039
total convertible trade	5689	6951	7493	9313	5746	6205

Source: Calculated by the author from data of *Oficina Nacional de Estadísticas*

Assuming a rough number for cash remittances of around US$1 billion per year[68] and US$0.8 billion from freezing of foreign accounts, then cash flow from Venezuela was US$5.2 billion in 2008, the peak year of the recent crisis, and some US$2.4 billion estimated for 2011. At an average price of near US$98 per barrel, Venezuelan shipments of petroleum in 2011 are worth US$3.9 billion. On this basis oil and cash flow from Venezuela in 2011 reached US$5.4 billion or close to 9 percent of GDP at official exchange rates but a much higher percentage at a far lower peso exchange rate that a unified equilibrium exchange rate imply.

Liquidity available to the Central Bank and other Cuban banks is represented by the assets held at BIS reporting banks, which amounted to US$5.7 billion in

---

[67] Barter trade comprises trade with Angola, Brazil, Bolivia, China, Ecuador, Nicaragua, Russia, Venezuela and Vietnam.

[68] This is the figure roughly estimated by Orozco, op. cit., for 2006 and 2007. He estimates it at $1.2 billion for 2008. Overall remittances are likely higher in 2010 and 2011 but with most of the increase probably being remittances in kind.

September 2011 and US$4.1 billion in December 2011. Lacking data on international reserves from the Central Bank of Cuba, the BIS data represents the best estimate available of Cuban international liquidity. It forms the basis for the analysis of Cuba's first line of defense regarding potential external shocks.

There are two major forces driving the value of trade. One is the rise of international oil prices. This is reflected immediately in the barter import data as Cuba relies on Venezuela for nearly all its oil import requirements. The second element is the austerity measures taken by Cuba in 2008 and continued since then. This affected imports of capital goods more than proportionally since they are largely sourced through convertible trade. Capital goods imports in 2010 were 44 percent below the level of 2008 and were even below the figure for 2005.

Barter trade is self-financed.[69] This has provided Cuba with immense sustenance in recent years. It means, looking at it from a different angle that Cuba can center on financing its convertible imports. However, the future could well look different. What about a shift in Venezuelan policy regarding Cuba and a reduction or suspension of current oil barter arrangements? Below is a look at the implications of potential external shocks for Cuba's international liquidity.

International Liquidity and Shocks

In this section we examine policy towards international liquidity using a simple model. Ordinarily one would want to focus on policy towards international reserves. The lack of data for official international reserves means that it is necessary to center the analysis on total international liquidity. This

---

[69] In strict terms not every barter transaction is financed by some form of official credit or grant and some trade with China, Russia and other barter partners may take place in cash. There is no way to separate cash trade from that tied to official finance so all trade with China and Russia is considered to be barter.

alternative focus provides a valid substitute as liquidity is entirely in the hands of official financial institutions.[70]

A simple model starts with the objective function of the government (or more narrowly of the central bank). The objective function is a quadratic function expressing that the government will use international liquidity (L) for two purposes, to support trade transactions (R) and to dampen the impact of external shocks (Z). R* and Z* represent target levels of the two kinds of liquidity and the objective function is:

$$U = -\tfrac{1}{2}\,\mu\,(L - R^* - Z^*)^2 \tag{1}$$

It means the government finds it undesirable when actual liquidity, L, deviates in any direction under or over (from) the sum of the target levels. Government policy implies optimizing (1)."[71] This can easily be done. Defining,

$$R^* = \gamma\,Mc \tag{2}$$

and

$$Z^* = Pr(S)\,Mb \tag{3}$$

These relationships mean that the target liquidity to back-up trade, R*, is a proportion, $\Lambda < 1$, of the level of convertible imports, Mc. Ordinarily a country can look at its reserve policy as a function of overall imports but as barter imports are self-financed, cover is only required for imports that need to be paid in cash or financed through ordinary commercial bank channels.[72]

---

[70] International reserves on the other hand would be indispensable for a complete analysis of the balance of payments and monetary policy.

[71] An article which looks at optimal international reserves in terms of designing a hedging strategy is R. Caballero and S. Panageas, "Contingent Reserves Management: An Applied Framework." Cambridge, Massachusetts: National Bureau of Economic Research, 2004

[72] Central banks may also want some liquidity for operations in the foreign exchange market. Pervasive capital controls in Cuba are a rough way to reduce this need.

Target liquidity needed to dampen the impact of potential shocks, Z^*, is equal to the probability of a shock here referred to as the stop of barter trade, Pr(S), times the level of barter imports. In the literature, a critical shock facing an emerging country is taken to be the sudden stop of capital flows.[73] In the Cuban case, because of default and arrears on external debt going back to the early 1960s, there are few capital flows to be stopped. The critical shock to be guarded against is that of an end or sharp reduction of barter imports, which are obtained at highly concessional terms. Alternatively, barter imports plus additional transfers or lending from barter partners can also be used to gauge the size of a prospective shock. In any case, the government will want to assess the likelihood of a shock in the form of a stop of barter trade in its design of a reserve or liquidity policy.

Substituting (2) and (3) into (1) and maximizing the objective function, the optimal level of liquidity, $L^\wedge$, is obtained:

$$L^\wedge = \gamma \, Mc + Pr(S) \, Mb \tag{4}$$

Using a similar procedure by redefining (1) in a more detailed form[74] the optimal level of liquidity associated with convertible trade, $R^\wedge$, and the mitigation of shocks, $Z^\wedge$, would be equal to the target levels defined above. So,

$$Z^\wedge = Z^* = Pr(S) \, Mb \tag{3'}$$

This result follows the form of the objective function, which can be modified to represent a variety of government preferences. A constraint on the availability of external liquidity can also be imposed on the objective function.

---

[73] See Sebastian Edwards, "Thirty Years of Current Account Imbalances, Current Account Reversals and Sudden Stops," *Staff Papers*, IMF, Volume 51 (10), pp. 1–49, 2004; Dani Rodrik, "The Social Cost of Foreign Exchange Reserves." Cambridge, Massachusetts, National Bureau of Economic Research, 2006; and Caballero and Panageas, op. cit.

[74] In this case we can define $U = -\frac{1}{2}\mu(R-R^*)^2 - \frac{1}{2}\alpha(Z-Z^*)^2$, where R and Z are current levels of the two types of liquidity, and μ and α are parameters expressing the government's sensitivity to liquidity targets. Substituting (2) and (3) and optimizing in regards to R and Z we obtain $Z^\wedge$ in (3') and the corresponding expression for $R^\wedge = R^* = \gamma Mc$.

This is shown in the Appendix, which derives $Z^\wedge$ under a budget constraint from the convertible trade balance as a function of the exchange rate and capital flows. In this section the unconstrained objective function is used which yields a range of interesting results for $Z^\wedge$ and $R^\wedge$ set against available data on international liquidity.

The variables above could be interpreted as one period variables. That is, $Pr(S)$ could be taken as the probability of a stop of barter trade in one year. More realistically, the government has a longer policy horizon, encompassing several years. In this case, we can rewrite (3') in the following multi-period form:

$$Z^\wedge = \sum \beta^n \, Pr(S) \, M_{b,n} \tag{5}$$

This means that optimal liquidity needed to mitigate the effects of a stop in the barter trade will be the sum of expected values of barter import losses over the policy horizon where $\beta < 1$ is the discount factor per period n and $M_{b,n}$ is barter imports in year n. We can calculate the value of $Z^\wedge$ at the beginning of the policy horizon.[75] For example for $Pr(S) = .3$ and $\beta = .8$, $Z^\wedge$ will be equal to 1.5 times barter imports.

It will be useful to examine Cuba's international liquidity in the context of the framework outlined above. The key question involves the adequacy of liquidity to meet convertible trade needs and as a cushion against a stop of barter trade.

Table 3 shows the result of a simulation that yields optimal international liquidity for Cuba for 2005–2010. In this simulation actual liquidity obtained from the BIS is compared to the optimal results. The latter assume three yearly probability levels, 0, .1 and .2, for the end of barter trade caused by a stop or

---

[75] Over a long planning horizon the value of $Z^\wedge$ at period 0 will be approximated by $Pr(S)M_b/(1-\beta)$. We do not make $\sum \beta^n Pr(S) = 1$, so that $Z^\wedge$ can exceed one year of barter imports. M_b is in constant year 0 dollars.

disruption of Venezuelan shipments of oil and additional finance. Throughout the calculations $\Lambda = .8$. This factor discounts future import flows and adjusts for the use of a constant annual probability of a stop of barter trade.

The first column of optimal liquidity shows results at $Pr(S) = 0$ meaning that optimal liquidity is derived only from the need to cover convertible imports. Here the assumption is that the import coverage ratio is equal to six months' imports ($\gamma = 0.5$), a level that would allow the government to assure collateralized trade finance for convertible imports by pledging its assets in BIS banks. Under this calculation Cuba experienced a shortage of liquidity in 2005–2008 and an excess of liquidity for 2009 and 2010.[76] But why does Cuba maintain this apparent excess liquidity?

The answer is that $Pr(S)$ is greater than zero in 2009–2010. The second and third columns of optimal liquidity use values of 0.1 and 0.2 for $PR(S)$. A higher probability of a stop of barter trade raise liquidity needs. Table 3 shows that with a probability of .1 per year actual liquidity is close to optimal liquidity. Is it that the government expects the probability to be around .1 per year? Note that at .1 per year over a long policy horizon, the discounted cumulative probability of a stop in barter trade nears ½. Any serious observer would agree that the cumulative probability of an end to the Venezuelan subsidy over a long horizon is at least close to one. Analysts reckon that the Venezuelan subsidies are economically and politically unsustainable for Venezuela.[77]

---

[76] This result should be adjusted for the changes in actual trade finance from BIS banks, but doing this does not substantially alter the outcome. For example a US$0.5 billion increase in trade finance in 2005–2007 still would leave Cuba with a shortage of available liquidity. In addition, a US$0.2 billion decrease in 2008–2011 would also make little difference.

[77] R. Castañeda op. cit., and Castañeda, "La Ayuda Económica de Venezuela a Cuba: Situación y Perspectivas — Es Sostenible?." *Cuba in Transition — Volume 19*, ASCE, 2009.

Table 3. Actual and Optimal Liquidity
(million US$)

	Actual	Optimal		
		Pr(S)=0	Pr(S)=.1	Pr(S)=.2
2005	874	2067	3802	5538
2006	1457	2456	4749	7042
2007	1836	2673	5040	7406
2008	2849	3435	7117	10799
2009	4288	2064	4453	6842
2010	5402	2084	5324	8564

At an annual Pr(SBT) = .2, the sum of discounted probabilities over a long period approaches 1, and it is .74 over five years. In this case the observed Cuban liquidity is clearly insufficient. The government is unable to raise liquidity because of the weakness of convertible trade, poor financial access and alternative needs among them the urgency to import essential foodstuffs.

Undoubtedly the Cuban government has in mind other strategies to provide a cushion against a Venezuelan shock. There is some evidence that Cuba is trying to diversify its barter trade with agreements with other nations, among them Angola and possibly Algeria. Cuba would presumably obtain oil in exchange for health services. At present, trade with those two countries is very small.

Rather than relying on deep structural reform to make the economy more internationally competitive, the government's main approach to guard against a major shock is to develop offshore oil and gas that can ease dependence on Venezuelan barter arrangements.[78] Offshore oil development is now in an exploratory stage and many analysts believe that it will take at least five years to bring production so that it can cover the bulk of domestic needs.

---

[78] Larry Luxner, "Jorge Piñón: Cuba's enormous oil and gas potential." *Cuba News*, April 1, 2009.

Reforms and External Shocks

Deep reforms to change the structure of the economy to provide a substantial role for private enterprise and markets that would improve investment and international competitiveness are not yet in the cards.[79] Reforms announced at the VI Party Congress in 2011 and measures by the Council of Ministers accompanying them relegate the external sector to a secondary role.[80] The approved guidelines referring to the external sector are mostly a statement of good intentions devoid of specific policy mechanics. The new decrees and laws announced in 2011 and through April 2012 are geared towards improving the fiscal situation and boosting parts of the domestic economy particularly small-scale business and the secondary market for houses and cars but have little to do with establishing competitive and flexible market structures that will provide an adequate response to external shocks. Only new agricultural policies designed to boost small farms and cooperatives will have a positive impact on the external accounts by helping to raise foodstuff production. Below two important areas for reform, exchange rate policy and state enterprises are discussed.

Exchange Rate Policy

Dual currencies, exchange controls and foreign exchange allocation to ministries and state companies result in multiple exchange rates and engender anti-export distortions, misallocation of capital, extra fiscal taxation and corruption. Previous experience during the Special Period and into the last decade indicates that external shocks are dealt with administratively by rationing foreign exchange and import controls creating a new set of distortions, hindering economic efficiency.

---

[79] In April 2012 Cuban Vice President Lazo said that in four or five years, 40% to 45% of GDP would be in the non-state sector, but he did not specify what "non-state" means. "Cuba Plans Massive Shift to Non-State Sector." Reuters, April 23, 2012.

[80] For a summary of reform measures see Jorge F. Pérez-López, "Cuba's External Sector and the VI Party Congress," *Cuba in Transition — Volume 21*, ASCE, 2011.

It should be a priority to unify the currency and enabling a market clearing exchange rate, which will likely be within the range of the two existing exchange rates of CUC 1 = US$1 and CUP 25 = US$1. The data on international liquidity suggests that at an exchange rate of, let us say, CUP 10 = CUC 10 = US$1, foreign currency assets of the Central Bank will provide coverage of the monetary base. According to a summary balance sheet of the Central Bank of Cuba at end 2009, the monetary base was CUP 34.4 billion.[81] Gross international assets of the Cuban banking system at that date at CUP 10 = US$1 amounted to CUP 42.9 billion.[82]

So from the monetary side there is room for moving up (depreciating) the official exchange rate of CUC 1 = US$ 1. Equally critical is implementing complementary reforms to go along a new unified exchange rate system, which at first would involve either a fixed rate or some form of controlled sliding rate. Among the needed complementary reforms the following are the most important: 1) wide liberalization of prices in the economy to improve the allocation of consumption and investment; 2) easing convertibility restrictions on the holding of foreign exchange by enterprises and individuals; 3) fiscal reforms needed to substitute implicit foreign exchange taxes by explicit revenue measures; 4) gradual lifting of import and exchange controls.[83]

Movements towards a market clearing exchange rate would help provide a cushion against potential shocks in several ways. First, it would contribute to an increase in liquidity available to dampen disturbances by raising convertible exports and improving the allocation of imports. Second, it would improve domestic allocation of production. Third, a flexible exchange rate policy would contribute to offset the impact of shocks.

---

[81] *Banco Central de Cuba*, Financial Statements, December 31st, 2009. Interaudit, 2010.

[82] The *Banco Central*'s summary balance sheet does not provide a breakdown between CUP and CUC liabilities. Presumably they are properly consolidated as CUPs.

[83] Ernesto Hernández-Catá, "Macroeconomic Effects of Exchange rate and Price Distortions: The Cuban Case," *Cuba in Transition — Volume 21*, ASCE, 2011, discusses the economic effects of controls and the output gains from liberalization.

It appears Cuban officials are reluctant to undertake monetary and exchange rate unification afraid of the negative impact on basic consumption by the population. The system as it now operates provides an implicit subsidy for the purchase of basic foodstuffs that are imported by a state agency at a highly overvalued exchange rate. This points to the need to consider explicit subsidies for foodstuffs to replace those operating through the exchange rate mechanism as unification takes place.

State Enterprises

State enterprises are key players in Cuba's external sector as they are involved with the bulk of exports, imports and tourism as direct participants and as trading companies on behalf of the government and its agencies. On the other hand, as described above, the reforms in motion over the last two years leave the new private enterprises without a meaningful role in international transactions.

Cuba's main exports nickel, medical products, petroleum distillates, and tobacco are controlled by state companies directly or by tightly structured joint production agreements with foreign corporations. State corporations control the import of foodstuffs, capital goods and technology.

At this time there are few signals that 1) a competitive market environment for products, labor and capital is being developed in which state enterprises can flourish and 2) that either substantial reforms of management and governance of these enterprises is being contemplated or, preferably, privatization measures to create independently operating entities. Turning some weaker state enterprises into worker cooperatives, as has been signaled by party officials, without meaningful reforms in management and incentives will not suffice. The experience of emerging market economies, including socialist states such as China and Vietnam, strongly point to the need to tackle the deep productivity problems engulfing the Cuban state sector.

Conclusion

Cuba's external accounts include sizable barter trade with Venezuela and a few other countries where trade transactions do not match payments and now account for some 60 percent of all Cuban merchandise trade. In this context, it is useful to examine Cuba's external cash flow. It denotes a strong flow of finance and transfers to Cuba that peaked at US$ 7 billion in 2008 and has oscillated around US$4 billion per year in 2009–2011. Simultaneously, Cuba accumulated external financial assets in major international banks that at the end of 2011 reached US$ 4.1 billion. A simulation using a policy model attributes a substantial part of this liquidity to the need to ameliorate a potential shock from the stop of barter trade with Venezuela. Major policy reforms directed towards improving international competitiveness would provide protection against shocks, but are not yet in sight. Exchange rate policy and reform/privatization of state enterprises are key policy areas essential to strengthen the external sector.

Appendix

Optimal Shock-Dampening Liquidity with Budget Constraint

This Appendix examines the government's objective function towards international liquidity when constrained by a budget. The government wants to optimize the objective function subject to an external sector liquidity constraint. Λ is the constrained objective function.

$$\Lambda = - \tfrac{1}{2}\, \mu\, (R{-}R^*)^2 - \tfrac{1}{2}\, \alpha\, (Z{-}Z^*)^2 + \lambda(g + he^{\theta} + K{-}R{-}Z) \qquad \text{(A1)}$$

where $g + he^{\theta}$ is the sensitivity of the convertible trade balance to deviations of the exchange rate from the market clearing rate, θ is the sum of elasticities of exports and imports with respect to the exchange rate and g and h are constants expressing initial conditions of the balance on convertible trade and tourism. Here, e = E/E* where E is the exchange rate or, in Cuba's case, a weighted average of the multiple exchange rates expressed as CUPs per US$, and E* is the market clearing rate. At a unified exchange rate at equilibrium, E = E* and e = 1. K is the given net cash capital flows and transfers. As previously defined, R and Z are the liquidity to back up trade and to dampen shocks. λ is the Lagrange multiplier.

Substituting values for R* and Z* from (2) and (3), first order conditions for maximization of (A1) are:

$$- \mu(R-\gamma Mc) - \lambda = 0 \qquad (A2)$$

$$- \alpha(Z-Pr(S)Mb) - \lambda = 0 \qquad (A3)$$

$$\theta \lambda he^{\theta-1} = 0 \qquad (A4)$$

$$g + he^{\theta} + K-R-Z = 0 \qquad (A5)$$

Solving these four equations by substitution, $\mathbf{Z}^\wedge$, the optimal liquidity to dampen the impact of a shock (S, stop of barter trade) subject to a budget constraint is obtained:

$$\mathbf{Z}^\wedge = 1/(\alpha+\mu)\{\mu(g + he^{\theta}) + \mu(K-\gamma Mc) + \alpha Pr(S)Mb\} \qquad (A6)$$

The three terms in brackets in equation (A6) express the liquidity derived (or needed) from the convertible trade balance at given exchange rates, the liquidity from net capital inflows after coverage of convertible imports, and liquidity needed for the expected value of a stop of barter trade. In Cuba's current situation e<1 and there is a slight surplus (2010) of US$ 0.1 billion in convertible trade plus tourism according to official Cuban data.

Policies that enhance liquidity derived from convertible trade will ease the budget constraint and allow an increase in $\mathbf{Z}^\wedge$. One such policy is unifying the exchange rate near market equilibrium. The size of the impact will be greater in proportion to the elasticities, θ, that reflect the sensitivity of exports and imports to a movement of the exchange rate.

There is insufficient data to calculate the value of θ and other parameters in equation (A6). Data on specific imports and exports indicates that they face low price elasticities of demand and supply, which in turn suggest low elasticities with regard to the exchange rate. Foodstuff demand and nickel exports are price inelastic. We estimate the price elasticity of nickel exports at 0.7 on data for 1986–2010 and price elasticity of demand for imported foodstuffs at -0.1. However, non-traditional exports will be more responsive to prices if vigorous structural reforms of markets and finance are undertaken.

7

CUBA: ACCESS TO CAPITAL MARKETS, EXTERNAL DEBT BURDEN, AND POSSIBLE AVENUES FOR DEBT RELIEF

Lorenzo L. Pérez[84]

This paper analyzes Cuba's financial relations with the rest of the world with a focus on Cuba's external debt. In a world of globalization, countries do not have a choice but to try to integrate their economies as much as possible to the rest of the world in order to grow and improve their living standards. An important aspect of a country's relations with the rest of the world is the amount and the quality of financing a

[84] The author thanks Ms. Mandana Dehghanian and Mrs. Heather Huckstep for excellent research and administrative assistance and Jorge Pérez-López for making available current account estimates for Cuba. The views expressed in this paper are those of the author and should not be attributed to the International Monetary Fund, its Executive Board, or its management.

country receives from its partner countries. This paper tries to analyze the degree to which Cuba has been successful in mobilizing external financing when compared with other developing countries; assesses its external debt burden; discusses the type of analysis that needs to be done to determine the debt relief that Cuba would need to reach external debt sustainability; and discusses possible alternatives that may be opened to Cuba in the future to address its external debt arrears.

Cuba defaulted on its external debt in the 1960s. The information available to the author suggests that Cuba did not try to renegotiate its external debt for about 20 years. This situation was made possible in part by Soviet economic aid. Since the early 1980s, Cuba has been renegotiating its outstanding debt with some of its creditors on a bilateral basis and has generally honored the obligations acquired under that debt restructuring as well as the new debt obligations acquired from those creditors after bilateral restructurings.

Cuba's External Debt

The analysis of Cuba's external debt is hindered by lack of detailed official economic data. This section of the paper presents information on Cuba's external debt from various sources and derives some working estimates of the stock of Cuba's external debt. The Central Bank of Cuba (CBC) reports information on Cuba's external debt in the *Anuario Estadístico de Cuba*, published by the *Oficina Nacional de Estadisticas*. This information is reported in Table 1 (tables are at the end of the paper). Contrary to international practices, the information is reported in Cuban pesos and, for purposes of this study, it is assumed that the exchange rate that was used to convert to Cuban pesos was an official exchange rate of Ps1 = US$1. The latest published information is of a stock of active (performing) debt of US$7.8 billion. Three-fourths of the debt is medium- and long-term debt. This is the debt that the Cuban government is currently servicing. In addition, the CBC reports a stock of immobilized (nonperforming) debt of US$7.6 billion, which is the external debt that probably has not been serviced for some time.[85] Sixty percent of this debt is due to Paris Club creditors. Apparently, the stock of the nonperforming debt includes past due interest (PDI).[86] If it does not, the debt could be considerably larger and the PDI will be subject to negotiations in a future restructuring.

There are other estimates available on Cuba's external debt, reported in Table 2. The Economist Intelligence Unit (EIU) reports a total of US$16.6 billion for end-2006, slightly higher than the official numbers. The Cuba Transition Project of the University of Miami reports a number of US$23.8 billion at the end of 2007. This estimate has been put together using newspaper reports and it has valuable creditor information. It indicates that Venezuela is by far the main external creditor of Cuba with some US$8 billion in credits.[87] Another report from the Cuba Transition Project notes that since 2005 Cuba has received the equivalent of approximately $1.2 billion in credits from Iran. That would put Iran ahead of Russia and Mexico in the list of the main external creditors of Cuba.[88] Unfortunately, it is not possible to reconcile the various sources of information. Information available from the Bank for International Settlements (BIS) on bank credits from some 24 countries with large bank

---

[85] The debt defaulted in 1986 was that of the *Banco Nacional de Cuba* (the former monetary authority) and of the Republic of Cuba. The CBC makes the point that the new debt it has acquired since 1986 or the restructuring agreements negotiated by Cuba since that time have been serviced on the agreed terms.

[86] This is not clear from the CBC data, but Stuart Culverhouse provides an estimate of PDI of US$1.8 billion as part of the stock of nonperforming debt in "Cuba: Closer but still no cigar," September 4, 2006, Sovereign Fixed Income Research, Exotix Limited.

[87] It would not be surprising that official external debt statistics of Cuba do not include the debt to Venezuela given that this is likely to have arisen from Venezuela's oil shipments to Cuba. Unfortunately, official data do not provide detailed information to allow a cross check with the University of Miami data. Information available from audited statements of *PDVSA* (the state petroleum company of Venezuela) indicate that shipments of petroleum to Cuba are likely to amount to over $7.5 billion during 2006-2008. These oil shipments are financed by Venezuela at highly concessional terms.

[88] "Islamic Investment in Cuba," Cuba Transition Project of the University of Miami, Staff Report, Issue 99, August 11, 2008.

centers shows similar information regarding Cuba's short-term external debt (less than one year) to that provided by the CBC.

Finally, there is the debt of Cuba to the former Soviet Union that Russia inherited after the breakup of the Soviet Union in the amount of some 21.5 billion rubles. The question here is: what exchange rate should be used to convert the stock of debt to U.S. dollars or to any other convertible currency. This is an issue that Russia will bring up in future multilateral debt restructuring negotiations but this debt will have to be subjected to a huge discount and/or an exchange rate favorable to Cuba, if not completely written off, to make an agreement possible.[89] Interestingly, this has not stopped Russia from providing credits to Cuba in recent years. The data of the Cuba Transition Project of the University of Miami reports that Russia's credits to Cuba in the post-Soviet period already amount to some US$800 million.

It is useful to compare Cuba's external debt to its economic size and the value of its foreign trade. This analysis can be put in an international perspective to determine the degree that Cuba is integrated into the world economy. For purposes of this analysis, the paper uses the figure for the external debt of Cuba in 2006 of US$16.6 billion published by the EIU (thus ignoring Russia's claims from the Soviet time) and the GDP number in U.S. dollars also published by the EIU of US$41.7 billion. This indicates that Cuba's external debt is about 40 percent of its GDP. If one were to use a figure of US$51 billion for the GDP of Cuba in PPP terms published in the Central Intelligence World Fact Book for Cuba, the ratio declines to 33 percent. Table 3 shows that Cuba's external debt in terms of GDP at market prices and in PPP terms is not very different from that of a sample of Asian, Central Asian, Eastern European, Caribbean, and Central American countries that have gone through similar experiences as that of Cuba or have similar types of economies. The share of imports of Cuba financed by short-term credits

---

[89] For a discussion of Cuba's debt to the Soviet Union, see "External Debt Problems and the Principle of Solidarity: The Cuban Case" by Alberto Martinez-Piedra and Lorenzo L. Pérez, pp. 33–34 in *Cuba in Transition*, Volume 6, 1996, Association for the Study of the Cuban Economy.

from the sample of banks of the BIS compares favorably to the other countries—about 12 percent at the end of 2006 (Table 4).

When the comparison of external debt stocks is done in terms of exports of goods and services, the conclusion is strikingly different. Cuba's ratio is considerably higher than that of other countries. Table 5 shows that Cuba's external debt in relation to exports of goods and services (although declining in recent years, as the value of export services has increased) at 173 percent, is one of the highest of the countries in the sample. Indeed, only Latvia, the Dominican Republic and El Salvador have higher ratios. This is an important result. This ratio considers how large is the debt in terms of the foreign exchange generating capacity of the country and indicates that Cuba has a large external debt burden.

Comparing directly Cuba's external debt service burden—in terms of exports of goods and services—confirms that the country is at a relative disadvantageous situation. No information is available regarding the amortization schedule of Cuba's external debt or the interest rate that is charged on these loans. We assume two scenarios: one with a 5-year amortization schedule and another with a 10-year amortization schedule for both performing and non-performing debt. Under both scenarios we assume an interest rate of 5 percent (this may be an optimistic assumption). In 2006, Cuba would have had a debt service ratio of 20 percent on the performing debt under the 5-year repayment scenario or 12 percent under the 10-year repayment scenario. However, if the same assumptions are applied to the non-performing debt, this would essentially double the debt service ratio, to 40 percent of exports of goods and services and 24 percent, respectively. The latter results are really the more relevant if one is trying to assess Cuba's creditworthiness in capital markets. Table 6 shows that the debt service ratio of the comparator countries range from single digits to the mid 20's, with only a few countries showing a debt service burden exceeding 30 percent.

Another important indicator of the external debt burden is the share of government revenues that have to be dedicated for this purpose. External debt service of Cuba's performing and nonperforming debt in terms of total state budget revenues in 2006 was 12 percent under the 5-year amortization scenario and 7 percent in terms of the 10-year scenario. These are not relatively large ratios.[90] This compares favorably to the ratios of the comparator countries (Table 7). However, this is converting the government revenues to U.S. dollars at the official exchange rate of Ps 1 = US$1. The Cuban peso is probably seriously overvalued, and at a more realistic exchange rate, the debt service in terms of government revenues would indicate a very different situation. Assuming that the exchange rate were to be Ps 10 = US$1, about the mid-point between the official rate and the level that the parallel market rate has been hovering around in recent years, the external debt service would have been the equivalent of 120 percent of total state budget revenues in 2006.

An analysis of the debt relief that Cuba needs to attain external debt sustainability is beyond the scope of this paper, particularly in light of the lack of reliable data. Debt sustainability can be defined as a situation in which a borrower is expected to be able to continue servicing its debt without an unrealistically large correction to the balance of income and expenditure. Sustainability thus encompasses the concepts of solvency and liquidity, without making sharp distinctions among them. Assessing debt sustainability is highly sensitive to the assumptions underlying projections of growth, inflation, interest, and exchange rates. For Cuba to come up with a defensible debt relief proposal, it would be necessary to put together a macroeconomic scenario for the medium to long term showing how the economy would grow (at a politically acceptable rate that permits a significant increase in living standards), how its external current account balance will evolve, and the degree of foreign exchange receipts that could be expected to be available during this period to service the external debt. On the domestic side of the economy, such a scenario will need to show that a sufficiently high fiscal primary balance would be generated by the government to service its debt.[91]

---

[90] State budget total revenues for 2006 are reported as Ps 31.9 billion in the *Anuario Estadístico de Cuba*.

[91] The fiscal primary balance is total revenues minus government expenditures excluding interest payments on government debt.

Cuba's Attempts to Re-structure its External Debt and Options open under existing Practices by The International Community

As noted above, Cuba has negotiated some restructuring agreements with bilateral creditors, and some export credit agencies of industrialized countries provide cover for short-term transactions. Medium-term coverage is available on a case-by-case basis from some countries such as Germany. In 1983 and 1984, medium-term "Credit Lyonnais" loans and short-term non-trade loans originally denominated in various currencies were rescheduled. These rescheduled loans have guarantees from the Republic of Cuba and have the advantage of an official agent (Credit Lyonnais). These are Cuba's obligations that are traded with some degree of regularity in the secondary market.[92] In 1998, Cuba negotiated some loans with Japan amounting to some ¥ 100 billion and in recent years there have announcements of debt restructuring with Mexico, Spain, and other countries.

Recently, the CBC attempted to improve the creditworthiness of Cuba by establishing a presence in the international bond market by issuing one-year bonds in the London market for a value of Euros 400 million on February 14, 2006, at a nominal interest rate of 7 percent. The prospectus of the bond issue made it clear that the bonds were issued by the CBC without a guarantee by the Republic of Cuba and that the proceeds of the bonds would be used to redeem two bonds issued on December 5, 2005 and February 5, 2006.[93] The offer was undermined by the limited economic information provided in the prospectus. For example, the balance sheet of the CBC did not have information on net international reserves and this was justified by the existence of the "commercial and financial blockade" of the United States and the risks that it means for Cuban assets held in foreign countries. At the end, these bonds were reportedly bought by banks in Cuba owned by the government and the bonds

---

[92] *Exotix Emerging Market Debt Guide 2005.*

[93] The author does not have information on how these two bonds were issued or on whether other bonds were issued prior to 2005.

were redeemed on time. This type of financial operation did not appear to improve Cuba's creditworthiness in financial markets. In August, 2008, there were press reports that Cuba was having difficulties in paying off its short term debt to Japan and that the export credit agency of Japan might withdraw insurance coverage to Cuba. Problems regarding Cuba's paying for the oil extracted by a Canadian company in Cuban territory and delivered to Cuban companies have also been reported.

It is not clear whether Cuba has negotiated a multilateral debt restructuring on its nonperforming debt with Paris Club creditors.[94] There is documentation of an exchange of information between Cuban officials and representatives of the Paris Club regarding a possible rescheduling of the obligations falling due to Paris Club creditors in 1983. In these documents a reference is made to apparently existing rescheduling of the obligations falling due in 1982. Apparently, the negotiations for the 1983 rescheduling were not concluded successfully.

Given Cuba's external debt service burden, it is clear that a multi-creditor, multi-year debt restructuring agreement would need to be worked out. This will undoubtedly improve the terms under which Cuba can have access to international capital markets. Although the servicing of external debt is being facilitated by the increase in service receipts, particularly from the tourist sector, it would best serve Cuban interests if the country were able to negotiate a comprehensive restructuring agreement, including the Soviet era debt.

Paris Club creditors have two preconditions for debt restructuring under their aegis: the creditors must be convinced that a debtor country would be unable to meet its external payments obligations unless it receives debt relief (financing need); and that the debtor country seeking a restructuring take the steps necessary to eliminate the causes of its payments difficulties in order to

---

[94] The Paris Club is an informal group of creditor governments (mainly from industrialized countries) that has met regularly in Paris since 1956 to reschedule bilateral debts. The French Treasury provides the Secretariat. The core creditors are mainly OECD countries, but other creditors relevant for a particularly debtor country are frequently invited to participate. Russia became a full time member of the Paris Club in September 1997.

achieve a durable improvement in its external payments position. Thus, the country is expected to undertake an adjustment effort, typically in the context of a program supported by the International Monetary Fund (IMF). The terms of a Paris Club restructuring (i.e., grace period, maturity profile, interest rate) typically depend on the income level of the debtor country, as well as the category of debt involved, for example commercial debt with market-related interest rates, Official Development Assistance (ODA), debt on concessional terms. Paris Club creditors decide on a case-by-case basis whether a specific country receives non-concessional or concessional terms largely on the basis of the income level of the debtor country.

Cuba's income per capita using the EIU data is about US$3,800 and would not qualify Cuba to receive debt relief in highly concessional terms. Rescheduling terms for low-income countries have become increasingly concessional over time. A reduction in the present value of eligible debt (NPV) of 67 percent has been done in recent years under the so-called Naples terms. In addition, the international community recognized in 1996 that the external debt situation for a number of low-income countries (Highly Indebted Poor Countries—HIPC), mostly in Africa, had become extremely difficult and influenced the prospect for economic development. For these countries, even full use of traditional mechanisms of rescheduling and debt reduction (Naples terms), together with continued provision of concessional financing and pursuit of sound economic policies, may not be sufficient to attain sustainable external debt levels within a reasonable period of time and without additional external support. In the context of the HIPC Initiative, creditors agreed in November 1996 to increase the NPV reduction up to 80 percent on eligible debt (also known as Cologne terms). Creditors can choose from a menu of options to implement debt relief: debt reduction option, debt-service reduction option, and capitalization of moratorium interest option.

More recently, in October 2003, Paris Club creditors established the Evian approach, which is the new framework for treating debts of non-HIPC countries. This approach aims to tailor better debt treatment to the specific circumstances of the debtor country. Creditors consider the debtor's economic potential, fiscal adjustment effort, the existence and magnitude of external shock, and previous as well as future recourse to the Club. Creditors take into account whether the country requesting a debt treatment is facing a liquidity problem in which case debt-service reduction and/or capitalization of moratorium interest may be more appropriate or a solvency one that may require a debt reduction option (this is to be granted on exceptional circumstances). To decide on what type of debt relief to offer, creditors develop their own view on the debt sustainability situation, in close coordination with the staff of the IMF and based on the IMF's debt sustainability analysis (DSA).

Nine countries have benefited from debt treatment under the Evian approach so far: Kenya and Moldova faced liquidity problems and received debt service reductions; Iraq and Nigeria were judged to have unsustainable debt and were provided with upfront debt stock reduction. For the Dominican Republic, Gabon, Georgia, Kyrgyz Republic and Grenada, the Paris Club followed a phased debt reduction approach. In these cases, a "goodwill clause" stating that creditors would reconsider the debt sustainability situation at a later stage was included in the agreed minutes of the original Paris Club agreement that granted the initial debt relief. The income per capita of these countries ranged from $6,600 for Gabon to $900 for Kenya and the Kyrgyz Republic.

The best strategy for Cuba to become creditworthy would appear to be to seek a comprehensive debt restructuring from the Paris Club under the Evian approach that provides complete flexibility to Paris Club creditors. To do this, Cuba would need to take significant steps to improve its relations with the United States and become a member of the IMF. Short of this, the only avenue open to Cuba is to try to continue to restructure its external debt on a bilateral basis. The Paris Club members have recognized that there may be circumstances under which the conditions of the Paris Club for debt relief are not met, in particular whether a country has a relationship with the IMF. If this situation is formally recognized by the Paris Club, Paris Club members are free to pursue bilateral negotiations. It appears that this has been the case of Cuba and that some Paris Club members are willing to negotiate with Cuba on a bilateral basis. For Cuba, however, this approach is not optimal because it is likely to be more costly and will continue to delay universal access to capital markets.

This paper has shown that Cuba has been able to obtain external financing in the last 20 years. While no information is available on the terms of the financing, Cuba's borrowing costs are likely to be high given the existing external debt arrears which have limited its access to capital markets.

Conclusions

The external debt burden appears to be high, particularly if measured by debt service payments as a percentage of exports of goods and services or as a percentage of government revenue. To have a sustainable debt service situation, Cuba needs to achieve debt relief. So far the revolutionary government has been trying to negotiate debt restructuring agreements on a piecemeal basis that does not address the problem in a comprehensive way and continues to limit the efficient participation of Cuba in international capital markets. An optimal approach would be a comprehensive debt restructuring with Paris Club creditors, but this is not possible unless dramatic changes in policy occur in Cuba. In the foreseeable future, the piecemeal approach is likely to continue.

◆ ◆ ◆

Important events have occurred and new information has become available since 2008, when this article was written. Luis R. Luis (2012) estimated Cuba's foreign debt at the end of 2011 at $43, compared with about $16 billion reported in this article for 2006. (See Luis, "Cuba's External debt and Finance in the Context of Limited Reform, in *Cuba in Transition*, Vol., and "Cuba's External Debt Problem: Daunting Yet Surmountable" in ascecuba.org//blog). Luis based his estimate on data from a variety of sources: lending to Cuba by banks reporting to the Bank for International Settlements (BIS); the Paris Club; project lending by non-members of the BIS (like Brazil and China);

Cuban debt to suppliers reported by the Cuban authorities; and information on defaulted bonds and commercial loans carried at face value by foreign creditors. Most of the difference between the two estimates reflects the inclusion in the Paris Club data used by Luis of the debt in arrears to Russia (which the Cuban authorities do not include in their tables) and the accumulation of new liabilities between 2006 and 2011.

In October 2013, Cuba and the Russian Federation signed an agreement to write off 90% of Cuba's $30 billion debt to Russia, with the remaining $ 3.2 billion to be repaid over 10 years. There are also reports that some debt relief has been granted by Japan and Mexico. Following these agreements, Luis projected Cuba's debt at the end of 2014 at $24 billion. This estimate does not include debt to Venezuela arising for the bilateral agreement which provides for the shipment of oil and oil products to Cuba. This debt carries an interest rate of 1 percent per annum and a grace period of 30 years.[95]

---

[95] An alternative interpretation of the Accord is that Venezuelan oil shipments are barted against Cuban professional services rendered to Venezuela. See article 1 in this book.

Table 1. Cuba: Official External Debt Statistics, 2004–06 1/
(In millions of pesos)

	Total	Short Term	Percent	Medium and Long Term	Percent
2004					
Total debt	5,806.0	1,578.8	27.2	4,227.2	72.8
Government credits	2,573.0	797.9	31.0	1,775.1	69.0
Banks' credits	1,311.6	423.7	32.3	887.9	67.7
Suppliers' credits	1,921.4	357.2	18.6	1,564.2	81.4
2005					
Total debt	5,898.2	922.1	15.6	4,976.1	84.4
Government credits	2,787.3	261.0	9.4	2,526.3	90.6
Banks' credits	1,147.1	346.2	30.2	800.9	69.8
Suppliers' credits	1,963.8	314.9	16.0	1,648.9	84.0
2006					
Total debt	7,793.7	1,947.6	25.0	5,846.1	75.0
Government credits	3,945.2	733.7	18.6	3,211.5	81.4
Banks' credits	1,371.2	317.5	23.2	1,053.7	76.8
Suppliers' credits	2,477.3	896.4	36.2	1,580.9	63.8

Source: Central Bank of Cuba.

Note: The Central Bank of Cuba notes that there is inactive debt in the amount of 7,591.7 million pesos. This is debt that has not been serviced since 1986 when Cuba started restructuring its foreign debt.

1/ Includes active external debt (debt currently being serviced by the Cuban government). While there is no mention of the exchange rate used to convert the external debt to pesos, one of the official exchange rates that was probably used is Ps 1 = US$1 or Ps 0.93 = US$1.

Table 2. Cuba: Unofficial Estimates of External Debt
(In billions of U.S. dollars)

	2003	2004	2005	2006	2007
Total external debt	11.3	13.8	14.5	16.6	16.8

Source: The Economist Intelligence Unit

	2007
Total external debt	23.8
Main creditors	
Venezuela	8.0
Spain	3.2
Japan	2.4
Argentina	2.0
China	1.8
France	1.7
Russia (post-Soviet)	0.8
Mexico	0.5

Source: Cuba Transition Project, Institute for Cuban and Cuban-American Studies, University of Miami

	2000	2005	2006	2007
Consolidated foreign claims of reporting				
banks (immediate borrower basis)	1.6	1.8	1.9	2.2
Of which:				
France	0.5	0.5	0.5	0.7
Germany	0.1	0.2	0.2	0.3
Mexico	...	0.3	0.3	0.3
The Netherlands	0.3	0.2	0.2	0.1
Spain	0.3	0.3	0.4	0.4
By maturity				
Up to and including one year	1.3	1.4	1.1	1.4
Over one year up to two years	0.1	0.1	0.2	0.3
Over two years	0.3	0.6	0.8	0.8
By borrowing sectors				
Banks	...	0.6	0.8	1.1
Public sector	...	0.2	0.2	0.2
Nonbank private sector	...	0.5	0.5	0.5

Source: Bank for International Settlements

Table 3. External Debt as a Percentage of GDP in 2006 for Cuba and Selected Countries

(In percent of U.S. dollar GDP)	
Cuba	40
Asian countries	48
Central Asia and Eastern Europe	57
Caribbean and Central American countries	48
(In percent of U.S. dollar GDP in PPP terms)	
Cuba	33
Asian countries	21
Central Asia and Eastern Europe	29
Caribbean and Central American countries	25

Memorandum item:

The sample of Asian countries comprise Cambodia, Maldives, Philippines, Sri Lanka, and Vietnam.

The Central Asian and Eastern European countries comprise Albania, Armenia, Bulgaria, Czech Republic, Estonia, Georgia, Kyrgyz Republic, Latvia, Poland, and Romania

The Western Hemisphere countries comprise Barbados, Belize, Costa Rica, Dominican Republic, El Salvador, Guatemala, Honduras, Jamaica, Nicaragua, and St. Lucia.

Source: World Economic Outlook database of the International Monetary Fund.

Table 4. Consolidated Claims of Reporting Banks - Immediate Borrower Basis on Individual Countries by Maturity and Sector / Amounts Outstanding and In Percent of the Value of Imports

(International claims over - up to 1 year)

	December 2000	December 2006	December 2007
	In millions of US dollars		
Cuba	1,300	1,100	1,400
Asia			
Cambodia	4	2	7
Maldives	8	11	17
Philippines	810	547	973
Sri Lanka	94	185	138
Vietnam	152	272	507
Central Asia and Eastern Europe			
Armenia	10	13	29
Georgia	15	2	37
Kyrgyz Republic	2	1	16
Latvia	1268	1989	3906
Albania	19	69	190
Bulgaria	578	862	1572
Czech Republic	1082	1409	2178
Estonia	1212	1823	2165
Poland	2451	2569	4734
Romania	1103	2560	4984
Western Hemisphere			
Barbados	40	245	282
Belize	13	26	15
Costa Rica	188	188	313
Dominican Republic	246	141	217
El Salvador	162	97	79
Guatemala	152	172	120
Honduras	51	30	79
Jamaica	97	42	62
Nicaragua	15	23	16
St. Lucia	6	5	40
	In percent of imports of goods		
Cuba	--	11.6	--
Asia			
Cambodia	0.10	0.04	0.12
Maldives	1.22	1.35	1.82
Philippines	1.69	1.03	1.69
Sri Lanka	1.06	1.80	1.21
Vietnam	0.44	0.64	0.85
Central Asia and Eastern Europe			
Armenia	0.63	0.68	1.04
Georgia	0.55	0.05	0.74
Kyrgyz Republic	0.18	0.06	0.61
Latvia	15.09	17.73	26.42
Albania	0.76	2.37	5.01
Bulgaria	3.35	3.91	5.51
Czech Republic	1.43	1.53	1.87
Estonia	12.50	14.48	15.14
Poland	2.47	2.06	2.97
Romania	2.94	5.42	7.74
Western Hemisphere			
Barbados	2.73	16.88	18.26
Belize	2.34	4.25	2.34
Costa Rica	2.03	1.73	2.56
Dominican Republic	2.49	1.17	1.61
El Salvador	2.48	1.34	0.98
Guatemala	1.77	1.74	1.04
Honduras	0.78	0.41	0.92
Jamaica	2.28	0.90	1.10
Nicaragua	0.51	0.67	0.39
St. Lucia	1.43	0.96	8.80

Source: Bank for International Settlements (BIS).

Table 5. External Debt: Cuba and Comparator Countries
(In percent of exports of goods and services)

	2003	2004	2005	2006
Cuba	243	400	220	173
Asia				
Cambodia	68.6	60.2	52.7	45.1
Maldives	49.6	48.3	100.6	105.2
Philippines	162.1	142.8	137.5	114.2
Sri Lanka	175.8	175.8	165.4	167.3
Vietnam	57.0	50.3	46.7	41.1
Central Asia and Eastern Europe				
Armenia	107.9	105.2	82.7	83.7
Georgia	136.8	111.4	78.9	68.7
Kyrgyz Republic	240.9	205.9	200.4	159.2
Latvia	200.1	222.3	201.4	271.4
Albania	118.5	97.6	81.3	74.6
Bulgaria	126.8	121.4	109.4	116.9
Czech Republic	61.8	58.8	51.8	53.5
Estonia	93.4	103.8	108.4	122.3
Poland	148.6	136.2	117.9	122.6
Romania	97.0	99.7	118.7	134.1
Western Hemisphere				
Barbados	55.9	54.9	54.4	50.3
Belize	191.6	195.0	177.2	147.9
Costa Rica	68.0	63.3	61.3	59.5
Dominican Republic	75.6	78.7	78.1	65.4
El Salvador	209.0	199.6	199.9	190.7
Guatemala	150.7	166.8	173.9	171.6
Honduras	115.0	102.7	76.3	55.6
Jamaica	118.4	131.3	132.5	130.5
Nicaragua	560.9	376.4	153.6	140.3
St. Kitts and Nevis	194.4	176.3	163.3	153.2
St. Lucia	87.3	79.8	80.6	93.2

Source: World Economic Outlook (WEO) for Asia, Central Asia and Eastern Europe, and Western Hemisphere. For Cuba, the external debt stocks of the Economist Intelligence Unit are used and the information on exports of merchandise and services are obtained from Jorge F. Pérez-López, Recent Cuban Foreign Trade patterns (manuscript).

Table 6. Debt Service
(In percent of exports of goods and services)

	2000	2001	2002	2003	2004	2005	2006	2007
Asia								
Cambodia	0.7	1.0	0.9	1.0	0.8	0.7	0.6	0.5
Maldives	4.8	4.8	4.6	3.8	4.1	6.7	5.5	6.1
Philippines	14.9	19.1	19.7	20.6	19.7	18.5	18.6	17.9
Sri Lanka	13.2	14.3	12.3	10.9	10.1	7.4	11.5	12.0
Vietnam	10.5	10.6	8.6	7.8	6.0	5.6	5.3	5.4
Central Asia and Eastern Europe								
Armenia	10.6	9.7	9.9	11.2	5.7	4.2	4.1	3.3
Georgia	9.6	9.1	7.2	5.8	10.3	7.7	7.1	5.4
Kyrgyz Republic	21.7	21.4	14.0	14.3	8.7	7.1	6.0	5.3
Latvia	16.6	22.8	16.6	20.6	21.2	36.2	36.2	43.9
Albania	4.1	4.4	6.8	5.3	4.5	4.5	6.1	5.9
Bulgaria	16.3	20.0	15.9	14.0	21.6	42.2	24.0	29.5
Czech Republic	37.7	32.1	31.9	32.9	31.0	26.6	24.8	25.1
Estonia	7.5	13.4	16.3	20.5	26.0	27.1	30.6	37.9
Poland	19.0	26.9	22.9	23.7	17.1	14.7	17.0	12.8
Romania	13.2	16.6	17.9	14.9	14.1	18.1	20.6	19.7
Western Hemisphere								
Barbados	5.7	6.2	10.4	10.6	9.9	8.5	9.8	7.5
Belize	11.7	18.0	35.3	26.2	40.6	37.8	19.3	13.6
Costa Rica	8.2	7.9	7.4	10.3	7.5	5.4	4.1	3.6
Dominican Republic	6.4	9.7	10.8	11.6	8.6	10.3	15.7	13.6
El Salvador	14.2	16.4	20.6	24.0	33.5	25.9	25.9	27.0
Guatemala	10.1	8.3	9.0	9.9	11.5	13.5	17.7	15.2
Honduras	12.5	4.9	4.4	4.3	3.8	4.2	3.2	2.4
Jamaica	13.4	17.6	24.7	23.0	20.4	21.1	22.3	19.1
Nicaragua	14.9	23.0	13.5	8.9	5.5	5.0	5.1	5.1
St. Kitts and Nevis	14.1	18.8	21.0	25.5	26.2	24.1	25.1	25.3
St. Lucia	9.3	9.2	20.5	12.9	15.7	14.4	18.9	23.5

Source: World Economic Outlook (WEO).

Table 7. Debt Service

(In percent of government revenue and grants)

	2000	2001	2002	2003	2004	2005	2006	2007
Asia								
Cambodia	2.8	4.1	3.8	4.9	4.4	3.8	2.9	2.5
Maldives	11.0	10.7	10.8	9.1	10.7	8.9	6.4	10.8
Philippines	51.8	58.8	67.4	68.7	66.9	55.9	51.4	44.1
Sri Lanka	30.5	32.9	26.1	24.1	23.2	14.2	20.1	20.0
Vietnam	29.8	28.4	22.9	20.8	16.1	15.8	15.4	17.2
Central Asia and Eastern Europe								
Armenia	15.0	14.4	15.5	20.3	10.4	7.3	5.6	4.2
Georgia	20.5	16.8	13.0	10.7	16.4	13.1	10.9	7.8
Kyrgyz Republic	59.9	46.2	29.2	32.4	20.5	14.6	13.0	10.8
Latvia	24.9	35.5	25.2	31.9	33.5	58.5	53.8	60.1
Albania	3.3	3.5	5.8	4.8	4.3	4.4	6.4	6.3
Bulgaria	23.4	28.6	22.6	19.7	31.8	63.1	39.6	45.0
Czech Republic	86.2	73.3	67.8	69.8	73.6	67.8	68.5	73.4
Estonia	34.4	59.1	61.6	71.5	93.1	101.1	109.9	122.4
Poland	28.2	40.2	36.9	43.7	38.1	29.8	36.8	26.2
Romania	13.9	18.5	21.3	18.1	16.9	19.8	21.3	19.2
Western Hemisphere								
Barbados	9.1	9.7	15.6	16.3	15.7	14.5	18.3	14.2
Belize	28.0	37.4	72.9	63.0	93.0	89.5	48.4	33.5
Costa Rica	31.9	24.6	23.5	34.4	25.4	18.8	14.2	11.4
Dominican Republic	18.0	22.5	24.7	39.1	26.9	19.9	30.4	22.0
El Salvador	32.9	35.7	43.7	49.5	74.0	51.3	49.6	49.7
Guatemala	20.7	15.6	16.2	16.4	19.8	23.2	29.6	28.9
Honduras	43.3	15.3	15.0	14.1	13.0	14.4	9.7	6.7
Jamaica	20.7	27.0	35.7	35.5	29.6	30.2	32.1	31.6
Nicaragua	23.5	35.8	20.8	15.2	10.0	9.6	10.5	11.5
St. Kitts and Nevis	21.7	29.1	26.1	34.6	37.1	28.8	28.1	28.2
St. Lucia	19.7	18.1	35.3	25.4	34.7	32.3	34.2	38.3

Source: World Economic Outlook (WEO).

8

IF IT WERE JUST THE MARABÚ...
CUBA'S AGRICULTURE 2009-10

G.B. Hagelberg [96]

"We face the imperative of making our land produce more. ... the needed structural and conceptual changes will have to be introduced," Raúl Castro famously proclaimed on 26 July 2007, a few days short of a year after provisionally taking over the reins of Cuba's government from his incapacitated older brother. Nine months later, now formally confirmed in power by the National Assembly, he told a plenary meeting of the Central Committee of the Cuban Communist Party on 28 April 2008 that food production had to be their top concern as a matter of national security.

In countries otherwise so very diverse as the United States, Russia and Nigeria, Germany, Iran and the Dominican Republic, Sweden, Brazil and

[96] I am grateful to Brian H. Pollitt as well as to José Alvarez, Marc Frank, William A. Messina, Jr., and Jorge F. Pérez-López for useful comments on earlier drafts but am solely responsible for remaining shortcomings.

Honduras, the four years that Raúl Castro has de facto presided over Cuba would constitute a full term of office, towards the end of which supporters and opponents of an administration argue over its record during a general election campaign. While Cuba's one-party regime marches to the beat of a different drummer, its people — like people across the world — respond to the thrice-daily call of their stomachs. Cuba is no exception to the applicability of the time dimension in politics and economics, and the passage of time is a necessary yardstick for judging this government's effectiveness.

What brought the food situation to the fore of the government's agenda were the ballooning cost of food imports and an alarming deterioration of the food export-import balance pressing on the merchandise trade balance, now that foreign exchange earnings from sugar exports no longer offset imports of other agricultural products. Other countries also felt the impact of sharply increased international commodity prices in 2007–08. Cuba's government, however, could not blame soulless world markets alone if people did not have enough to eat. The downsizing of the sugar industry — more demolition than restructuring — had created hundreds of thousands of hectares of idle land, on which dense thickets of *marabú* (*Dichrostachys cinerea*) bore highly visible evidence of the state's mismanagement of the island's resources. Fifteen years or so into the "Special Period in Time of Peace" that began with the end of Soviet-bloc support for the Cuban economy, the government was faced with the specter of a return to the drop in food availability, if not the nutritional deficits, experienced in the first half of the 1990s — a double dip in current economic recession parlance.[97]

---

[97] Raúl Castro inherited a stagnant farm sector. After rising by 3.6% in 2003, crop and livestock agriculture and forestry GDP (at constant 1997 market prices) successively fell by 0.2%, 12.4% and 7.5% in the next three years. Growth of 19.6% in 2007, 0.6% in 2008, and 3.3% in 2009 just about restored it to its previous level (ONE, 2009 and 2010, Table 5.8). Short of hard currency, the government slashed food and live animal imports by almost a third from 2.2 billion pesos in 2008 to 1.5 billion pesos in 2009, slightly below the 2007 level (ONE, 2010, Table 8.11). But roughly the same quantity of milk powder, for instance, cost 22% more in 2009 than it had in 2007, and 4% more money bought nearly 13% less rice (ONE, 2010, Table 8.13).

So what has the government done in the farm sector in the first four years of Raúl Castro's stewardship?

- Debts amounting to tens of millions of pesos owed by state agencies to cooperative and independent farmers have been paid. However, the revelation that barely had the old debts been settled when new debts began to accumulate (Varela Pérez, 2009a) undermined claims that the deficiencies which allowed such arrears to arise had been eliminated (cf. Hagelberg and Alvarez, 2007).

- A reorganization of the agriculture ministry begun in 2007 reportedly resulted in the closure of 83 state enterprises and the transformation of 473 loss-making units, with 7,316 workers transferred to other jobs. Analysis of 17 enterprises selected in a second stage showed the possibility of cutting the number of employees in management by more than half. Overall, the ministry counted some 89,000 "unproductive" workers in the state sector — not including Basic Units of Cooperative Production (UBPCs), undertakings that "after many ups and downs and ambiguities have still not fulfilled the mission for which they were created" (Varela Pérez, 2009b). More recently, agriculture minister Ulises Rosales del Toro[98] stated that more than 40,000 "indirect workers" in the sector had to be relocated (Pérez Cabrera, 2010).

- Controls formerly exercised directly by the agriculture ministry from Havana have been shifted down to municipal level. To what extent this actually reduced the bureaucratic apparatus and made life easier for producers is uncertain. The Cuban economist Armando Nova González expressed doubt, arguing that the functions of government and of business management were still being confused: while one structural level had been eliminated, two had been created by introducing a chain of service enterprises to supply production inputs. That was all very well, but how were the producers to acquire the inputs? Through a market or, as hitherto, by central allocation, which for years had been shown not to be the best way? (Martín González, 2009)

---

[98] Rosales del Toro was subsequently replaced as head of the agriculture ministry by its first vice minister and put in overall charge of the agriculture, sugar and food industry ministries (*Granma*, 12 June 2010), a move that possibly presages a merger of these bodies.

- Shops selling hand tools and supplies for convertible pesos (CUC) have been opened in some municipalities. The degree to which this has created direct access to production inputs has so far been limited by the small number of such outlets and the range of goods on offer. Some fraction of farmer income from produce sold to the state and otherwise is also denominated in CUC. But for the acquisition of larger items and bulk quantities, bank loans in that currency would have to become available (Nova González, 2008).
- Sharply increased state procurement prices — some, notably for milk and beef, to double and more their former level — have, by all accounts, been an incentive to raise output.

But these measures did not amount to structural or conceptual changes, though they could awaken hopes that those would come.

Small is Beautiful

At the end of the first four years of Raúl Castro's watch, the one structural change worthy of the name in agriculture was the mass grant in usufruct of idle state land mainly to small farmers and landless persons. Although these transfers are surrounded by conditions, Decree-Law No. 259 of 10 July 2008 is deeply revisionist in concept since it implies — more clearly than the conversion of state farms into -UBPCs in 1993 — the abandonment of the long-held doctrine of the superiority of state or parastatal, large-scale, mechanized agriculture reliant on wage labor, of which Fidel Castro had been the foremost exponent in Cuba. Over the signature of Raúl Castro as President of the Council of State, it was decreed that landless individuals could obtain up to 13.42 hectares and existing landholders could bring their total area up to 40.26 hectares under licenses valid for up to 10 years and successively renewable for the same period. Existing state farms, cooperatives and other legal entities could apply for the usufruct of an unlimited area for 25 years, renewable for another 25 years.[99]

---

[99] For the text of Decree-Law No. 259 of 10 July 2008 and of the implementing regulations, Decree No. 282 of 27 August 2008, see *Granma*, 18 July 2008, and *Gaceta Oficial No. 30*

No detailed statistics of operations under Decree-Law No. 259 seem to have been published since mid-2009 (González, 2009; cited in Hagelberg and Alvarez, 2009). The information on land areas by type and tenancy in the most recent yearbook of Cuba's National Office of Statistics stops at 2007 (ONE, 2010, Table 9.1). Different global figures can be found in media reports. Raúl Castro informed the National Assembly towards the end of 2009 that around 920,000 hectares had been transferred to more than 100,000 beneficiaries, which represented 54% of the total idle area (*Granma*, 21 December 2009). This would put the magnitude of the total idle area at the outset at 1.7 million hectares. Almost five months later, Marino Murillo Jorge, minister of economy and planning, gave the congress of the *Asociación Nacional de Agricultores Pequeños* (ANAP), the national association of small farmers, the same figure of 920,000 hectares as the land transferred under Decree-Law No. 259, adding that around half of the areas so assigned remained idle or insufficiently exploited (*Granma*, 17 May 2010).

From the second half of 2009 onwards, the reportorial focus in the state-controlled mass media has shifted noticeably from implementation of Decree-Law No. 259 to advancing a so-called *Agricultura Suburbana* program. Raúl Castro gave the cue in a speech to the summer 2009 session of the National Assembly (*Granma*, 3 August 2009):

Let us forget tractors and fuel in this program, even if we had them in sufficient quantities; the concept is to execute it basically with oxen, because it is about small farms, as a growing number of producers are doing with excellent results. I have visited some and could verify that they have transformed the land they are working into true gardens where every inch of ground is used.

Extraordinaria, 29 August 2008, respectively. The provisions are summarized in Hagelberg and Alvarez (2009). As noted there, already prior to this legislation, the agricultural land owned or leased by private farmers had grown by 25% from 970,000 hectares to some 1.2 million hectares between 1989 and 2007, according to official statistics, with the cultivated land in that sector increasing by more than 50% from 520,000 hectares to 800,000 hectares. Subject to certain conditions, Ministry of Agriculture Resolution No. 223/95, dated 29 June 1995, authorized grants of up to one *caballería* (13.42 hectares) of idle state land in indefinite usufruct to small farmers having sufficient family labour and equipment to exploit the land (http://faolex.fao.org/docs/pdf/cub4795.pdf).

Raúl Castro entrusted this new initiative specifically to Adolfo Rodríguez Nodals, the head of the National Group of Urban Agriculture (since renamed National Group of Urban and Suburban Agriculture) in the agriculture ministry. The group, he declared, "has obtained outstanding results in urban agriculture, fruit of the exactingness and systematicity expressed in the four controls that it carries out annually in all the provinces and municipalities of the country" (*Granma*, 3 August 2009). This suggests that Raúl Castro still prized centralized control over operational functionality, evidently unconscious of the fact that it is wholly unsuitable for the management of small-scale mixed farming.

While the idea of the *Agricultura Suburbana* plan may indeed have come from the experience of the *Agricultura Urbana* program created in the 1990s (Rodríguez Castellón, 2003) and shares some of its policy objectives and features, such as high labor intensity, the two schemes are as distinct as town and country, horticulture and agriculture. *Agricultura Urbana* rests, in the main, on patios (domestic gardens), plots (empty lots planted to vegetables) and so-called organopónicos — low-walled beds filled with soil and organic matter, with or without drip irrigation, in the open air or in shade houses, their high-tech name derived from hydroponic installations that could not be maintained after the collapse of the Soviet Union. The system, now reportedly embracing around 10,500 *organopónicos* alone and occupying more than 300,000 workers (Luben Pérez, 2010), no doubt contributes substantially to the food supply and has other advantages. Equally, Rodríguez Nodals's group undoubtedly fulfills some useful functions by providing advice and facilitating access to supplies in other countries easily available.[100] Its face to the wider public, however, consists of tedious reports of its quarterly inspections and the grades it bestows on its charges, rather in the manner of an elementary school teacher (e.g., Varela Pérez, 2010h).

In contrast, the basic structural model of *Agricultura Suburbana* is the *finca*, a small farm, most often in private hands, located in an eight-kilometer-deep ring between two and ten kilometers from urban centers. The plan is being

---

[100] The writer, residing in a small English city, gets the seeds, with instructions how to plant on the packets, for his little vegetable garden from a nearby supermarket.

rolled out in stages stretching over five years, some selected municipalities at a time. Its declared objective is to source the food supply of population concentrations as far as possible from nearby crop and livestock producers primarily reliant on animal power for field work as well as transport. Around the city of Camagüey, the test ground for the project, it will ultimately comprise some 1,400 units with a total area of roughly 65,000 hectares, 80% of which is agricultural land, the greater part devoted to cattle (Hernández Porto, 2009; Carrobello, 2010; and Frank, 2010). Introduced as an experiment in 18 municipalities at the beginning of 2010, the program would be progressively extended to some 600,000 hectares across the whole country, according to ANAP president Orlando Lugo Fonte (Bosch, 2010).

The emphasis was on narrowing the distance between producer and purchaser — distributor, processor or final consumer — on employing animals in place of internal combustion engines in field work and haulage, and on using compost instead of inorganic fertilizers. This shows that the *Agricultura Suburbana* program, like the government's other major agricultural policy initiatives in the last 20 years from the creation of the UBPCs to Decree-Law No. 259, is inspired above all by the need to reduce Cuba's dependence on imports, both food and production inputs, at a time of extreme economic stress.[101] To go by the official propaganda, were *Agricultura Suburbana* enterprises to be characterized by a logo, it would have to feature a pair of oxen. Hence it is disconcerting to find that Cuba's stock of draught oxen appears to have shrunk by a quarter from 377,100 to 284,700 between 2004 and 2009, in contrast to a growing equine population (ONE, 2010, Tables 9.15 and 9.24). If ONE's figures are right, the question can reasonably be asked: do the policymakers in Havana know what goes on down on the farm?

Regardless of whether it offers a perspective of more than a semi-subsistence agriculture, the shortage of material resources to back up the effort to return

---

[101] The expenditure on inorganic fertilizer imports was reduced by two-thirds from 171.3 million pesos in 2008 to 55.7 million pesos in 2009 (ONE, 2010, Table 8.13). Urea, the main item in quantitative terms in 2009, was probably used at least in part as an animal feed additive. Imports of herbicides, pesticides and plant growth regulators were also cut, but relatively less.

swathes of mostly *marabú*-infested land to production under Decree-Law No. 259 favored the more measured approach of the *Agricultura Suburbana* program. The authorities were admittedly overwhelmed by the flood of requests for plots triggered by Decree-Law No. 259 (Carrobello and Terrero, 2009a). Within barely more than a month of opening the door to submissions in the autumn of 2008, some 69,000 applications were received — 98% of them from individuals and 79% of these from persons without land — according to official figures (Nova González, 2008). Another month or so later and the number of applicants had swelled to some 117,000 (Carrobello and Terrero, 2009a). Was the notorious Cuban dislike for agricultural work another myth? If a fan of the Beatles, Raúl Castro may well have been reminded of the lyrics of *Eleanor Rigby*: "All the lonely people / Where do they all come from? / All the lonely people / Where do they all belong?" Declaring the distribution of idle land in usufruct one of the great challenges for the coming year, he rather optimistically told an interviewer on the last day of 2008: "We have already put behind us the first, initial obstacles we encountered because of atavistic bureaucratic habits" (González Pérez, 2009).

In fact, many successful applicants found that what they had signed up for was, as the trade union organ *Trabajadores* recalled later, *hacer de tripas, corazón* (summon up the guts to root out the *marabú*), "most often without the necessary tools and without a gram of herbicide, by sheer spirit alone" (Rey Veitia et al, 2010). An investigation by a team of *Juventud Rebelde* reporters in March 2009 unearthed multiple problems — lack of hand tools, machinery and fuel, insufficient financial support, uncertainty over whether even a shelter was permitted on the plot, shortage of fencing wire, and bureaucracy — along with concern over the technical unpreparedness of people new to farming (Pérez et al, 2009). In rebuttal of purported exploitation of the issues by foreign news agencies allegedly intent on defaming Cuba, *Trabajadores* sought to dampen down expectations: "It would be a delusion to think … that any agricultural process that begins with the request for the land could bring significant productive results in only nine months…. Bureaucracy? Yes, it is a process that implies steps and involves various agencies" (González, 2009).

Yet similar complaints of shortages, delays, irregularities, bureaucracy, and official incompetence have resurfaced again and again (e.g. "Efectuado pleno...," 2009; Rey Veitia et al, 2010). The persistent bureaucracy made the front page of *Granma* when farmers informed

José Ramón Machado Ventura, member of the Politburo and first vice president of the councils of state and of ministers, at an ANAP meeting in Havana, of the "diabolical" mechanisms holding back pig meat production in the metropolitan area (Varela Pérez, 2010e). And *Juventud Rebelde* quoted an outstanding young farmer (Martín González, 2010):

> For some time I have been supplying eggs to a school in the community. Until now I have done it with the hens I have, but they have to be replaced because they are getting old and don't produce. When I asked for replacements, there was so much paperwork that I am still thinking about it.

Lies, Damned Lies, and Statistics

A bane in the lives of the Cuban people, an incompetent bureaucracy constitutes a minefield for the country's leadership. In their efforts to devise agricultural reforms, Cuba's policymakers labor under a big informational handicap. The government is ill-served by its statistical apparatus. A cardinal case in point is a monograph survey of land use, released by the National Office of Statistics in May 2008, which put the idle agricultural land at 1,232,800 hectares, equal to 18.6% of all agricultural land, as of December 2007 (ONE, 2008). Presumably, this was the figure that guided the framers of Decree-Law No. 259 of 10 July 2008. The number was repeated in ONE's statistical yearbooks for 2008 and 2009 (Table 9.1), published in 2009 and 2010 respectively, and is still the most recent available from that source. However, as casually revealed in *Trabajadores*, it appears to have been a gross understatement: "A study of the idle state lands arrived at 1,691 thousand hectares" (González, 2009). The provenance of this study has remained unidentified, as far as is known, but a figure in the order of 1.7 million hectares is now evidently the accepted magnitude of the idle land area existent on the eve of Decree-Law No. 259.[102]

Hagelberg and Alvarez (2009) underlined the scope for statistical manipulation offered by a metric of land utilization that allows inclusion of areas merely

---

[102] To put this in perspective, the 1.7 million hectares of idle land exceeded by 350,000 hectares the sugarcane area harvested in 1988/89 for a crop of more than 8 million metric tons of sugar.

earmarked for a crop, as officially employed in Cuba in respect of sugarcane. Carrobello and Terrero (2009a) subsequently pointed to another possibility — there may have been no second study, merely a reclassification of categories that moved the goalposts: "But if we add [to the figure of 1,232,800 hectares] the pastures of doubtful utility, 55% of the agricultural area was not cultivated." Agricultural statistics everywhere must, by the nature of things, be granted a margin of error and should not be interpreted too closely. But this is a discrepancy of a different order. In a matter as sensitive as idle land, pollution of the statistical process by political or ideological considerations cannot be excluded. In addition, a century-old practice of maintaining grassland reserves in sugar plantations to expand the cane area when profitable to do so conjures up an image of turf wars between the agriculture and sugar ministries.

However, ONE publications also contain numerous infelicities hard to ascribe to political contamination. For instance, the most recent ONE statistical yearbooks (ONE, 2009 and 2010) report tonnages of sugarcane processed in each season since 2002/03 (Table 11.3) greater than those produced for delivery to the mills in the respective season (Table 9.4). Though perhaps not on a par with the biblical miracle of the loaves and fishes, the magnification amounts to as much as 900,000 metric tons in 2002/03 (4.1%) and 800,000 tons in 2006/07 (6.7%). Examination of earlier editions of the yearbook indicates that this inconsistency began in 2002/03, the first crop following the restructuring of the industry. The technical indicators displayed in Table 11.3 — cane milled, sugar produced, yield and polarization — are a farrago of incongruities and plain error. Unusually, ONE references these solecisms to the sugar ministry, but that does not absolve it of responsibility since it is the controller of the national system of statistics and guarantor of their quality.

The question-mark hanging over ONE's integrity, competence and professionalism notwithstanding, it is for outside analysts the only source of the data necessary to present more than an anecdotal picture of Cuban agricultural performance. Accurately weighing the impact of the three major hurricanes and a tropical storm that occurred in 2008 — described as the most destructive hurricane season in Cuba's recorded history (Messina, 2009) — both on that year's output and regarding after-effects, is an additional problem.

Messina noted miscellaneous reports of damage and losses in tree and arable crops, chicken and egg production, and sugar factories. But the expected high levels of loss were not reflected in the official data. Discussing the possible reasons for the lighter than anticipated losses recorded, Messina thought the most plausible explanation was that particularly in perennial and tree crops the greater part of the harvest takes place in spring and was largely completed before the hurricane season. The full impact of the 2008 weather events would therefore not become apparent until the spring harvest of 2009 and would have to be taken into account in looking at the previous year' year's figures. Table 1

Table 1. Cuban Food Crop and Livestock Production, 2009

	Production (1000 m.t.)	Change from 2008 (%)	Non-state share (%)	
			2008	2009
Tubers and roots	1565.6	12.4	86.6	86.1
Bananas and plantains	670.4	-11.6	82.7	84.5
Horticultural crops	2548.8	4.5	82.1	80.4
Paddy rice	563.6	29.3	87.5	85.8
Corn	304.8	-6.4	93.4	91.8
Beans	110.8	14.0	97.0	94.5
Citrus fruits	418.0	6.7	37.9	38.8
Other fruits	748.0	1.3	92.2	90.8
Deliveries for slaughter, ive weight				
Beef	130.0	4.9	na	na
Pigs	271.0	-7.2	41.0	44.8
Poultry meat	42.6	<0.5	77.8	77.9
Cow milk	600.3	10.0	86.4	86.4
Eggs	2426.8[103]	4.2	19.1	23.4

Source: ONE, 2010, Tables 9.9, 9.11, 9.17, 9.18, 9.20, 9.22, 9.23. Percentages calculated by the author, in the case of the non-state shares of pigs delivered for slaughter, poultry meat and eggs, indirectly by subtraction of the output of state enterprises from total production.

---

[103] Million units.

summarizes the official data on 2009 performance in the major crop and live-stock categories. The information for the non-state sector is said to compre-hend Basic Units of Cooperative Production (UBPCs), Agricultural Production Cooperatives (CPAs), Credits and Services Cooperatives (CCSs), as well as dis-persed private producers and estimates for house patios and plots (ONE, 2010, Chapter 9, Introduction). No breakdown into its components is provided in the yearbook. Given the hybrid character of the UBPCs (Hagelberg and Alvarez, 2009), their assignment to the non-state sector is debatable. Interestingly, they are carried on a separate government register from CPAs and CCSs (ONE, 2010, Chapter 4, "Institutional Organization," Methodological Notes). The estimates for patios and plots may also include self-provisioning patches of state enterprises, UBPCs and CPAs; but it is reasonable to suppose that the majority are in private hands. In any event, it is understandably difficult to capture the full volume of production in this category (Messina, 2009).

With the sole exception of rice, recorded 2009 outputs in the major crop lines listed in Table 1 were below — in some cases, far below — their levels in 2004, the first year shown in this edition of the yearbook. Average yields per hectare (ONE, 2010, Table 9.12) were the lowest for the six-year period 2004–2009 — except citrus fruits, in fourth place from the best, higher than expected, and other fruits, in fifth place. The record is better in livestock prod-ucts, with only poultry meat not reaching the 2004 figure. Except in egg and poultry meat production (ONE, 2010, Tables 9.22 and 9.23), there are also clear signs of improved efficiency, with average beef and pig live weights at slaugh-ter and milk yield per cow on rising trends, although still at very low levels (ONE, 2010, Tables 9.17, 9.18 and 9.20).

Not so much legacy effects of the 2008 weather as badly distributed and over-all low rainfall the following year (ONE, 2010, Table 2.3) was probably at least in part responsible for lackluster 2009 crop yields, alongside of more secular factors. Messina (2009) surmised that citrus output may still be affected by the bacterial citrus greening or *Huanglongbing* disease, a conjecture confirmed by Varela Pérez (2010c). Growing corn in Cuba is constrained by low yields and high production costs. Some of the output swings in either direction are easily traceable to official actions on prices and resource allocation. Potato producers enjoyed priority in the supply of imported seed, fertilizer and plant chemicals. Rice and beans are focal points of the policy of import substitution. Milk production mirrors the effect of price incentives and the increase in small-scale stock farming as a result of Decree-Law No. 259, among other factors. On the other hand, the drop in the delivery of pigs for slaughter suggests a classic hog cycle farmer response of herd reduction after encountering marketing difficulties in 2008.

Unsurprisingly in an sector as exposed as Cuba's agriculture to governmental intervention as well as the vagaries of the weather, there is scant evidence of stabilization in domestic food production. A greatly expanded area planted was the principal factor behind a comparatively large tomato harvest, the main contributor to the smallish rise in the horticultural crop total. Memories of losses due to the inability of *Acopio*, the state procurement agency, and of processing plants to handle last year's tomato crop are likely to be reflected in 2010, if the large decreases in area planted and production in the first quarter, compared with the same period in 2009 (*ONE, Dirección de Agropecuario*, 2010) are a guide. Compared with the same period in 2009, the first three months of 2010 saw bananas and plantains up 75.1%, but tubers and roots down 9.0%; horticultural crops down 25.1%; corn up 4.9%; beans down 30.5%; paddy rice up 45.5%; citrus fruits down 21.7%; other fruits up 16.1%; live weight beef and pig deliveries for slaughter down 3.2% and 3.3% respectively; cow milk down 6.0%; and eggs down 1.1% (*ONE, Dirección de Agropecuario,* 2010). Unless the 2010 rainy season breaks the severe drought that began in late 2008, the government could easily find itself again between the Scylla and Charybdis of a national food crisis or a huge food import bill.

Private Enterprise to the Rescue of the State

If there is a clear message from the data, it is Cuba's dependence on the non-state sector — and to a greatly increasing extent on the truly private sub-sector— for the national food supply. The gradual 245,000–hectare (25%)

expansion of the agricultural land owned or leased by private operators that took place between 1989 and 2007 (Hagelberg and Alvarez, 2009) was dwarfed by the structural change in land tenancy within the space of a few months by the implementation of Decree-Law No. 259.

This is too recent a development to have made an impact on the non-state shares in output shown in Table 1, most of which were already of a high order. However, it is reflected in the non-state shares in crop areas harvested and in production — in seven out of eight categories higher in 2009 than in 2008 (Table 2).

Table 2. Non-Sugar Food Crop Areas Harvested and in Production, 2009

	Area (1000 ha)	Change from 2008 (%)	Non-state share (%) 2008	2009
Tubers and roots	246.0	25.4	87.8	90.8
Bananas and plantains	106.4	27.2	82.7	88.8
Horticultural crops	278.6	7.5	86.7	88.4
Paddy rice	215.8ta	38.7	88.0	87.6
Corn	204.0	57.9	91.2	95.5
Beans	150.6	58.0	94.9	96.3
Citrus fruits	47.9	5.0	54.0	62.2
Other fruits	91.7	10.4	85.6	88.1

Source: ONE, 2010, Tables 9.6, 9.8. Percentages calculated by the author.

Overall, the total area harvested and in production of the crops listed here grew by 293,353 hectares from 1,047,559 hectares in 2008 to 1,340,912 hectares in 2009 (ONE, 2010, Table 9.6), an increase of 28.0%. The expansion of the non-state share was greater, both absolutely and relatively, amounting to 296,571 hectares from 906,981 hectares in 2008 to 1,203,552 hectares (ONE, 2010, Table 9.8) — an increase of 32.7%.

Indicative of the impaired state of Cuba's agriculture, however, is that while the 2009 areas of all these crops exceeded the previous year's, those of bananas and plantains, horticultural crops and citrus fruits had yet to recover their 2004 levels. The total 2009 area of 1,340,912 hectares exceeded the corresponding figure for 2004 by just 114,279 hectares, or 9.3%.

Another measure of the enhanced role of the non-state sector — in this case excluding UBPC affiliates who are considered ineligible to belong to it — is the growth of the organization representing private farmers, although there is a confusion of numbers. Towards the end of 2009, a member of the national bureau of the *Asociación Nacional de Agricultores Pequeños* reported that nearly 57,000 new producers had joined the organization and that a further 3,000 new entrants were expected, with an equal growth in the membership of credits and services cooperatives (Carrobello and Terrero, 2009b). The figure of some 60,000 new farmers was subsequently confirmed by Orlando Lugo Fonte, ANAP's president (Hernández, 2010). But Lugo Fonte has also reportedly said that the small farmer sector had grown by "more than 100,000 new members" as a result of the transfer of idle lands under Decree-Law No. 259 (*"Destacan potencial . . ."* 2010; Fernández, 2010). However, on the eve of the 2010 ANAP congress he spoke of 362,440 members in CPAs and CSSs, organized in 3,635 base units (Varela Pérez, 2010g). This figure would be roughly consistent with the addition of 40,000 new members to the 327,380 reported in 2005, which was the influx Lugo Fonte had initially expected in 2009 to result from Decree-Law No. 259 (Hagelberg and Alvarez, 2009).[104] While a large fraction of the new producers undoubtedly had previous farming experience

---

[104] The official employment statistics (ONE, 2010, Tables 7.2 and 7.3) do not clarify the issue. The total number occupied in agriculture, hunting, forestry and fishing — not broken down — reportedly rose by 26,500 from 919,100 in 2008 to 945,600 in 2009, but was still below 2004–06 levels. However, the number of cooperativists — UBPC and CPA members — fell by 2,200 from 233,800 to 231,600. Total private sector employment is put at 602,100 in 2008 and 591,300 in 2009, a drop of 10,800, while the number of self-employed workers, included in this category, increased by 2,200 from 141,600 to 143,800. Excluding these, presumably mostly urban, self-employed workers, private sector employment — under which heading come small independent farmers — thus appears to have shrunk by 13,000 from 460,500 in 2008 to 447,500 in 2009. Possibly, a high loss rate by retirement and death among farmers, given their advanced average age, more than offset the number of new entrants.

as agricultural laborers or technicians — the personnel made redundant by the downsizing of the sugar industry alone constituting a big pool, the fact that the bulk of the applicants for land under Decree-Law No. 259 were previously landless led Armando Nova, an academic and member of the *Centro de Estudios de la Economía Cubana*, to speculate on "the beginning of a process of 'repeasantization'" (Carrobello and Terrero, 2009b).

Recognition at the apex of Cuba's leadership that Decree-Law No. 259 had created new economic and social "facts on the ground," with political implications to be closely watched, would explain the participation of first vice president and Politburo member José Ramón Machado Ventura in ANAP regional meetings in preparation for the association's tenth congress in the spring of 2010. In a conspicuous display of political manpower, agriculture minister Ulises Rosales del Toro, Politburo member and a vice president of the council of ministers, and ANAP president Lugo Fonte, member of the Communist Party's central committee and of the council of state, were regularly outranked at the presiding table of these gatherings by the No. 2 in the national hierarchy.

Reality — up to a Point

In his speech to the National Assembly in July 2008, Raúl Castro himself returned to his oft-quoted 1994 statement, near the nadir of Cuba's fortunes following the collapse of central and east European communism, that "beans are more important than cannons." Previously, in April, his focus on food production (together with the announcement that the long overdue sixth Communist Party congress would be held towards the end of 2009) had ensured that the subject would continue to figure prominently in the debates about Cuba's future that the regime had organized throughout the country. As it turned out, the congress was again postponed in July 2009 and the prospect then offered of a party conference has also still to materialize. But whatever the authorities gained from the debates in gauging the popular mood, identifying hot spots, preparing the citizenry for cuts in public services and state jobs, and providing a safety valve for discontent, there is one visible result: the greatly increased reflection in the mass media of the raw reality that people have long talked about in the street.

A notable example is the acknowledgment by the veteran chief spin-doctor of the sugar and (more recently) of the agriculture ministries, Juan Varela Pérez, of the defects of the UBPCs (Varela Pérez, 2009c):

> "Time showed that, not having been recognized as true cooperatives, many remained halfway between the state farm and the CPA [collective farm composed of former private holdings]. [Their members] were neither *cooperativistas* nor wholly agricultural workers; a limbo was created, but moreover factors deforming their essence arose, to the point of maintaining intact the structure of the original enterprises, to the control of which they were subordinated."

In a subsequent article, Varela Pérez (2010b) listed the differences between genuine cooperatives and the UBPCs that had worked to the latter's detriment. But the new realism goes only so far. The UBPCs failed, with few exceptions, because "they strayed from the essential principles approved by the Politburo ... the approved basic principles were forgotten" and because of "the violation of the concepts that brought the UBPCs to life." Yet it was the regime's penchant for centralized decision-making and micromanagement that dominated in the creation of the UBPCs in 1993.[105] "We are so accustomed to disguise ourselves to others that in the end we become disguised to ourselves," La Rochefoucauld wrote long ago. As long as this is the case, the new openness cannot progress from description of symptoms to diagnosis of causes and thought-through response.

---

[105] Decree-Law No. 142 of 20 September 1993 placed the UBPCs "within the present enterprise structures of the ministries of sugar and agriculture" (Article 1) and prescribed that while "they will be owners of the production" (Article 2b), "they will sell their production to the State through the enterprise or in the form the latter decides" (Article 2c). For a list of critical papers — almost all from authors on the island and affiliated with Cuban institutions — see Hagelberg and Alvarez (2006).

Recognition that beans are more important than cannons has not so far led the government to more than tinker with two major issues that weigh on the overall performance of Cuba's agriculture: the debacle of the sugar agroindustry and the flawed system of state controls over farm inputs and outputs.

For the sixth year running — and, ironically, when world market prices reached their highest point since 1981—Cuba has produced less than 1.5 million metric tons of sugar in 2009/10, a fall of more than 80% from the average annual output of the 1980s. In the last days of the harvest, Reuters (3 June) put the final figure at 1.1–1.2 million metric tons.

In early May, a note from the council of state announced a change of sugar ministers, the outgoing having asked to be relieved of his responsibilities "on recognizing the deficiencies of his work which were pointed out to him" (*Granma*, 4 May 2010). An agronomic engineer, he had been promoted from first vice minister less than 18 months before, after a 38–year career in the sugar sector. His replacement, a chemical engineer, had similarly risen from first vice minister, after more than 30 years in the sugar sector. The new incumbent will not be a minister for long, however, if the knowledgeable Reuters and *Financial Times* correspondent in Cuba, Marc Frank, was right that the sugar ministry would soon be transmuted into a corporation (Reuters, 7 April 2010).

The day after this announcement, Varela Pérez (2010f) blamed what he called the poorest sugar crop since 1905 on bad organization, overestimates of the available cane, and "a high grade of imprecisions and voluntarism." But if this had to be the main tenor of a story put out to explain the defenestration of the minister,[106] disclosure that 55% of the crop area had not been fertilized, only 3% irrigated (down from up to 30% in the 1980s) and that sugarcane was

---

[106] The council of state's action itself was not mentioned in an article of more than 1,000 words bearing all the earmarks of having been officially briefed. The dismissal of the minister also went unnoticed in the 714–word review of the 2009/10 sugar crop disaster by another prominent journalist who, in addition to a price policy that made sugarcane uncompetitive with other crops, pointed to the handicap of a system of centralized allocation of hard currency financing, said to have been only recently made more flexible (Terrero, 2010).

"today the lowest paid [product] in agriculture", made implausible the pretense that "disciplinary measures" and "perfecting the system of administration" were all the answer required. In calling for the restoration of sugarcane to the place corresponding to its continued significance economically and as "part of Cuba's patrimony," Varela Pérez either forgot or hoped his readers would have forgotten Fidel Castro's denunciation in 2005 of sugar as the "ruin" of Cuba's economy and belonging to "the era of slavery" that was the cue to reduce the industry to its present penury. With the 2009/10 harvest having starkly demonstrated "the effects of the cane crisis" to the point where continued decline could end in the industry's extinction, there was an echo of the old Cuban saying, *Sin azúcar, no hay país* (without sugar, there is no country), in the way Varela Pérez (2010i) asked how to begin restoring sugar's "noble and economic tradition" that "has distinguished Cubans historically."[107] The repeated emphasis on the unremunerative cane price — responsibility of the ministry of finance and prices — suggests that the Cuban regime is not exempt from the inter-departmental differences regularly seen in other governments.

The other big issue — the state's control over what goes into and comes out of agriculture — lies at the heart of the Cuba's command economy, which explains the regime's reluctance to tackle it in a fundamental way despite the record of its vices stretching over decades.

In what is until now the most recent attempt to make the system more efficient, the distribution and marketing functions of *Acopio* in Havana city and province passed from the Ministry of Agriculture to the Ministry of Domestic Commerce (MINCIN) in August 2009. But within barely more than a month, it was clear that MINCIN "was not sufficiently prepared for the task," with the result of "significant losses" of perishable products (Varela Pérez and de la Hoz, 2009a). Anxious to find some progress, *Granma*'s reporters returned to the scene again and again (Varela Pérez and de la Hoz, 2009b, 2009c, 2009d), faith triumphing over experience: "However many difficulties, the socialist

---

[107] We have been here before. The regime's love-hate relationship with sugar began 50 years ago with the demolition of 10,000 *caballerías* (134,000 hectares) of cane, followed not long after by a plan to produce 10 million tons of sugar in 1970 (Hagelberg and Alvarez, 2006).

market has to be a mission possible," they wrote. It remained just a hope. In the first two months of 2010, the state food markets in the capital received only 62% of the supplies they were supposed to get from the farmers in the province. Among the reasons: growers had been left without the fertilizer and plant protection chemicals they needed in the last quarter of 2009, and MINCIN still had not got its act together. Bizarrely, a regulation prohibited trucks carrying produce from other provinces to enter the city, even with the proper documentation, and with MINCIN company buyers no longer picking up various kinds of horticultural produce, Havana province farmers were reducing plantings (Varela Pérez, 2010d).

Across the island, apparatchik interference with supply and demand has at different times and in different places thrown a variety of spanners into the works. Farmers who have heeded government calls to produce more have pitched up against a worn-out infrastructure. In Granma province, an unspecified amount of rice was lost, some was processed below quality, and growers still held 1,000 tons dried manually owing to insufficient industrial drying, milling and storage capacity, and these were not the only problems (Sariol Sosa, 2009). In a Villa Clara municipality, the government got itself into a tangle with farmers who, urged to plant a larger area of garlic than contemplated, produced about double the crop it had contracted to buy (Pérez Cabrera, 2009). In Camagüey, the state lactic products company was not ready to cope with the increased volume of milk deliveries, and the milk spent, on average, four and a half hours on the road between producer and processor, to the detriment of its quality (Febles Hernández, 2009). Mangoes similarly overwhelmed the infrastructure in Santiago de Cuba (Riquenes Cutiño, 2009). A cross-country survey of the non-citrus fruit situation (Carrobello and de Jesús, 2010) found some improvements, notably the appearance of roadside sales points and ambulant vendors; but production and distribution continued to be hampered by lack of irrigation facilities, input shortages ranging from fertilizer and plant chemicals to gloves and boxes, difficulties in obtaining bank credits, and the rigidities of the state procurement apparatus. Yet though he grumbled about various deficiencies and incongruities, *ANAP*'s

Lugo Fonte still thought that the cure lay in rigorous contracting between parties and was not prepared to identify the monopsonistic and monopolistic position of state enterprises in relation to the farmer as the root of the problem (Barreras Ferrán, 2010).

A whiff of oligarchic factionalism came from a Lugo Fonte interview in which he recounted the conditions that had depressed cattle farming in the private sector. Small farmers had been allowed to sell their animals only to state companies, most of which did not have scales and bought the cattle "on the hoof," based on the color of the hide, the tail and the horns, and with a high charge for slaughtering — all in accordance with regulations. These rules had been dumped and beef prices sharply raised. But, in order to preserve their margin, the companies were now hindering producers from sending animals directly to the abattoir by refusing to rent vehicles (Varela Pérez, 2010a). And while ANAP members were being encouraged to send raw milk straight to retail outlets, Lugo Fonte lamented that this practice had not been extended to other products, such as eggs (Varela Pérez, 2010g).

If *Acopio* was provoking "downpours" of criticism, the mechanisms of supplying farmers with inputs were causing a "tempest", as reported by *Juventud Rebelde*, the Communist Party's youth organ, on the weekend of the *ANAP* congress (Varios Autores, 2010). More was to come at the congress itself. Entitled "For greater farm and forestry production," much of the 37–point report of its commission on production and the economy was given over to a somewhat unselective survey of the gamut of products, from rice to medicinal plants, and from beef to honey, in which greater output could replace imports and enhance exports (*Granma*, 17 May 2010). But coupled with this were demands on government to resolve a host of functional issues: credit provision; water usage approval; allowing producers to sell directly to retailers, tourist facilities and slaughterhouses; promoting local micro and mini-industries; seasonal price differentiation; crop insurance; tax reform; access to building materials; freeing the cooperatives from restrictions and empowering them to enter into contracts; and reforming quality norms. Of sufficient importance to deserve a point by themselves were the "innumerable concerns" raised by the delegates from Havana city and province concerning the system of commercialization piloted in these territories — excessive product handling, crop losses, arguments over quality, retail outlet permits, state company margins, cartage, container return, and trucks owned by cooperatives being barred from delivering straight to the city's state markets.

Market Deregulation? Not yet

Closing the congress from the government side, minister of the economy and planning Marino Murillo Jorge made it clear that there would be no relaxation of the state's control of food marketing (*Granma*, 17 May 2010). In the sole reference to what he admitted was "one of the subjects most discussed in this congress," he claimed consensus on the need to improve the quality and compelling force of contracts, so that the parties meet their obligations and the quantities agreed are planted, harvested and marketed, avoiding the sale in the supply-and-demand markets of produce not certified as surplus to contract or allowed free disposal. Government and *ANAP* had to collaborate "to solve as soon as possible the problem of illegal intermediaries who artificially raise prices without contributing to society."

Concerning market reform, Murillo Jorge had but one announcement — the government would "organize the creation in the majority of the municipalities of the country of an input market where producers could acquire directly the resources necessary for crop and livestock production, replacing the current mechanism of central allocation." The price policy governing this market, he spelled out, "must guarantee, on the one hand, recognition in the *acopio* price [the price at which the state acquires products] of the real costs of production and, on the other, the elimination of the great number of subsidies that the state pays today through the budget." Whether this market will amount to something more than adding to the small number of existing stores selling tools and supplies for convertible pesos and how it will obtain its merchandise, if not by central allocation, was left in the dark.

Altogether, it is hard to resist the impression that this was a holding operation at which ANAP delegates could let off steam, but from which they emerged none the wiser about key government policy areas that affect the private farm sector. A number of subjects, Murillo Jorge said, were "in process of analysis and study within the context of the updating the Cuban economic model," naming taxation (of both farmers and their workers), the contracting of outside labor (stating that more than 100,000 wage workers were employed by cooperatives), and the prices of inputs and of *acopio*.

Speaking to the congress of the Communist Party's youth organization in April 2010 (*Granma*, 5 April), Raúl Castro acknowledged the existence of voices urging a faster pace of change. Whether the regime's tempo is dictated by the magnitude and complexity of the problems facing Cuba, as he claimed, by divisions among the leadership, by lack of the cash needed to jump-start major reforms, by incompetence, or by all these, is an unknown — certainly to outsiders. Specifically in the area of farm policy, the twists and turns over half a century invite the following question: do the policy-makers really understand agriculture and how it develops? When it comes to the effective application of scientific and technological advances — highlighted by Murillo Jorge as "an aspect that requires the greatest immediate attention"—are Cuba's policymakers sufficiently versed in the agricultural history of other countries to appreciate the interactions of market forces, farmer-boffins, equipment manufacturers, chemical companies, plant breeders and agribusinesses, alongside of public institutions such as experiment stations and extension services, that drive innovation?

Although located, broadly speaking, towards the opposite end of the spectrum from the extensive model of agroindustry growth that hit the buffers in the second half of the 1980s, before the fall of the Berlin Wall, the concept now being promoted is similarly extensive in several respects. In pursuit of the goals of replacing imports and increasing exports of agricultural products, the government campaigns to substitute human muscle and animal power for engines, compost for inorganic fertilizers, home-grown animal feedstuffs for concentrates, and prioritizes the expansion of land under cultivation over raising yields.

Understandable, up to a point, as fire-fighting in the midst of current economic and financial woes, can these methods generate a serious improvement in Cuba's agricultural trade balance? While the application of idle land and labor will surely increase the domestic food supply, can it make the country anywhere near self-sufficient? Is this model viable in the longer run?

Disturbingly, in all the hype in favor of using oxen for field work and transport, there is nary an indication that either the costs of breeding, rearing, training, feeding and appareling the animals, or the productivity of a team, including its driver, taking into account speed of locomotion and length of working day, have been factored in. Likewise missing from the hymns to the benefits of compost are signs of awareness that to make enough compost for general application entails industrial-scale production techniques with specialized equipment.

To project the picture of a new mentality gestating in the countryside, *Juventud Rebelde* located, for its edition on the weekend of the ANAP congress, a few young farmers earning several times the average national wage (◊Varios Autores, 2010). "In my case," said one, "when I get the money together, I'll buy myself a cellphone, because I need it; tell me about it, as, like other presidents of cooperatives, I don't have anything with which to communicate." Twenty-first century aspirations in Cuba, as elsewhere. For his part, Raúl Castro — spookily bringing to mind Churchillian rhetoric[108] — proclaimed before the National Assembly on 1 August 2009: "They didn't elect me president to restore capitalism in Cuba or to surrender the Revolution. I was elected to defend, maintain and continue perfecting socialism, not to destroy it." For that, he realized, beans are more important than cannons. Does he understand that they are more important than command and control?

---

[108] *Winston Churchill:* "I have not become the King's First Minister in order to preside over the liquidation of the British Empire." Speech at Lord Mayor's Luncheon, Mansion House, London, 10 November 1942.

References

Barreras Ferrán, Ramón. 2010. "Mirada a lo profundo de la tierra." *Trabajadores*, 16 January.

Bosch, Hernán. 2010. "Amplia incorporación campesina a la Agricultura Suburbana." *Granma*, 17 February.

Carrobello, Caridad. 2010. "Agricultura Suburbana: Abrazo productivo a la ciudad." *Bohemia*, 11 March.

Carrobello, Caridad, and Ariel Terrero. 2009a. "Agricultura: Cuando el surco suena…," *Bohemia*, 23 December.

Carrobello, Caridad, and Ariel Terrero. 2009b. "Contra la peor de las plagas posibles." *Bohemia*, 23 December.

Carrobello, Caridad, and Lázaro de Jesús. 2010. "Controversias en almíbar" and "¿Quién quiere comprarme frutas…?" *Bohemia*, 18 June.

"Destacan potencial productivo del sector campesino cubano." 2010. *Granma*, 15 January.

"Efectuado pleno del Comité Provincial del partido en la capital." 2009. *Granma*, 9 November.

Febles Hernández, Miguel. 2009. "Empresa Láctea en Camagüey: La ruta crítica." *Granma*, 5 October.

Fernández, William. 2010. "Congreso campesino trazará pautas para elevar rendimientos." *Granma*, 11 May.

Frank, Marc. 2010. "New agricultural reforms: Cuba looks to suburban farms to boost food output." *Reuters*, 7 February.

González, Ana Margarita. 2009. "Entrega de tierras (I): Realidades y manipulaciones." *Trabajadores*, 6 July. "Entrega de tierras (II): Con premura, pero sin chapucerías." *Trabajadores*, 13 July.

González Pérez, Talía. 2009. "Estos 50 años fueron de resistencia y firmeza del pueblo." *Granma*, 5 January.

Hagelberg, G.B., and José Alvarez. 2006. "Command and countermand: Cuba's sugar industry under Fidel Castro." *Cuba in Transition — Volume 16*, pp. 123–139. Washington: Association for the Study of the Cuban Economy.

Hagelberg, G.B., and José Alvarez. 2007. "Cuba's dysfunctional agriculture: The challenge facing the government." *Cuba in Transition — Volume 17*, pp. 144–158. Washington: Association for the Study of the Cuban Economy.

Hagelberg, G.B., and José Alvarez. 2009. "Cuban agriculture: The return of the *campesinado*." *Cuba in Transition — Volume 19*, pp. 229–241. Washington: Association for the Study of the Cuban Economy.

Hernández, Marta. 2010. "Aumenta número de productores agrícolas en Cuba." *Granma*, 6 May.

Hernández Porto, Yahily. 2009. "Desarrollan en Camagüey Agricultura Suburbana." *Juventud Rebelde*, 10 October.

Luben Pérez, Lino. 2010. "Laboran más de 300 mil cubanos en la agricultura urbana." *Granma*, 22 June.

Martín González, Marianela. 2009. "Los pies en el suelo ¿y el grito en el cielo?" *Juventud Rebelde*, 23 August.

Martín González, Marianela. 2010. "Alerta joven desde el surco." *Juventud Rebelde*, 6 June.

Messina, William A., Jr. 2009. "The 2008 hurricane season and its impact on Cuban agriculture and trade." *Cuba in Transition — Volume 19*, pp. 421–28. Washington: Association for the Study of the Cuban Economy.

Nova González, Armando. 2008. "El microcrédito en las nuevas condiciones de la agricultura." *Centro de Estudios de la Economía Cubana, Universidad de la Habana — Boletín Cuatrimestral*, December.

ONE. 2008. *Uso y Tenencia de la Tierra en Cuba — Diciembre 2007*. La Habana: Oficina Nacional de Estadísticas

ONE. 2009. *Anuario Estadístico de Cuba 2008*. Havana: Oficina Nacional de Estadísticas.

ONE. 2010. *Anuario Estadístico de Cuba 2009*. Havana: Oficina Nacional de Estadísticas.

ONE, Dirección de Agropecuario. 2010. *Sector Agropecuario. Indicadores Seleccionados, Enero-Marzo 2010*. May.

Pérez, Dora, et al. 2009. "La necesidad no tiene ciclo corto". *Juventud Rebelde*, 22 March.

Pérez Cabrera, Freddy. 2009. "Contratar bien, esa es la clave." *Granma*, 2 October.

Pérez Cabrera, Freddy. 2010. "Anuncian medidas para elevar la eficiencia en la Agricultura." *Granma*, 15 March.

Rey Veitia, Lourdes, et al. 2010. "Contrapunteo más allá del marabú." *Trabajadores*, 3 May.

Riquenes Cutiño, Odalis, 2009. "¡Le zumba el mango!" *Juventud Rebelde*, 1 November.

Rodríguez Castellón, Santiago. 2003. "La agricultura urbana y la producción de alimentos: la experiencia de Cuba." *Cuba Siglo XXI*, No. 30 (June).

Sariol Sosa, Sara. 2009. "Pleno del Partido en Granma: Provechoso examen sobre la producción arrocera". *Granma*, 29 September.

Terrero, Ariel. 2010. "Caña perdida." *Bohemia*, 17 May.

Varela Pérez, Juan. 2009a. "Impago a los productores agropecuarios: Fantasma que vuelve a rondar." *Granma*, 28 September.

Varela Pérez, Juan. 2009b. "La agricultura necesita poner en orden sus fuerzas." *Granma*, 10 November.

Varela Pérez, Juan. 2009c. "Aciertos y desaciertos de las UBPC." *Granma*, 4 December.

Varela Pérez, Juan. 2010a. "Ligero aumento de la producción de alimentos." *Granma*, 8 January.

Varela Pérez, Juan. 2010b. "Unidades Básicas de Producción Cooperativa: Ni trabas ni tutelaje." *Granma*, 19 January.

Varela Pérez, Juan. 2010c. "¿Volverán los cítricos a llenar tarimas?" *Granma*, 22 February.

Varela Pérez, Juan. 2010d. "Baches en las tarimas ¿pudieron aminorarse?" *Granma*, 3 March.

Varela Pérez, Juan. 2010e. "Frena la burocracia producción de carne porcina en la capital." *Granma*, 29 March.

Varela Pérez, Juan. 2010f. "Faltaron control y exigencia en la zafra." *Granma*, 5 May.

Varela Pérez, Juan. 2010g. "Campesinos traen un soplo de aire fresco." *Granma*, 12 May.

Varela Pérez, Juan. 2010h. "¿Despega la agricultura suburbana?" *Granma*, 1 July.

Varela Pérez, Juan. 2010i. "Cortar de raíz la indisciplina cañera." *Granma*, 9 July.

Varela Pérez, Juan, and Pedro de la Hoz. 2009a. "No dejar que nos sorprenda el majá." *Granma*, 8 September

Varela Pérez, Juan, and Pedro de la Hoz. 2009b. "No puede haber lugar para demoras." *Granma*, 18 September.

Varela Pérez, Juan, and Pedro de la Hoz. 2009c. "Misión posible." *Granma*, 2 October.

Varela Pérez, Juan, and Pedro de la Hoz. 2009d. "Comercialización de productos agrícolas en la capital: El espejo todavía está invertido." *Granma*, 2 November.

Varios Autores. 2010. "Los

9

SCHOOLING VS. HUMAN CAPITAL: HOW PREPARED IS CUBA'S LABOR FORCE TO FUNCTION IN A MARKET ECONOMY?

Luis Locay

A transition to a market economy is always challenging, especially when it also involves the struggle out of underdevelopment. Sometime in the future Cuba will probably be involved in such a transition. Almost everyone agrees the task will be most difficult, but many observers of the Cuban economy point out that one thing the Island has going for it is a fairly well-educated labor force. Increases in education and literacy are among the "achievements of the revolution" that are frequently proclaimed by the Cuban regime and its supporters.

High education coexists, however, with low productivity. In 2001 the United States government ranked Cuba above only Haiti in all of Latin America and the Caribbean in purchasing power adjusted per capita income (*World Factbook*, 2002). These two apparently contradictory characteristics of Cuba's labor force are normally reconciled by attributing the low productivity to the misuse of productive resources, including labor, by government planners. Under this view Cuba has high levels of human capital, so the earning potential of its labor force in an efficient market-oriented system is high. This conclusion is based on an extrapolation to Cuba of the relationship between schooling and earnings observed in market economies. The forces that have shaped the skills of Cuba's labor force, however, are much different than in those market economies, so this extrapolation may be unwarranted.

Formal education and informal on-the-job training are the primary ways individuals acquire the various skills that are collectively referred to as human capital. As with physical capital, the return to human capital can be in the form of direct consumption or it can be indirect through higher earnings. In market economies individuals (or their families) receive most of the benefits and face many of the costs (including opportunity costs) of their investments in human capital. It is not surprising therefore, that in making schooling and occupational choices (how long to stay in school, what field to study, what occupation to go into) potential earnings plays an important role. The end result is that proxy measures of human capital such as years of schooling and years of work experience are strongly related to earnings.

The formation of skills in Cuba's command economy has been guided by a very different process from that found in more market-oriented economies.[109] Decisions have not been made by individuals guided by market-determined wages and prices. Cuba's distributions of skills and occupations have, for the most part, been shaped by the same planners who have either been uninterested in using Cuba's resources efficiently, or unable to do so. Presumably they have been guided by the same political concerns that have guided their production decisions, so it may well be the case that Cuba's current distributions of skills

---

[109] Madrid-Aris (2000) finds that increases in education, though large, contributed little to economic growth in the period 1963-88.

and occupations are quite different from the distributions that will prevail once Cuba makes a transition to a market economy. If the two distributions are very different, and it is difficult to transition from one to the other, then it amounts to saying that Cuba's current levels of schooling and work experience overstate the country's human capital.

As an example, consider a twenty-year professional in the area of physical education. This is a field whose high current numbers are almost certainly not sustainable in a future market-oriented economy. Such an individual may not find employment in his profession in a post transition Cuba. His basic education is a general form of human capital that is useful in most jobs in a modern economy, but his post-secondary education and on-the-job training may have generated fairly occupation-specific human capital. If this is so, even though our hypothetical individual may be a college graduate with 20 years of work experience on paper, his human capital is really closer to that of an 18-year-old high school graduate.

To suspect that there may be a mismatch between current skills and those that will prevail in a future market economy is quite different from knowing what specific fields will expand and which will contract. Knowledge of what the occupational and skill distribution will be *does not exist today*. To claim otherwise is to fall into the central planner's fallacy: the belief that armed with the "facts" an intelligent analyst can determine what markets will do. Yet it would seem that such knowledge is necessary if we are to compare Cuba today with what it will be in the future. This task is not possible, even with much better data than currently exists. We can, however, ask a related, but more modest question: does the distribution of occupations and skills in Cuba today resemble those in more market-friendly Latin American countries? More precisely, could we pick Cuba out from a sample of Latin American economies on the basis of broad occupational and schooling categories? If Cuba is not an outlier on the basis of broad categories, it does not necessarily imply that its skill and occupational distribution is close to what it will be under a market system, since it is possible that it is an outlier if narrower categories are used. But if Cuba is an outlier under such broad comparisons it would suggest that the necessary adjustments may be considerable, and that optimism for a future transition due to Cuba's high level of human capital should be tempered.

The first section of this paper describes some of the major changes in Cuba's labor market in the 1990s. The second section is the heart of the paper. There I compare Cuba's labor force with those of more market-oriented Latin American economies. The basic finding is that Cuba's skill and occupational distribution tends to be an outlier, so that its transition to a market economy may be more difficult than one would expect from looking at overall levels of education. I conclude with a few findings using more disaggregated data that support the conclusion that Cuba's levels of education overstate its levels of human capital, and I raise additional concerns about the quality of its labor force and the problems that may pose to a future transition.

The Cuban Labor Market in the 1990s

By the 1980s, Soviet assistance to Cuba was enormous, perhaps as much as one third of national output.[110] Between 1989 and 1992 this assistance came to an abrupt end, sending Cuba into its worst economic crisis since the Castro government came to power. Despite initial resistance to making any structural changes, toward the end of 1993 the government was forced to implement limited reforms in order to avert disaster. The events surrounding these reforms are well documented and will not be discussed here in any detail.[111]

In late 1993 the Cuban government began implementing a series of policies that would stabilize the economy and result in a modest recovery. The new

---

[110] Madrid-Aris (1997) reports that Soviet subsidies during 1980-84 accounted for 33% of Gross Material Product, while Hernández-Catá (2000) estimates that subsidized prices and credit averaged 15% of Gross Domestic Product during 1986-90 if converted at the official exchange rate of one peso per US$.

[111] For a good summary of the events and policies of this period see Hernández-Catá (2000).

policies de-criminalized the possession and use of hard currency and legalized transfers of dollars from abroad as well as a limited from of self-employment. State farms were converted into cooperatives and farmers' markets, where many products could be sold at free market prices, were legalized, Foreigners were allowed to own property, and government employment was reduced. In the period between 1993 and 2000 real GDP grew 29.3%, and per capita growth was almost 26%.

Table 1. Selected Cuban Labor Market Statistics
(*in thousands*)

	1989	1994	1995	1996	1997	1998
Total Labor Force	4,728	4,496	4,526	4,515	4,606	4,646
% of working age population	76.1	67.5	67.8	67.9	69.2	70.0
Civilian Labor Force	4,039	4,141	3,948	3,970	4,028	4,061
% of working age population	65.0	62.2	59.1	59.7	60.5	61.2
Total Government Employment	4,127	3,524	3,409	3,401	3,453	3,440
% of labor force	87.3	78.4	75.3	75.3	75.0	74.0
Civilian Government Employment	3,437	3,169	2,831	2,856	2,875	2,855
% of civilian labor force	85.1	76.5	71.7	71.9	71.4	70.3
Mixed Enterprises	-	82	72	85	109	131
% of civilian labor force	0	2.0	1.8	2.1	2.7	3.2
Cooperatives	65	324	349	348	339	329
% of civilian labor force	1.6	7.8	8.8	8.8	8.4	8.1
Total Private	164	264	326	312	357	418
% of civilian labor force	4.1	6.4	8.3	7.9	8.9	10.3
Unemployed	372	301	357	343	323	307
% of civilian labor force	9.2	7.3	9.0	8.6	8.0	7.6

Source: From data in ECLAC (2000) and *Anuario Estadístico de Cuba*, 2002.

Despite the modest nature of the reforms of 1993-94, the Cuban leadership became concerned about the expansion of the private sector, and in 1996 the process of liberalization ended and was even somewhat reversed. Taxes and fees were sharply increased, and fines were imposed. Economic recovery slowed. Many of the new entrepreneurs were driven out of business or into the informal sector. By 2000 GDP and GDP per capita were still 12% and 17% below their respective 1989 levels.[112] Since September 11, 2001 recovery appears to have slowed further.

After initial resistance following the collapse of the Soviet Union, the Cuban government reduced state employment and allowed the emergence of a small, but significant, private sector that could absorb some of the displaced workers. Other displaced workers were employed in government joint ventures with foreign firms, mostly in the tourism sector. These firms are required to hire their workers through a government employment agency. The salaries of such workers are paid in dollars to the government agency, which then pays the workers in pesos at an exchange rate of one-to-one. The market exchange rate has not fallen below 20 pesos per dollar since holding and using dollars was legalized, so the effective tax rate has been 95% or higher.[113] Some reduction in state employment also appears to have been achieved through early retirement and probably an increase in the informal sector.

Table 1 shows the behavior of the labor force and of government and private sector employment for the period 1989-98. From 1989 to 1998 total government employment fell by about 687,000 workers, and the civilian government workforce by about 583,000. The bulk of the decline followed the reforms of 1993-94.[114] The state sector's share of employment fell from about 95% to

---

[112] Again, according to Mesa-Lago (2001) GDP was 21% and GDP per capita 25% below their respective 1989 levels.

[113] This does not take into consideration under-the-table payments or gratuities the workers may receive.

[114] The figures in Table1 imply that a very sharp decline in the non-civilian government work-force occurred in 1994, followed by a large increase in 1995. I wonder if a reclassification of workers is partly responsible.

79%. This decline in government employment was accounted for mostly by increased employment in other sectors. Most state farms were converted into cooperatives (264,000). Although these are thought to have some autonomy, they are far from being private enterprises. Employment in mixed enterprises, the joint ventures between the government and foreign firms mentioned above, increased by 131,000 workers. ECLAC considers both of these sectors part of the private sector, while the government considers the bulk of the mixed enterprise employment part of the state sector.[115] I believe it is useful to keep them separate. The true private sector, consisting for the most part of the self-employed and of small farmers, increased by 254,000. The remaining decline in public sector employment was accounted for by declines in the labor force (82,000). Unemployment was actually lower in 1998 than in 1989 (a decline of 65,000).

The data in Table 1 does not adequately account for informal activity, so the relative decline of the state sector may be understated. During the period covered in Table 1, for example, the size of the working age population rose (by 424,000) and university enrollments fell (by 140,000).[116] Together with the declining size of the labor force, these numbers suggest an increase in the informal sector. Furthermore, there is anecdotal evidence that at least some government employees work at their official job only a fraction of the day, devoting much of their time to informal market activity. Other observers claim, however, that this effect is modest. While they agree that underemployment is huge, they claim it is difficult for government employees to turn free time into informal market activity. It is also frequently claimed that the formal self-employed report only a fraction of their income (the usual number is one half), so that many in the formal sector may also be acting informally. Though it may not accurately measure the division of

---

[115] Political and social organizations are included in government employment.
[116] The data are from ECLAC (2000). Working age is defined as 17-54 for women and 17-59 for men.

employment between the public and private sectors, Table 1 probably does indicate general trends.

Prior to 1993 wages played a much smaller role in determining the occupational and skill distributions of the Cuban labor force than they would have if the country had had a market economy. This is because Cuba's command economy did not rely very much on prices to allocate jobs or schooling. The government decided what jobs would have to be filled, what fields of study would be offered, and so forth. The end result was a wage structure with little relationship to productivity, a characteristic of the public sector to this day. Mesa-Lago (2000), for example, reports ratios of highest to lowest wages of only 4.9:1 and 4.5:1 in 1979 and 1987, respectively. Table 2 shows monthly average product per worker by sector and monthly salary of public employees. In 1989 the public sector made up almost the entire economy. Even excluding financing, insurance, real estate and business services, which I suspect includes the rental value of owner-occupied housing, the two variables are negatively correlated, though not significantly different from zero.

While the wages of government employees appear to understate productivity differences in government enterprises, the difference in earnings between private sector and government workers after 1993 almost certainly exaggerates the productivity differences between the two sectors. According to Mesa-Lago (2002) the poorest private farmers tend to have incomes that are three or four times those of doctors or university professors, while owners of *paladares*, the small home restaurants, can make much more.[117] Such earnings disparities probably overstate the differences between wages in the two sectors. As stated previously, many public employees do very little actual work, and private economic activity, whether practiced formally or informally, has substantial risks and costs that require that a compensating differential be paid. Even taking these considerations into account, the earnings differences

---

[117] These salaries correspond to March and April of 2002. Some of the magnitudes appear implausible and may reflect confusion between gross and net earnings Nevertheless, the differences are so huge that even with considerable error they still suggest incredible distortions. Similar numbers are found in Mesa-Lago (2000).

between the private and public sector appear to be quite large. Such earnings differentials could not be maintained in the absence of severe restrictions on occupational choice. Most professionals, for example, are not

Table 2. Average Product and Salary, 1989
(*In pesos*)

Sector	Monthly Average Product per Worker	Monthly Salary
Agriculture, Forestry, Hunting, and Fishing	243	187
Mining and Quarrying	368	206
Manufacturing	578	183
Electricity, Gas, and Water	1024	200
Construction	331	199
Wholesale/Retail Trade, Restaurants, and Hotels	861	164
Transport, Storage, and Communications	485	207
Community, Social, and Personal Services	387	194
Financing, Insurance, Real Estate, and Business Services	2031	203
Average	463	188

Source: Computed from data in ECLAC (2000)

allowed to practice their profession in the private sector. It is widely believed that such restrictions, coupled with the distortions in wages between the two sectors, have contributed significantly to the sharp decline in university enrollments that will be mentioned below.

Comparisons with other Countries in Latin America

I begin the comparison of Cuba with other Latin American countries by looking at the distribution of employment by sector. Countries can differ considerably in their distribution of employment by sector due to their levels of economic development and their comparative advantages. To mitigate this problem, the comparison below excludes the two sectors most sensitive to the level of economic development and to comparative advantage: (1) agriculture, forestry, hunting and fishing, and (2) mining and quarrying. Table 3 shows the distribution of employment for selected countries and years among the remaining sectors. Data availability, completeness and consistency determined the choice of countries and years. As can be seen, Cuba in 1997 had lower than average employment in trade and in financial and other services.[118] The last column of Table 3 shows the sum of the *relative* deviations (not including the "not specified" category) from the mean occupational distribution of the countries in the table, excluding Cuba's state sector. Let s_{ij} be country j's share of employment in sector i, and s_i be the sample average share in sector i. The relative deviation for country j in sector i, is defined as $d_{ij} = |s_{ij} - s_i|/s_i$. The sum of the d_{ij}'s over all sectors is the measure of total relative deviation that appears in the last column of Table 3. As can be seen, Cuba's economy deviates the most from the sample mean. Cuba's state sector deviates even more than the economy as a whole.

The results of Table 3 may be just a fluke. After all, employment by sector could vary considerably even among market economies. Table 4 shows similar results, however, for major occupational categories. As can be seen, Cuba is heavy with professional and administrative personnel, but relatively light on clerical and service workers. Once again Cuba deviates the most from the mean distribution of employment by sector using the same measure of total relative deviation used in Table 3.

The countries selected for Table 4 are the ones that had complete and consistent data. Table 5 shows employment distribution for a larger set of countries, but only for three occupations for which complete and compatible data were available. Again, Cuba deviates the most from the sample average.

---

[118] I chose 1997 for comparison because it was the year for which data for the other countries was most commonly available.

Table 3. Employment Distribution By Sector

(% EMPLOYED, EXCLUDING (1) AGRICULTURE, FORESTRY AND FISHING, AND (2) MINING AND QUARRYING)

Country	Manufacturing	Electricity, Gas, and Water	Construction	Wholesale/ Retail Trade Restaurants, and Hotels	Transport Storage and Communications	Financing, Insurance, Real Estate and Services	Community, Social, and Personal Services	Not Specified	Deviation from Sample Average
Chile (1997)	19.1	0.7	10.8	21.6	8.9	8.3	30.6	0.0	1.8
Colombia (1997)	20.7	0.6	6.3	25.8	7.5	9.5	29.3	0.4	1.62
Cuba (1997)	21.5	1.9	8.7	16	6.9	2.4	42.5	0.00	2.53
Ecuador (1997)	16.7	0.4	6.5	30.6	6.2	4.9	34.6	0.10	1.3
El Salvador (1997)	21.9	1	9.1	29.1	6.3	2.0	30.6	0.00	1.17
Honduras (1997)	27.6	0.5	6.7	30	3.6	3.2	28.5	0.00	2.16
Paraguay (1996)	15.1	0.7	7.3	35.3	5.5	5.0	31	0.00	1.16
Uruguay (1995)	18.9	1.4	7.6	20.6	6	6.5	38.9	0.00	1.31
Venezuela (1995)	15.9	1	9.5	26.4	7.3	6.6	33.2	0.20	0.83
Average	20.2	1	8.1	25	6.3	5	34.2	0.10	1.54
Cuba, Public Sector (1997)	24.4	2.2	8.7	14.4	5.3	1.8	43.3	0.00	3.34

Source: *Statistical Abstract of Latin America*, Vol. 36 and ECLAC (2000)

Table 4. Employment Distribution by Major Occupational Category
(in percent employed)

Countries	Professional, Technical and Related Workers	Administrative and Managerial Workers	Clerical and Related Workers	Service Workers	Other Workers	DDeviation from Sample Average
Chile (1997)	9.0	3.5	14.4	13.0	60.1	1.06
Colombia (1997)	14.1	1.8	12.6	17.8	53.6	1.25
Cuba (1997)	21.4	7.8	4.6	15.4	50.8	2.32
Honduras (1997)	6.4	2.3	4.1	10.4	76.8	2.15
Panama (1997)	12.9	6.3	10.3	16.2	54.4	0.75
Paraguay (1994)	8.9	4.0	8.1	17.8	61.1	0.66
Uruguay (1995)	11.5	4.1	14.2	18.2	52.1	0.80
Venezuela (1995)	12.3	3.4	10.2	14.8	59.4	0.29
Average	12.1	4.1	9.8	15.5	58.5	1.16

Source: *Statistical Abstract of Latin America*, Vol. 36 and ECLAC (2000)

Given the importance the Cuban government places on the training of doctors, it is not surprising that Cuba has by far the highest number of majors in health care. Perhaps not as well known is that it also has the highest percentage of education students. Together, health care and education accounted for over 60% of post-secondary students. At the other end, Cuba had the lowest percentage of business students, again not a surprising result. As with the occupational distributions, Cuba's distribution of majors deviates the most from the average distribution of Latin American countries in the sample. What's more, Cuba's deviation is likely to be understated because the "other or not specified" category was not used in the calculations. This was the fourth largest category for Cuba (almost 8% of enrollment), and it is thought to consist entirely of physical fitness majors.

During the 1990s, post-secondary school (mostly university) enrollments in Cuba fell dramatically. They went from 242,434 in 1990 to only 102,598 by 1998. The decline in enrollments, together with a distribution of majors heavily skewed toward education, medicine and physical education, as shown Table 6, means that in some fields Cuba will be producing few professionals. If we rank the countries in Table 6 from lowest (1) to highest (16) in majors per person, we find that Cuba's weighted average rank, where the weights are the fraction of each major in the entire sample of countries, is only 5.2. In several fields only Haiti had fewer majors per person, and the Haitian data is for 1989. In two fields that many would consider important for a successful transition to a market economy, business and technology, Cuba ranks second and third lowest, respectively.

Table 5. Employment Distribution by Major Occupational Category
(in percent of enrolled)

Countries	Professional, Technical and Related Workers	Administrative and Managerial Workers	Clerical and Related Workers	Deviation from Sample Average
Bolivia (1996)	13.9	4.1	4.2	0.93
Chile (1997)	9.0	3.5	14.4	0.97
Colombia (1997)	14.1	1.8	12.6	1.28
Costa Rica (1997)	10.9	4.5	7.4	0.44
Cuba (1997)	21.4	7.8	4.6	2.67
Dominican Republic (1997)	4.7	1.4	4.5	1.61
El Salvador (1997)	8.9	2.1	4.6	1.01
Honduras (1997)	6.4	2.3	4.1	1.26
Mexico (1997)	13.4	2.1	5.8	0.88
Panama (1997)	12.9	6.3	10.3	1.26
Paraguay (1994)	8.9	4.0	8.1	0.39
Peru (1997)	9.2	0.8	5.9	1.20
Uruguay (1995)	11.5	4.1	14.2	0.96
Venezuela (1995)	12.3	3.4	10.2	0.35
Average	11.0	3.4	8.2	1.1

Source: Political Abstract for Latin America, Vol. 36 and ECLAC (2000)

Table 7 compares post-secondary enrollments in Cuba with those of the most market-oriented economy in Latin America, that of Chile. The data for the two countries are not exactly comparable. Cuba's include all post-secondary students, while Chile's exclude graduate students and post-graduates. Consequently, Chile's numbers are undercounted by about two or three percent. Fields are not defined exactly alike, though for the ones shown there are considerable similarities in the titles used.

Cuba's big lead in education and medical students declines throughout the 1990's, so that by 1998 both countries are close in terms of enrollments per 1,000 persons in these two fields. In technology and business, however, Chile's lead in 1990 grows dramatically, so that by 1998 Chile has more than six times as many students per capita than does Cuba in these two fields. In total students Cuba's slight lead in 1990 is completely reversed by 1998. In that year Chile had almost three times as many undergraduates per 1,000 persons as Cuba had post-secondary students per 1,000 persons.

Table 6. Distribution of University Enrollments by Major
(in % of enrolled)

Country	Education	Humanities	Art and Architecture	Law	Social Science and Mass Communication	Commercial and Business Administration	Natural Science	Health Care	Technology	Agriculture Forestry and Fishing	Deviation from Sample Average
Argentina, 1994	1.6	8.3	7.0	16	5.9	20.1	9.4	13.7	13	3.4	4.6
Bolivia, 1991	0.7	2	3.1	12	9.2	17.7	7.6	19.8	18.6	2.5	3.3
Brazil, 1994	11.6	8.3	2.1	12	12.8	19.1	8.4	9.3	10.2	2.4	3
Chile, 1996	7.7	6	6.6	5	14.3	18.9	2.4	5.6	25.7	7.7	5.8
Costa Rica, 1994[a]	15.6	3.8	3.1	5.4	7.2	18.6	5.6	6.1	9.2	2.2	2.6
Cuba, 1996	34.2	1.7	1.4	2	2.6	4.0	2.6	26.3	12.7	4.9	7.8
Ecuador (1990)	24.8	0.6	2.9	8.2	14.8	17.5	3.6	11.5	12.5	2.7	3.7
El Salvador, 1996	0.2	10.9	4.4	7.1	9.8	23.6	14.9	12.5	14.7	1.7	5.1
Haiti, 1989	3.4	14.1	0	15	2.4	30.3	6.3	12.4	11.8	4.4	6.5
Honduras, 1994	12.6	1.4	1.3	12	5.3	22.5	5.3	11.7	15.7	3.8	2.6
Mexico, 1994	11.7	1	5.2	9.9	9	24.4	7.3	7.9	20.8	1.4	3
Nicaragua, 1995	11.6	1.2	2	16	6.3	19.6	9.2	11.1	18.7	2.0	3.3
Panama, 1994[a]	12.1	7.6	5.8	5.1	12	29	5.1	4.2	17.7	1.1	4.3
Peru (1991)[a]	11.4	1.5	1.7	9.2	13.2	19.2	5.4	11.4	17.3	4.6	2.4
Paraguay, 1996	17	0	9.1	15	21.9	5.6	6.2	13.5	7.6	3.7	6.2
Venezuela, 1988	21.1	1.1	1.5	7.0	7.5	21.2	4.9	9.5	15.9	3.8	3.3
Average	12.3	4.3	3.6	9.8	9.6	19.5	6.5	11.7	15.1	3.3	4.2

Source: Computed from data in Statistical Abstract for Latin America, Vol. 36

It can be argued that in a market economy there will tend to be under-investment in education in general and in medical training in particular. This is why a high number of doctors in a developing economy is usually viewed as a good thing. It shows that such a country is successfully countering this tendency toward under investment. Beyond a certain point, however, the social return to an additional doctor is lower than the social cost. With a level of doctors per capita that is several times that of richer countries in the region with comparable or better levels of life expectancy, Cuba almost certainly has gone well beyond the point of optimality (ECLAC, 2000).[119] Rather than an indication of success, the high number of doctors is a sign of pathology. Regardless of efficiency, Cuba's high number of doctors will likely not be sustainable in a more market-oriented economy.

Table 7. Enrollments per Thousand persons, Chile and Cuba

		1990	1991	1992	1993	1994	1995	1996	1997	1998
Technology	Chile	5.1	4.9	5.4	5.8	5.8	6.0	6.5	6.7	7.4
	Cuba	3.5	3.3	3.1	2.6	2.0	1.6	1.4	1.3	1.2
Business	Chile	4.2	3.8	4.3	4.8	4.8	4.8	4.7	4.4	4.5
	Cuba	1.3	1.1	0.8	0.6	0.5	0.4	0.5	0.5	0.7
Education	Chile	1.9	2.0	1.9	1.8	1.8	1.8	1.8	1.8	2.0
	Cuba	10.5	9.2	7.2	5.3	4.4	3.8	3.5	3.2	3.2
Agricultural Sciences	Chile	1.4	1.4	1.8	2.0	2.0	1.9	1.9	2.0	1.9
	Cuba	1.0	0.9	0.8	0.8	0.7	0.6	0.5	0.4	0.4
Natural Sciences and Math.	Chile	0.5	0.5	0.5	0.5	0.5	0.5	0.6	0.6	0.6
	Cuba	0.6	0.5	0.5	0.5	0.5	0.5	0.4	0.4	0.4
Medicine	Chile	1.1	1.1	1.1	1.1	1.2	1.2	1.4	1.5	1.6
	Cuba	3.6	3.5	3.6	3.4	3.1	2.7	2.5	2.3	2.2
Total	Chile	18.7	18.5	20.7	22.5	23.0	23.8	24.8	25.4	26.5
	Cuba	22.8	20.9	18.3	15.2	12.9	11.1	10.1	9.5	9.2

Source: Computed from data in *Statistical Abstract of Latin America*, Vol. 36

a. Universities only.

---

[119] Cuba has more than twice the number of doctors per capita than the United States has, and more than four times as many as Barbados, Chile, and Cost Rica, all of which have equal or higher life expectancies.

Conclusions

We saw in the previous section that Cuba's employment distributions by very broad industry and

occupational categories deviate more from the means of a group of Latin American economies than any other country in the sample. Because of the broad definitions used here, it is to be expected that differences between Cuba and the other countries are actually greater. I do not know of the existence of more disaggregated data that could be used to explore this proposition, but there is some evidence on the allocation of professional talent that supports it.

Another example of Cuba's peculiar allocation of professional and technical talent is found in the number of scientist, engineers, technicians and auxiliary personnel devoted to research and development. In 1995 Cuba had 44,119 such persons engaged in non-military research and development (*Statistical Abstract of Latin America*, 2001). This may well be the highest level in Latin America, though we cannot be certain because the data differ somewhat across countries. It is certainly the case, however, that Cuba has by far the highest number of research personnel per 1,000 inhabitants. When one considers the very low productivity of the Cuban economy, it appears likely that once again the Cuban government is pursuing an agenda with respect to its occupational assignments that has little to do with economic efficiency.

In the previous section we saw that Cuba's distribution of post-secondary fields of study also deviated the most from the average for a sample of Latin American countries. Cuba had an unusually high concentration of students studying medicine, which is consistent with its extremely high number of doctors per capita. The most common major has been education, and not surprisingly, Cuba has a very high number of elementary and secondary schoolteachers. ECLAC (2000) reports that in 1996 Cuba had the lowest and second lowest number of students per elementary and secondary schoolteacher, respectively, in all of Latin America and the Caribbean. Medicine and education, along with physical fitness, have accounted for much of post-secondary education in Cuba. While the fraction of students in these fields has declined slightly, it remains high. In 1990 69% of post-secondary students were in one of these three fields. By 1998 it had only declined to 65%. The absolute number of students in these fields fell sharply, of course, because post-secondary enrollments fell by more than 50% over this period.

The high number of professionals in these three fields poses some significant problems for a future transition to a market economy. First, the numbers of persons in these fields are almost certainly unsustainable in a more market-oriented system. Second, the training in these fields is probably not easily applied to other occupations. Together, these two conditions suggest that professionals in these fields may become a serious obstacle to future market-friendly reforms. This is especially true of the field of education. The profession is one of the most ideologically sensitive in Cuba, in which Marxist ideology is an important part of the educational content. This "knowledge" is not very useful in teaching outside a Marxist society, it is useless in any other profession in a market economy, and it is likely to be a hindrance in a future democratic Cuba. Many teachers produced by the current regime, therefore, are of suspect quality and have training which may not be very desirable in a future Cuba even in the field for which they were trained. Doctors, on the other hand, may find that being able to practice in a the private sector, even in one with enormous excess supply, is still better than working for the public sector under current conditions. Unlike teachers, Cuban doctors are likely to have skills that are valuable in other countries. I expect many Cuban doctors to emigrate if the opportunity presents itself.

The high number of professionals in medicine, education and physical education, along with sharply declining post-secondary school enrollments, implies that professionals in other fields are few in number and falling or not growing very rapidly. This is especially important in business and technology, where a comparison with the most market oriented economy in Latin America, Chile, highlighted Cuba's lack of students in these areas. Business education is a particular concern, not only because of the low number of students and the low number of trained personnel, but also because one cannot but be skeptical of the quality of business education they are receiving. Opportunities for on the job training are probably also very limited. Anecdotal evidence confirms the scarcity of persons trained in business administration, especially in marketing, finance, management, and to a lesser degree accounting, where recent efforts are being made to increase the number of accountants. Not surprisingly Cuba's distribution of employment by industry (excluding agriculture and mining) shows it to have below normal percentage of workers in trade and finance (Table 3). At the same time Cuba has an unusually high percentage of administrative personnel, something not unusual for bureaucratic systems. The number of administrators and managers will almost certainly fall in a transition to a market economy. More problematic is that their managerial and administrative skills, like those of many teachers, may not transfer well to the private sector. From the ranks of public managers and administrators may well come some of the strongest opposition to future reform.[120] What is more, they will be in positions to sabotage the reform process from within.

Besides the question of the disparity between the current skill distribution in Cuba and the distribution that would prevail in a market economy, there is the question of the quality of the existing skills. In some professions ideological purity is the paramount consideration. The classic example is probably teaching. When a characteristic other than ability is used in the selection process, ability suffers. In some fields, such as business, the educational expertise may be lacking, and the opportunities for practicing severely limited. Depreciation of skills for lack of use may be a serious problem, even in professions where the initial skills acquired were fine. This is happening not only to those professionals who have abandoned their fields to work in the private sector, but also to many in the public sector. Extensive underemployment has led many professionals to do the work of mid-level technicians—electrical engineers doing the work of electricians is an example—which also leads to a depreciation of human capital. A related problem arises because in some fields Cuban industry is quite primitive and there are insufficient opportunities to apply and

---

[120] See Locay and Ural (1995).

develop new knowledge. A good example of this problem is agriculture, which because of a lack of inputs, especially fuel, has been reverting to a pre-industrial state. According to knowledgeable observers, two industries where Cuban workers are well trained by international standards are mining and tourism. These are two industries subject to international competition and under foreign management.

Some economists outside of Cuba also worry to what extent fundamental skills and values useful in a market economy may have been eroded. Many of the features that have characterized the Cuban economy under the Castro regime—the lack of connection between performance and pay, the evasion of responsibility, the lack of incentives for risk taking, the view of the law as something to be gotten around—have led to patterns of behavior that would be highly dysfunctional in a market economy. The question that cannot be answered at this time is to what extent these harmful attitudes that have developed over the past forty years will linger once a transition to a market system begins in earnest.

One of the supposed bright spots in Cuba's future prospects, its well-educated labor force, does not seem so bright on closer inspection. This should come as no surprise, for why should we expect a system that has failed miserably in terms of efficiency in every other aspect of the economy to have done a good job in educating and allocating its workforce?

References

Economic Commission for Latin America and the Caribbean (ECLAC), 2000. *La economía cubana: Reformas estructurales y desempeño en los noventa. Fondo de Cultura Económica*, Mexico, D.F.

Hernández-Catá, Ernesto, 2000. "The Fall and Recovery of the Cuban Economy in the 1990's: Mirage or Reality." *Cuba in Transition—Volume 10*. Association for the Study of the Cuban Economy, Washington, D.C.

Locay, Luis and Ural, Cigdem, 1995. "Restitution vs. Indemnification: Their Effects on the Pace of Privatization." *Cuba in Transition—Volume 5*. Association for the Study of the Cuban Economy, Washington, D.C.

Madrid-Aris, Manuel, 1997. "Growth and Technological Change in Cuba." *Cuba in Transition— Volume 7*. Association for the Study of the Cuban Economy, Washington, D.C.

Madrid-Aris, Manuel, 2000. "Education's Contribution to Economic Growth in Cuba." *Cuba in Transition—Volume 10*. Association for the Study of the Cuban Economy, Washington, D.C.

Mesa-Lago, Carmelo, 2000. *Market, Socialist, and Mixed Economies: Comparative Policy and Performance—Chile, Cuba, and Costa Rica*. The Johns Hopkins University Press, Baltimore.

Mesa-Lago, Carmelo, 2001. "The Cuban Economy in 1999-2001: Evaluation of Performance and Debate on the Future." *Cuba in Transition, Volume 11*. Association for the Study of the Cuban Economy, Miami, FL.

Mesa-Lago, Carmelo, 2002. "Crecientes disparidades económicas y sociales en Cuba: Impacto y recomendaciones para el cambio." *Cuba Transition Project*. Institute for Cuban and Cuban-American Studies, University of Miami, Coral Gables, FL.

Statistical Abstract of Latin America, vol. 37, 2001.James W. Wilkie, ed.. UCLA Latin American Center Publications, University of California, Los Angeles.

World Factbook 2002. http://www.cia.gov/cia/publications/factbook/

BIOGRAPHICAL NOTES

Gabriel di Bella earned Ph. D. in economics from the University of Wisconsin in 2003. He joined the International Monetary Fund in 2002, where he currently serves as Mission Chief to Haiti, and has participated in IMF missions to Latin American, African countries, the United States and Canada. Prior to joining the IMF, he worked for eleven years as an economic consultant for Arriazu & Associates in Buenos Aires, Argentina. He is a member of the Association for the Study of the Cuban Economy, and has published a number of articles on the Cuban economy in *Cuba in Transition* and other outlets.

After receiving his doctoral degree in agricultural economics, **Ed Canler** went to work in private business that took him to every Latin American country bar one, his native Cuba. This omission was remedied in 1994 after a 33-year absence. Following several trips to the island and meeting with high officials there, he began writing *Cubanalysis*, an internet newsletter on the Cuban economy and writing occasional articles, some of which were presented to the Association of the Cuban Economy. He later appeared in a documentary about Operation Peter Pan which spirited some 14,000 children out of Cuba in the early 1960's. Broadening his scope of work, he has just finished a book on the history and geography of the country intended for the visitor, *Just the Right Place*, awaiting publication.

G.B. (Jerry) Hagelberg passed away on September 2, 2011. This is what his friend and colleague José (Pepin) Alvarez wrote about him. "The *Financial Times* called Jerry 'one of the most astute observers', and the commodity trading and research house F.O. List's 'one of the most prominent sugar analysts [who] had an intimate knowledge of the Cuban sugar industry and agriculture in general.' Besides numerous and comments for both outlets, he authored the book *The Caribbean Sugar Industry: Constraint and opportunities* (1974), several book chapters, and articles in *Cuba in Transition* and *Cuban Affairs*. He was a research fellow at the Academy of Sciences and the Institute for the Sugar Economy in Berlin, and held appointments at Yale University and the University of Glasgow. From 1980 to 1986 he was sugar adviser to the government of Barbados, receiving the Honorary Silver Crown of Merit in the Order of Barbados".

Ernesto Hernández-Catá received his *Licence* from the Graduate Institute of International Studies in Geneva, and his Ph.D in Economics from Yale University. He spent most of his career at the International Monetary Fund where he served as Associate Director for the African and Western Hemisphere departments, manager of the World Economic Outlook, head of the North American Division, and chief negotiator with the Russian Federation. From 1976 to 1979 he was an Economist in the Division of International Finance of the Board of Governors of the Federal Reserve System. He taught macroeconomics and monetary policy at the Latin American Program in Applied Economics of The American University; and economic development at the School of Advanced International Studies of the Johns Hopkins University. He is co-author of *The U.S. Economy in an Interdependent World,* and author of *War, Justice and Infamy. He also* wrote extensively on the economies of the United States, Russia, Sub-Saharan Africa, and Cuba, and on transition issues in the former Soviet Union.

Luis R. Luis, an international economist specializing in international finance and investments is a co-founder of International Research and Strategy, a firm centered on emerging markets finance and investments. Previously he was Managing Director at Scudder Investments in Boston where he directed international research and helped manage international fixed income and equity portfolios, including emerging markets and country funds in Argentina, Brazil, Mexico and Venezuela. He was Director of the Latin America Department at the Institute of International Finance in Washington, D.C., head of international economics at Midland Bank in London and Crocker Bank in San Francisco, and Chief Economist at the Organization of America States in Washington. Earlier he was in the economics faculty at the US Naval Academy in Annapolis and at The American University, and held a Fulbright visiting professorship at the Universities of Trujillo and Pacifico in Peru. He has lectured on international economics at universities and research institutions in England, Spain, Argentina, Brazil, Chile, Colombia and several other Latin American countries. An author of articles on international economics and finance and a contributor to several books on emerging markets and portfolio management, Luis holds a PhD degree in economics from the University of Notre Dame.

Lorenzo Pérez earned Ph. D. in economics from the University of Pennsylvania in 1972. Worked as an international economist at the U.S. Treasury and at the Agency for International Development from 1972 to 1978. He worked at the International Monetary Fund from 1978 through 2009, leading missions to Latin American, Middle East, Central Asia and African countries. He taught international and development economics at The George Washington University, a founding member and former President of the Association for the Study of the Cuban Economy, Pérez is currently consultant for is the Independent Evaluation Group for the World Bank. He has published a number of articles on the Cuban economy in *Cuba in Transition* and other outlets.

Joaquín P. Pujol, graduated from the Wharton School of Finance and the University of Pennsylvania where he taught and conducted research under Professor Lawrence Klein. He worked for the International Monetary Fund for 29 years, and was Assistant Director in both the Policy Review Department (where he had responsibility for overseeing the IMF involvement with over 60 countries) and the Western Hemisphere Department where he headed negotiating teams to a number of Latin American countries. He was IMF Resident Representative in Uruguay 1970-72, and was a member of the IMF's negotiating team in Mexico during the debt crisis in 1982-87. After retiring from the IMF, he served as Advisor on Monetary Policy and Banking Supervision to the Central Banks in the CARICOM Region and the Government of Trinidad and Tobago. Pujol was one of the founding members of the Association for the Study of the Cuban Economy (ASCE), and edited two books, *Cuba: Políticas Económicas para la Transición*, and *Cuba: Revolución o Involución* by Oscar Espinosa Chepe (Aduana Vieja).

Rafael Romeu earned a Ph. D. in economics from the University of Maryland in 2002. He is currently the Managing Director at DevTech Systems, Inc., a development economics consulting firm located in Arlington, Virginia. He worked at the International Monetary Fund from 2001 through 2014, and held positions at the Board of Governors of the Federal Reserve and the Central Bank of Venezuela prior to working at the IMF. He has taught financial theory at the Department of Economics of Yale Univeristy in New Haven, Connecticut, and is a former President of the Association for the Study of the Cuban Economy. He has published a number of articles on the Cuban economy in *Cuba in Transition* and various other outlets.

Jorge A. Sanguinetty, a PhD. in Economics from CUNY, worked in Cuba until 1966 at the National Institute of Tourism, the Central Planning Board and the Ministry of the Sugar Industry. He studied economics at the *Instituto Juan Noyola* of the University of Havana, coinciding with Oscar Espinosa Chepe. In 1967 he worked at Merrill Lynch, the National Bureau of Economic Research and the Manufacturers' Hanover Trust in New York City. After his postdoctoral fellowship at Yale University, he joined the Brookings Institution as a research associate in Washington, D.C., later coordinating research projects in education and economic development in Latin-America under United Nations, while teaching economics at the Catholic University of Rio de Janeiro. In 1978 he directed the Latin-American Program in Applied Economics at American University in Washington, D.C. In 1984 he founded *DevTech Systems, Inc.*, a consulting firm with headquarters in Washington, D.C. and Miami. A co-founders of the Association for the Study of the Cuban Economy, many of his articles and papers can be seen in www.cubafuturo.net and *Cuba in*

Transition's www.ascecuba.org. He is the autor of *Cuba: Realidad y Destino Presente y Futuro de la Economía y la Sociedad Cubanas.*

Andy Wolfe earned Ph. D. in economics from the University of Wisconsin in 1983. He briefly taught economics at Bowdoin College in Brunswick, Maine, before joining the International Monetary Fund, where he worked from 1987 through 2014, leading missions to Latin American, Central Asia and African countries. He has taught international and development economics at American University, and is a member of the Association for the Study of the Cuban Economy. He has published a number of articles on the Cuban economy in *Cuba in Transition* and other outlets.